LIBERATION NARRATIVES

Books by Haki R. Madhubuti

Non-Fiction

Freedom to Self-Destruct: Easier To Believe Than Think — New And Selected Essays

YellowBlack: The First Twenty-One Years of a Poet's Life, A Memoir

Tough Notes: A Healing Call for Creating Exceptional Black Men

Claiming Earth: Race Rage Rape, Redemption:
Blacks Seeking a Culture of Enlightened Empowerment

Dynamite Voices: Black Poets of the 1960s

Black Men: Obsolete, Single, Dangerous? The Afrikan American Family in Transition

From Plan to Planet: Life Studies; The Need for Afrikan Minds and Institutions

Enemies: The Clash of Nations

A Capsule Course in Black Poetry (co-author)

African Centered Education (co-author)

Kwanzaa: A Progressive And Uplifting African American Holiday

Poetry

Run Toward Fear: New Poems and A Poet's Handbook

Heartlove: Wedding and Love Poems

Ground Work: New and Selected Poems of Don L. Lee/Haki R. Madhubuti from 1966-1996

Killing Memory, Seeking Ancestors

Earthquakes and Sunrise Missions

Book of Life

Directionscore: New and Selected Poems

We Walk the Way of the New World

Don't Cry, Scream

Black Pride

Think Black!

Anthologies

Releasing the Spirit: A Collection of Literary Works from Gallery 37 (co-editor)

Describe the Moment: A Collection of Literary Works from Gallery 37 (co-editor)

Million Man March/Day of Absence: A Commemorative Anthology (co-editor)

Confusion by Any Other Name: Essays Exploring the Negative Impact of
The Black Man's Guide to Understanding the Black Woman (editor)

Why L.A. Happened: Implications of the '92 Los Angeles Rebellion (editor)

Say that the River Turns: The Impact of Gwendolyn Brooks (editor)

To Gwen, With Love (co-editor)

Recordings: Poetry and Music

Rise Vision Comin' (with Nation: Afrikan Liberation Arts Ensemble)

Medasi (with Nation: Afrikan Liberation Arts Ensemble)

Rappin' and Readin'

LIBERATION NARRATIVES

New and Collected Poems 1966-2009

HAKI R. MADHUBUTI

With a Foreword by Houston A. Baker Jr.
an Introduction by Regina Jennings
and an Afterword by Lita Hooper

Chicago

Third World Press
Publishers since 1967
Chicago

First Edition
Printed in the United States of America

Library of Congress Cataloging-in-Publication Data

Madhubuti, Haki R., 1942-
Liberation narratives : new and collected poems 1966-2009 / Haki R. Madhubuti ; with a foreword by Houston A. Baker Jr. ; an introduction by Regina Jennings ; and an afterword by Lita Hooper.
p. cm.
ISBN-13: 978-0-88378-289-7 (cloth edition : alk. paper)
ISBN-13: 978-0-88378-314-6 (pbk. edition : alk. paper)
ISBN-10: 0-88378-289-8 (cloth edition : alk. paper)
ISBN-10: 0-88378-314-2 (pbk. edition : alk. paper)
I. Title.
PS3563.A3397L53 2009
811'.54–dc22

2009023258

14 13 12 11 6 5 4 3 2

Deepest gratitude and thanks to Gwendolyn Mitchell, Solomohn Ennis, Keir Thirus and Rose Perkins for their commitment and diligent work that contributed to the production of this book.

Special thanks to Houston A. Baker Jr., Regina Jennings, and Lita Hooper for their words of encouragement and critical grounding.

Dedication

For Barack Hussein Obama,
44th President of the United States,
and the millions of young people who
made it happen thus helping to
generate a new spirit in this
great country of ours.

and
Michelle Obama, Malia and Sasha

and
Adrienne Rich, Robert Bly, Wendell Berry
Mari Evans
Ruby Dee
Nora Brooks Blakely
Wesley Snipes
Lerone Bennett Jr.
Danny Glover
Margaret Burroughs
Carol D. Lee aka Safisha Madhubuti

and
Walter and Beverly Lomax, Joe Stroud,
Jon Lockard, Willis Bing Davis
Estella Conwill Majozo
Frank Madison Reid III

and my children
Don, Regina, Mariama, Laini, Bomani and Akili

and
always for the students and faculty of
Chicago State University
my intellectual home for over a quarter century

Remembering...

Gwendolyn Brooks
Barbara A. Sizemore
Mahmoud Darwish
John Hope Franklin
Richard Wright
Paul Robeson
Octavia Butler
Alice Rochon
Charles Burroughs
Sherley Ann Williams
Welvin Stroud
Nichole L. Shields
John Coltrane
Leon Despres
Addison Gayle Jr.

Studs Terkel
Ossie Davis
Toni Cade Bambara
Malcolm X
W.E.B. DuBois
John O. Killens
Murry N. DePillars
Donda West
Dudley Randall
Hoyt W. Fuller
Louis Armstrong
Miles Davis
James Baldwin
Betty Shabazz
KoKo Taylor

John H. Johnson

Schanna Gayden and all children of senseless violence

Jeff Donaldson
Asa G. Hilliard III
Maxine Graves Lee

Special Thanks to

Naomi Long Madgett/Lotus Press
Paul Coates/Black Classic Press
Kassahun Checole, Africa World Press/Red Sea Press
Wade and Cheryl Hudson/Just Us Books
Earl G. Graves Sr./Black Enterprise
Jessica Care Moore/Moore Black Press
Nati Ntaki/Afrikan World Books
Lorene Cary/Art Sanctuary(Annual Book Festival)
Haile Gerima and Shirikiana Aina/Sankofa Video and Books
Maulana Karenga/The Organization Us
Max Rodriquez, Harlem Book Fair/Quarterly Book Review
Bill Cox, Black Issues Book Review/Diverse Issues
Howard Dodson/Schomburg Center for Research in Black Culture
Larry Robin/Moonstone Arts Center
Tony Rose/Amber Books
Robert Chrisman/The Black Scholar Journal
Brenda Greene/National Black Writers Conference
Quraysh Ali Lansana/Gwendolyn Brooks Center Chicago State University
Willie Williams/Broadside Press
Fred Hord/The Association of Black Culture Centers
Kelly Norman Ellis/MFA Program in Creative Writing, Chicago State University
Bakari Kitwana/Hip-Hop Generation Books
Patrick Oliver/Say it Loud! Readers and Writers Series
Kevin Coval/Young Chicago Author's Luder than a Bomb
Lisa Lee/Jane Addams Hull-House Museum
Susan L. Taylor/National CARES Mentoring Movement
Ron Daniels/Institute of the Black World 21st Century
Diane D. Turner/Charles L. Blockson Afro-American Collection, Temple University
Anthony Daniels-Halisi/Institute of Positive Education

and the Sisters and Brothers of the following organizations and publications

Johnson Publishing Co. (*Ebony* and *Jet*)
Carter G. Woodson Library
National Council of Black Studies
National Association of Black Social Workers
Third World Press
Third World Press Foundation
South End Books
Z Magazine
Nation Magazine and Books
In These Times Magazine
The Progressive Magazine
Mother Jones Magazine
National Conference of Artists
Betty Shabazz International Charter School
Barbara A. Sizemore Academy
DuSable Leadership Academy
New Concept School
The Black Church

Contents

Black Pride (1968) 39

Don't Cry, Scream (1969) 55

We Walk the Way of the New World (1970) 87

Directionscore (1971) 135

Book of Life **(1973)** **147**

Earthquakes and Sunrise Missions **(1984)** **199**

Heartlove: Wedding and Love Poems (1998) 347

Foreword

Houston A. Baker Jr.

Poetry entered my life in a Kentucky birthing room as my mother recited lyrics and ballads from English Bards to ease the pain of my first appearance. My mom never gave over reciting long stretches of verse from memory, and she spiced her classic British repertoire with Paul Laurence Dunbar, Langston Hughes, Baudelaire, and Villon. *Mais ou sont les neiges d'antan?*

How natural was it that in my early twenties when I entered graduate school I worked earnestly at English, French, and American poetry? I seemed almost destined to write my dissertation on the Aesthetic Movement in England. My advanced literary travels featured bold emphasis on poetry, from Chaucer to Eliot, Whitman to William Carlos Williams, the Pleiade to Rimbaud. But immediately after graduate study, a tectonic intellectual shift rattled my old certainties with redemptive grace. The shift occurred in three movements.

First, a group of brilliant Black graduate and professional students at Yale University snapped me out of my stupor of tweed jackets, expensive sherry, and Victorian literary isolationism. I allowed my hair to grow natural, donned dashikis, and began to dream different dreams.

Second, I received a publishing contract to compile an anthology of Black American Literature. Thus began my pursuit of texts derived from Middle-Passage-Americas and Plantation-to-Urban-Ghetto improvisational survival modes. I began to catch the breath and finer spirit of what was then called the "Black Experience."

Third, as part of my publishing contract I gained license and funds to travel to Manhattan for a week in order to access the resources of the old Schomburg Library, with its scratched yellow tables, hard chairs, and open windows in lieu of air conditioning. Mr. Earnest Kaiser, though quiet, was *the man* at the Schomburg; he was a Black Archive and resource with every breath. Sensing that I was in my Black Literature and Culture novitiate, he inquired: "Have you read the poetry of Don L. Lee?"

In late-afternoon sunlight of the Schomburg, I read *Think Black!*, *Black Pride*, and *Don't Cry, Scream.* Rhythms, chords, harmonies, and accents of Black Harlem floated in through open windows of the reading room as I experienced an epiphany. Reading Don L. Lee (who was already well on his way to reincarnation as Haki Madhubuti) completed my transition from an "old" — even a "new" — Negro to an emergent Black American Activist Scholar. The engaged voice of Haki endowed me with an expanded and revolutionary concept of *poetry*: its nature, function, rhythm, situation, and importance.

Haki's poetry stretched my conceptualization of and address to oppression and liberation, deprivation and desire, debilitating gender privilege and desperately abject ceremonies of survival. His work remains dedicated to social critique, honest and lyrical analyses of inequality, calls for commitment, tenderness, revolution, community, and love. Such nostrums anchor Haki's voice and compassion to a poetry fundamentally different in kind from classic English, American, and French repertoires. English, French, and American canons are often the only verse endorsed by literary critics and scholarly promulgators of so-called *universal* standards of poetic form and excellence. These self-fashioning "gate keepers" have sought to ignore or minimize Haki's indisputably formative role in creating space, techniques, audiences, and publishing venues for new forms of Black poetic articulation.

Haki's excellence as a poet is the *sui generis* literary correlate to his unique personal and social commitment to rigorous educational standards for the young, ending violence against women, and protesting genocidal conflicts that rage across our globe. Haki's poetry is a vessel and vehicle, an insistent, passionate call for social and redistributive justice. As poet, educator, and activist Haki has no leisure for or traffic with what might be termed a contemporary "poetry of decorum and anxious prizes" that passes itself off as "Black," or even more disingenuously, "post-black" creativity.

For a coterie of present-day Black academic critics and heady anthologists, the disastrous rupture of *politics* and *aesthetics* instituted by the West remains in play. They embrace this fissure in return for guaranteed cultural capital in mainstream media, and acclaim from dominantly white and useless "societies," "endowments," and "academies."

Haki's academy is, and has always been, *the streets.* In the streets, aesthetics and politics are irrevocably wed. Ancestral poets and prophets such as Du Bois, Woodson, Wells, Malcolm, and King have enjoined us that it is *only* from the streets and through our commitment to their well being and salvation that our redemption as a people will arise. In pages that follow ancient wisdom combines with promises of a better-resourced future for the Black Majority in poems that resonate with wisdom, hope, and love.

Houston Alfred Baker Jr. serves as a Distinguished University Professor at Vanderbilt University. His most recent book is *Betrayal: How Black Intellectuals Have Abandoned the Ideals of the Civil Rights Era.*

Preface
Art II: Reviewing A Life, A Calling

Among these senior words, this questioning and quieting narrative, art, and all its imperfections, contributed wonderfully to the defining history of my life. As a doer in this world, as a committed poet, political and cultural activist, educator, publisher, public intellectual, business man, husband, father, cultural father, word-organizer, editor, institution builder, protector of children and prostreet-fighter; I have swum in an ocean not of my making. After over sixty-seven years of an imperfected back stroke, I realize the many countless times I have been close to drowning, only to emerge stronger in part due to the thousands of special and not so special people I have encountered in this life, in this struggle.

I am here because of poetry. Poetry from all cultures in its multitudes of forms, laced with abundance—word-play, rhymes and unrhymes, metered, unmetered and off-metered, lines and stanzas defined and undefined, packed with knowledge, information, laughter and occasional wisdom. I am here because of a patched-quilt of voices that directed my younger life as I searched for all kinds of answers. Although I was surrounded by adults who could not manage their own lives, it was poetry and music that stopped me in my negative and ill directed tracks. Poetry and music slowly demanded that I change paths, contemplate the dangers before me with a limited understanding of the cultural forces that I was born into. These cultural forces were created to trap young people like myself, positioning in us a can't do philosophy that many carried into adulthood and for too many late eldership.

For me, reading and rereading and eventually studying the works of Wright, Hughes, Toomer, M. Walker, Brooks, Tolson, McKay, S. Brown, Bontemps, Fanon, Hayden, DuBois, Robeson, A. Locke, F.M. Davis, Cullen, Frazier, Woodson, Garvey, B.T. Washington, Davis and Dee, Dunbar, Douglass, Malcolm, H.W. Fuller, Baraka, Karenga and countless others in and outside of my culture confirmed in me that any people who control and define their own cultural and political imperatives and as a result of such intellectual influences should be about the healthy replication of themselves and the world they walk in. Implanting in me the recognition that without art in abundance there is little abundance.

During the absence of love and grits, during the years of bottomless lies, legal betrayals and enormous deaths, without the maintenance and nurturing of early spirits that art mandates, my life would have continued to evolve around reactions to: the alphabet of hourly timecards, fast walking urban street double-eyed locating identity in wearing labeled clothes, multicolored fingernails and pants below the crack of one's ass. Without wonder words, involved music, inviting visuals and flying feet children will drink sports, rapper's realities, mall hopping consumption, twenty-four hour cable surfing, all representing debilitating and limited information or knowledge needed to grow a superior intellect. Art activates the mind, drives the spirit and gives a unique definition to the participant and the receiver.

Yet, what continues to energize these overworked bones are children of all cultures who have—for the most part—not been captured by the many demons, daggers and multiple predators that populate this earth and the absolute necessity in me to listen to young people, their laughter, tears and loud silences continue to renew me.

But, quiet as it's kept, preceding all else, coming back to the stimulating juice that has fueled this life has been liberating language as poetry and ideas. Equal to poetry has been music and visual art all slapping saneness, Black perspective, a hunger for the unknown and a thousand questions into this yellow black boy, teenager, young man, mature drinker of knowledge, and elder confirming and affirming that art works.

To call oneself a poet or artist like that of the Black preacher, primary family doctor, veterinarian, farmer, or teacher of any branch of knowledge and to function at the highest order honoring one's choice is truly a calling. We are, indeed defined by our yesterdays, our here and now and tomorrows. To claim this calling finally acknowledges and accepts the little appreciated fact that we—the poets, musicians, fiction writers, visual artists, playwrights, wood and stone carvers, photographers, quilt makers, idea people, artists of all disciplines; the real lovers of civilization and the exceptional children that are formed by it—that we are here to stay. We have come to *change the conversation.*

Especially and lovingly in this era of the first Black president, which I, as many of my generation clearly thought impossible, it is time to acknowledge that artists and their art and the demand on progressive thinking/acting that all good art requires played a pivotal and decisive role in making possible the moving of the first African American family into the white house. And, representing the best commentary from the choicest and least of us we continue to influence and inspire our country's wholistic journey towards the inclusive ideas of liberation. And, yes, for most artists there is no retirement. The poems in *Liberation Narratives* represent my life—a poet's life who in the final words of those who care, "he has been around the block, several times." I'm ready for the next trip. Thank you!

Haki R. Madhubuti
2009

Introduction
The Poetry of Haki R. Madhubuti aka Don L. Lee

Regina Jennings

The poetry of Haki Madhubuti represents an epoch that radically changed the nature, art, and creative purpose for composing poetry. Constructed during the Black Arts/Aesthetic Movement, his poetry is a point of contrast for protest poetry from the Harlem Renaissance to the 1950s and it is an originator of contemporary spoken word and hip hop lyricism. The importance of his body of literature must not be understated, although some contemporary critics for curious reasons have attempted to do just that, which I will speak more on later. *Liberation Narratives,* Madhubuti's poetry from 1966 to 2009 still rings with the revolutionary/evolutionary potential begun during the Black Arts Movement of the 1960s and 1970s, and this continuity makes him reliable champion to his primary audience, Black people. His is the poetic voice that speaks for the repressed, the confused, and those stunned into subdued articulation based on the rigors of racism that have, since enslavement, diminished people of African descent. Like the oratory of Malcolm X, Madhubuti's poetry provides readers with a discussion and resolution for perplexing human issues that influence the psychology of Black people particularly in America. This is his credo in 1968:

> I
> seek
> integration
> of
> negroes
> with
> black
> people (*GroundWork,* 21)

How his poetry and that of the Black Arts Movement changed forever the nature of African-American artistry has more to do with its purpose: to stimulate a deconstruction of American injustices concerning those once misnamed Negro. Madhubuti's poetry like his name change from Don L. Lee to Haki R. Madhubuti was to deliberately supply instructions for a people in a stage of becoming self and race determined climbing from Negro to Black to African-American. Rooted in the ideology of Malcolm X, Marcus Garvey, W.E.B. Du Bois, Richard Wright, and Paul Robeson, this poetry vibrates with ancient Kemetic (Egyptian) propensity. Because early African writing is instructional, that topology begins the tradition of art with a purpose. Madhubuti's mentor Gwendolyn Brooks, the first African-American to receive a Pulitzer for poetry assisted in how he shaped the poignancy of English. This reciprocal relationship helped bring Gwendolyn Brooks to neo-Blackness that had already fired up his literary world, a world different from her 1950 "Negro" portraitures. His purposeful and pointed poetry from *Think Black* (1966) to *Run Toward Fear* (2004) not only holds up a mirror to Black people, but also brings useful transforming methods to shape shift any disturbing reflection.

BLACK	PEOPLE	THINK
PEOPLE	BLACK	PEOPLE
THINK	PEOPLE	THINK
BLACK	PEOPLE	THINK—
THINK	BLACK.	

(*GroundWork*, 17) (1966)

Redefining the meaning and image of "Black," he urged a redefinition of the self. Yet in this small poem titled "Awareness" composed of three words in a juggle of juxtapositions when carefully read the term "Think" is most used. Initially, because of its power "Black" shocks and consumes the imagination; however, Don L. Lee/Haki Madhubuti exhorts his readers and listeners to delve more into productive thought.

In his own thought, to specify his perspectives in art, he separated the genders before such divisions were instituted in academia, i.e. women's studies, Black women's studies. Regularly, without apology, he wrote poems to "brothers" and to "sisters," and in this categorizing he signaled two things: gender particularity for empowerment and once empowered the outreach to progress the family, community, society, and the world. By projecting African-American modes of thought, Madhubuti urged transformation in both people and society. In "Afrikan Men" he writes:

there is a certain steel-ness about you
the way u set the vision & keep it
the way u view the world & warn us.
the coming tomorrows the limited memory of what was
the image the reflection the realness of what is to be.

(*GroundWork*, 141) (1973)

In the above controlling image, he captures an admirable "realness" in men destined to carve a desired direction in leadership. The poet picks up and presents sober energies and masculine tendencies that he appreciates because the subjects are predictors of "coming tomorrows." They are purposeful to the community. In the next poem, "You Will Recognize Your Brothers," through his mastery of alliteration and repetition, he replicates this desire for intentional, authoritative maleness. Starting with the visual, he shapes the point of view of others in search of masculinity on the move.

You will recognize your brothers
by the way they act and move throughout the world.
there will be a strange force about them,
there will be unspoken answers in them.
this will be obvious not only to you but to many.
the confidence they have in themselves and in
their people will be evident in their quiet saneness.
the way they relate to women will be
clean, complimentary, responsible, with honesty and as
partners.

(*GroundWork*, 179) (1973)

The repetitive "will be" speaks the future into the present while honoring the now. Additionally, this instructional poem idealizes character traits for imitation and proliferation. His portrayal of women is in opposition to the defamation Black women find today in some contemporary rap. From a poetry series following an essay poem entitled "Women Black: Why These Poems," he writes:

woman black
I have tried to write about you
words
in a language strange & not of our making
words
refreshingly new
clean, lively, honest, & uncomplicatedly indepth
words
forging & fighting their way into meaning
knowing too that
words
are like people are like you
woman black
& if left to simple interpretation
could be twisted, misused & misunderstood.
I will write about you with loving care
my woman

(*GroundWork*, 197) (1984)

The "my woman" in this poem is every woman Black. Our legacy is in his heart and creativity, as he handles us with care, modifying the myth of the Black male female angst.

The enlargement and unification of Love like other themes is a weapon in the 1960's paradigm of poetry. That model designates the personal/political, designed to destroy centuries old institutions of unfairness, which had energized a deformed psychology of Black thought (and behavior)—Thus the unique, double-mouthed poetry of Haki Madhubuti that maintains the propulsion of yesterday and the Black Diaspora of today. Where many are seeking inclusion and non-ethnic visions and values, Madhubuti still speaks fluently and urgently the fire of the 1960s malcolmian ethic. In his poetic point of view, in the particular, he unearths the universal. Let's look closely at *HeartLove* (1998), where Madhubuti portrays a variety of amorous themes, specific to Black people, appreciated by everyone.

The major poet, Robert Bly refers to *HeartLove* as "elegant," with "some of the finest human poems in English." His use of "human" implies that he, a poet, non-Black, finds connection and value with the word pictures in *HeartLove.* Obviously, Madhubuti emotionally touched him, because Bly even cites his favorites. Lucille Clifton insists that *HeartLove* is a "necessary book" with poems that celebrate "our long history of loving and being loved." Like all great poets, Madhubuti writes descriptively about life as he experiences and views it. In the section, "Extended Families," "Rwanda: Where Tears Have No Power" appears, paralleling the lives of young males in Washington D.C. and in Rwanda. Here's a portion:

> across the planet in a land where civilization was born
> the boys of d.c. know nothing about their distant relatives
> in rwanda. they have never heard of the hutu or tutsi people.
> their eyes draw blanks at the mention of kigali, byumba
> or butare. all they know are the streets of d.c., and do not
> cry at funerals anymore. numbers and frequency have a way
> of making murder commonplace and not news (83)

From the 1960s Malcolm X spread the news of the cultural and biological link between Africans on the continent and those in the Americas. He called for the study and celebration of that connection in the collective mind of the then Negro people. Madhubuti heard him and in his first book *Think Black* (1966) he wrote about that African kinship relationship. In the above poem, written thirty-one years later, he again joins the American African to his continental counterpart. In this book about love, he portrays the decapitated history of American youth along with the contemporary murders of young males by young males. This global poem offers the results of the lack of love crafted by the designers of societies in Africa and America. This poem, structured in the contemporary conversational pattern with concise enjambment highlights the inhumanity of today and the readers' indifference outside of the lyrics. It is a well-honed indictment forcing all to consider how to stop the slaughter.

> modern massacres are intraethnic, bosnia, sri lanka, burundi,
> nagorno-karabakh, iraq, laos, angola, liberia, and rwanda are
> small foreign names on a map made in europe.

Broadening the idea from his personal international community and racial site to the ugly truth of international, contemporary slaughters, he bespeaks the spread of inhumanity. Yet, the courageous difference that marks Haki Madhubuti is that he "names the names." He mentions "europe." They are the makers of the new and old divide that assisted the many splits throughout the world. It is this truthful reminder that I believe causes this isolation in academia. It is this malcolmian penchant, search, and saying the most obvious that literally causes caution and fear about issuing his work. For example, Arnold Rampersad, the distinguished scholar, known for his outstanding biographies on Langston Hughes and currently Ralph Ellison, edited *The Oxford Anthology of African-American Poetry* (2006) and omitted the poetry of Haki Madhubuti. Madhubuti is mentioned in the introduction, in particular his book *Don't Cry, Scream* a best seller, but none of his poetry is included in the text itself. On the front cover, Henry Louis Gates, another esteemed scholar, writes that the anthology is a "definitive volume that captures in verse the history of African American life and culture." He goes on to say that the text is a "landmark publication for African American literature and a major contribution to American culture as a whole." Other key figures of the Black Arts Movement are visible in the volume, Amiri Baraka, Sonia Sanchez, Nikki Giovanni, and some of Madhubuti's students such as E. Etherbert Miller. None have published more than Haki Madhubuti although each is a fine poet. However to publish folk such as those mentioned and not to publish Madhubuti raises the concern of being erased from history. This is an egregious oversight, which is being questioned. Subtracting the poetry of Haki Madhubuti from this important source weakens the validity of the words of Henry Louis Gates because it disappears a powerful wordsmith and force in American letters. This subtraction attempts in my view to reinvent literary history for reasons I fail to understand. Madhubuti has eleven poetry books, actually more than eleven because even in his nine books of nonfiction, he includes poetry. Plus, his nonfiction text, *Black Men Obsolete, Single and Dangerous?* sold over a million copies. This man is a major American writer, an architect of the Black Aesthetic Movement. Yet, I continue to see Amiri Baraka, Sonia Sanchez and other creators of the Black Aesthetic Movement in tomes on Black literary figures, but not Haki. Take Henry Louis Gates' *Africana* (1999). In this highly anticipated and important resource, meant to finish the project started decades earlier by Du Bois, Gates and Kwame Appiah list Baraka, Sanchez, and Nikki Giovanni, but not Haki. Likewise, in the textbook, *Grace Abounding: Core Knowledge Anthology of African-American, Literature, Music, and Art* (2006), the editor Robert D. Shepherd published Baraka, Giovanni, Sanchez, Mari Evans yet no Haki Madhubuti! The others are published under the section "Civil Rights and Beyond" and no Haki Madhubuti, an independent Black male, poet, essayist, and publisher since 1966. Something don't smell right.

I have been teaching poetry since the 1990s, and my students absolutely adore the work of Haki Madhubuti. Normally, they have never heard of him and are surprised at the size of his literary corpus. Those who do know him discuss a heightened admiration beyond his poetry. They admire his public stance with language, and his building institutions—Third World Press, several charter schools—that benefit Blacks. My White, Asian, and intemational students consider him a hero.

His exclusion from literary texts is gate keeping, which is as nonproductive as the riff between Booker T. Washington and W.E. B. Du Bois, W.E.B. Du Bois and Marcus Garvey.

On another note, Gwendolyn Brooks included Haki Madhubuti when writing introductions to literary texts since 1972. At that time, in the anthology, *The Poetry of Black America,* edited by Arnold Arnoff, Brooks writes that she expected to find the poetry of Haki Madhubuti in that tome. She herself had heightened Madhubuti' s personal and poetic education, and he has written many tributary verses to her. She in a real sense allowed this motherless and fatherless young man to experience parental love again. His poem "Eighty Three is a Wise Number" showcases his poetic caring for a woman who enriched his life. He writes:

> The weather does not age, it
> changes
> bringing peach and hurricane,
> water
> and sun for planting, walking
> and smiles
> extending people to long life,
> maybe.
> I've grown up in your magic,
> shadows and words,
> I've seen you manage pens,
> papers, poor eyesight and gift
> giving.
> I've measured the recent dip in
> your walk,
> noting the way the wind leans
> you into its current
> and I worry.
>
> (*Run Toward Fear,* 33)

I believe Gwendolyn Brooks felt his "worry" and his guiding hand before she left the earth. I have been in her company and simply mentioned Haki's name, and her face became a smile. Clearly, he was her other sun. This warm glow extends in "Remembering Betty Shabazz," where he continues to venerate women while honoring and comparing himself to one of his heroes, Malcolm X:

i, a poet, a weaver of life, an unfinished soul in motion still
a closet dancer who greyhounded between
detroit and chicago
on the same roads
that Malcolm Little, Malcolm X, El Hajj Malik El Shabazz
traveled the identical highways
that Betty, Betty Shabazz, Dr. Betty Shabazz questioned still
i, a poet, an observer of life, met Betty,
giver and nurturer of black winds and earth,
airborne at 33,000 feet over pennsylvania in the year of 75

i, a poet, whose voice was confirmed, layered & enlarged
after hearing
a "young shining prince," before we knew
we had the sons of kings and queens among us whispering
African truths that gutted the whiteness in our bellies & minds

. . . .

i met a woman not a victim,

i met a sister not a tragedy

i met a warrior-teacher, not a professional widow,

(*Run Toward Fear*, 22-23)

Haki Madhubuti a "warrior-teacher" himself still holds up a mirror to Black people where we view our particular yet universal reflections. He, a major poet, highlights our existence and our history suggesting and presenting what we, and he, deem significant. He is a people's poet in the most humane and inclusive notion of the term; his words the metaphysical/physical of life. They are awareness in utterances.

The multiplicity alive in African-American discourse should be honored and duplicated so that the range of readers can enhance sensitivity and aesthetics through variations. Art appeals to people for contrasting reasons and some cannot appreciate art when they cannot visualize themselves within the creative production. Additionally, and more importantly, in order to fully explore the entire human condition, all voices deserve audibility.

An independent Black male voice that without precedent opened outlets for justified American rage is most needed in these perilous times where young Black males are killing one another in lyrics and in life. These males are sons, husbands, lovers, cousins, uncles, friends, brothers; thus, a vital part of the human family. They need to know a male poet who is hard, heroic, soft, courageous, and brilliant, one who found a number of avenues that allowed his/their particular expression to river and ocean. More than a poet, Haki Madhubuti is, but he is a poet. In his vision one finds unity, presenting us as multiples of the same essence.

I celebrate the forty-plus years of Third World Press, the institution that Haki Madhubuti built in order to publish during the 1960s his work and others who aimed words at racism and Black autonomy. I celebrate his being here, older, younger, wiser, more innocent singing the same and different pulsating songs that echo the sensations of the 1960s and 1970s.

Regina Jennings is the author of *Midnight Morning Musings, Malcolm X and the Poetics of Haki Madhubuti* and *Race, Rage and Roses.*

LIBERATION NARRATIVES

Liberation Narratives (2009)

The Last First

not the first heavyweight champion of the world,
airline pilot, quarterback in the NFL, college graduate,
doctor, teacher, big league baseball player, preacher-pastor,
ceo, mountain climber, university president, entrepreneur,
heart surgeon, inventor, governor or poet.
not the first mathematician, physicist, engineer, supreme court justice,
fastest man alive, publisher, reporter, ambassador, entertainer,
four-star general, best-selling author, executive chef, sergeant major,
scientist, basketball hall-of-famer, economist, secretary of state,
nobel prize winner, astronaut, law enforcer, chair of the joint chiefs,
senator, first responder or state legislator.
not the best trumpet player alive, bank president, husband, father,
organic farmer, rapper's rapper or coach's coach.
not an undefined question looking for an answer or
hidden agenda claiming the authority of one.
not an exploiter of the commons.
is the green hands nurturing fields, crops and rain forests.
is the water, food, education, clean energy, preventive health
and intellect required.
is the humanitarian connecting music and economy, writing political
notes
legible to professionals, novices, students and elders the world over.
is the community organizer maneuvering citizens' campaigns
expecting to implant knowledge, consent and saneness on
impracticability
as renegade* and renaissance* expand the *can* in *we* and *yes*
at the early-light of this promising century
not the last, is the first
barack hussein obama, president.

*Secret Service code names for President-Elect Obama and Mrs. Obama

Studs
(1918–2008)

as in metal,
confirmed loyalties and Farrell's *Lonigan*,
now, in the grandfather of your vision and giving
you have always understood the dominions of
words, money, privilege and organic liars.

you among the uncomfortable few,
an urban-tracker questioning influence and sovereignty,
questioning Texas spin, image and lineage,
used a worker's language to expose
the arrogance of the ultra-knowing wannabes
facing fear with your large heart
attached to the center of the people,
who are the colors of the planet
somewhat like southern quilts
the poor & poorer   landless   ownershipless
borderless tomato growers, green bean pickers,
indigenous fixers of anything with a motor,
hard workers of the muscular genre,
laborers, after 10-hour days 6 day weeks
tolling for people who do not like them,
also known as the working classes,
still able to smile as they will the best for their children and others
always seeking solutions without resources or library cards.
as obscenely paid lobbyist and economic hitmen
extend Washington's K Street on to the capitals &
side roads of Mississippi, the Sudan, Utah & Iraq
by-passing the culture of comprehension, caring & birth
in concert with the nation's healthcare for the rich, connected &
self-serving politicians who spit clichés
more numerous than hyper-producing roaches,
while legislating the work of mercenaries into law.

you taught us to hunt cleanly and carefully
the opposite of televised preachers whose
lies are honeyed metaphors
wide-netting the uninitiated hungry
looking for a home, answers and the truth

reading you is illumination & battle call
is flagless commitment to clean fire,
nutritious bread and comfort to the least of us.
it is not a paradox that children love you,
unlike bankers and agribusiness
you invest in co-ops, complex possibilities & dreams.

we grow observing the sun and language in your smile
the midnight musical moon that you ride,
the blues of your ideas & warnings
the manuscript from the opening of your hands
cupping the trumpet of your recognized voice

you the red shirted, boldly clear,
Robeson supporter & learned messenger   we
widely acknowledged that your children's children
populate the green fields, roads & spaces of the long marchers,
we are joyful that this is not an elegy or obituary.

your being among us is the rare, ripe, swinging musical
and we, the chorus, are still taking lessons, breaking only
to say thank you.

For Studs Terkel
October 31, 2008

Alice

she was birthed from light earth
a blend of mango and pineapple juices
anchoring a smile that could stop broadway.
i lived on the chicago and atlanta streets she frequented,
in and from a family not believing in family,
of pretty men and beautiful women with children
destined for great pain, disappointments and revelation,
most unable to discourse on culture, coltrane or bearden.

she inhibited memories and hunger with a
heart of a doll maker who could sew
always claiming possibilities without sound-bites.
her children were her mantra, imagination and journey,
they would do what it was too late for her to do.

she was born in the in-between times
like apartheid and brown v. board of education,
in between
black people not fully defined,
in between
south, down south, and up south,
in between
too pretty, too young and angry black men
despising themselves, the girl-women they caught
and the world that caught them.

but the girl could sew,
like sewing "don't ride" on the ass of a raging bull
or butterflies onto paper kites in flight.
too innocent to abuse others
she carried her scars privately with that smile
did I tell you, she loved reading, doll-making and
the colors purple, yellow and possibilities
stating quietly "don't forget me, now."

(For Alice Rochon, 1941-2009)

To the Graduates

dream no more about homework, after work or no work,
speak no more of the ineptitude of mumbling professors
captured by self-spin
it is now that you pave your own road,
forge your own steel-strength,
lay claim to the weight of your own ideas.
enter this century with conscience, smiles, and covenant,
with able melody, will and after words of why not?
prepare for penetrating confrontations and failures
expect rumors, falsehoods and fractured memories
all preceding wondrous expeditions
planting in you hope, heart, joy, love & unused questions

where do you belong?
i say chosen weather,
in best fields of cabbage and carrots,
in the breast of the first loved,
in the quiet contemplation of yes & yes,
in the accepted force of a learned & fighting history.
reach clearly, carefully and completely for the origin of
a challenged life of accomplished days & deeds
whistling merrily of possibilities & the acknowledgement
of laughing children.

for you, the hurried graduate
seeking hard fought considerations
of an uncertain road map,
an off course compass and culture
be mindful of ivory rat holes,
colored betrayals, rapid tongues in un-chartered terrain.
remain watchful of the palms of strangers.
smiling rulers in penthouses & gutters
are poised to redirect your dreams.
arrive battle ready and serious
wishing lately that you had not
slept through the lectures of mumbling professors.

(for Chicago State University Graduates and MFA class of 2005)

Thoughts on Bushism

1.
ignorant people
talking about how ignorant
other people are
reminds me of richard nixon, ronald reagan and
george w bush, in between their wars and
tax cuts to their friends,
eagerly initiating serious conversations
with their dogs.

2.
students in an advanced high school history class
upon viewing president george w. bush's
exit-press-conference asked their teacher:
does the president have a g.e.d. or
is he permanently stuck on stupid?

3.
people don't attack you
because
they don't like your
way of life
attacks come because you've
played a major, murderous role in
disrupting their
way of life.

4.
I am the decider,
Jesus Christ is my philosopher
we are a peaceful nation among nations
war on terrorism
I am a wartime president
evil, eviler, make them un-evil
democracy, freedom and justice is what they hate,
with us or with the terrorist
things evil men do
they don't like our freedoms,
we are fighting evil persons, evil doers, inventors of evil
we are a peaceful nation among nations
we are innocent, the American way is what they hate
God bless America
peace.

Now close your eyes and locate your brain
repeat each of the above words or phrases a 1000 times
borrow a dictionary
then look up the following in this order:
deliberate,
liar,
"f" minus
president.

Against the Grain

Do you remember what you were doing
the day that John F. Kennedy was shot?
Yes!
I was making love to the finest Black woman
in Little Rock, Arkansas.
I momentarily paused, as the
news interrupted quiet jazz
for the announcement—to cut the
radio off—and
I continued making love to the finest Black woman in
Little Rock, Arkansas.

America killing its own was not news or revealing,
It was business as usual.

Losing Honor

with misplaced masculinity, you claim the righteousness of your office,
with an "it is mine" addictive attitude, president for life and some
uttered as moral certainty. As the bones of Zimbabwe's children
dance hungrily against the sun, food exceeds the cost of wind
and ignorance is unblemished, rewarded, sought and praised.
history is reduced to the present not unlike the u.s. government's
lawyers, ceos, officers and cabinet members suffering failed memories
at testimony before congressional hearings on Iraq and the economy.
thousands of miles as the butterfly journeys enlightened governance
has given way to the patriarchy of "freedom fighters" and "glory days"
reinventing the tradition of
attributing to whites the debt and death of the nation,
for troubling weather, non functioning farms, diseased water, cholera,
million dollar loaves of bread and wheels that do not turn.
guns and nonsense are issued to old men and
babies without debate or reason.
as the world questions, the fathers of the nation raise their fist
again defying debate, reason and elections.
a generation of children and grandchildren are disenfranchised and
reduced to the bones of Zimbabwe,
too hungry to dream or study,
too fearful to speak or cry,
too angry to forget or forgive,
forcing the hopeful young,
the sorrowful few,
the parentless many to the streets
to train and reemerge as twenty-first century warriors
to confront and neutralize fathers
hell-bent on killing a nation.

(for Robert Mugabe)

Jews: A People and a Culture

religion, the one god concept. *medicine,* from their heart to ours. *law,* justice from the people of the book. practicing and teaching due process and equality. *journalism,* all the news that's fit to print. *tikkun,* to heal to repair, to make whole. *commentary,* never again, cultural literacy, defining and definite. *art,* in each decade multiple geniuses. *books,* as reader's readers and writer's writers. *science,* in all branches growing new leaves. *innovation,* refuse to stand still in new thinking, business, polling, advanced thought, original to the bone. *education,* indigenous to life and living, international knowledge distributors, importance and influence unmatched in the world, dominant in higher education. *literature,* reshaped modern forms in fiction, poetry, playwriting and literary nonfiction, creating new literary forms. *economics,* essential thinkers in capitalism, socialism, marxism, free markets and others. *money,* made, lost and remade to take care of their own people and others. *politics,* both sides of the question, the middle, and uniquely independent. *survivalists,* from the ashes of europe, to the creation of israel (1948), to the diaspora, as one people. *diplomacy,* reshaping policy and double watching the world. *agriculture,* made the desert bloom. *physics,* the law of relativity is only the beginning. *radio,* understood its potential before others. *film,* hollywood and the world dominated popular culture and popular thought. *television,* changed the landscape on both sides of the camera. *publishing* (books), little competition, percentage of writers per its small population is off the charts. *lobbyists,* for their numbers the most effective and strongest on the planet. *music,* classical, popular broadway show tunes, jazz, production—front office and as musicians and critics. *poverty* fought their way from penny to penny, from dime to dime into the middle class and redefined wealth. *human rights,* are the first to challenge inequities and respond unselfishly and effectively to their needs and that of others. *theater,* broadway, regional and university departments. *institutions,* sacred and secular at all levels of human need, most effective in defining and overseeing the survival and advancement of their own culture. *food,* made us all healthier. *finance,* great influence on all that is good and bad, percentage of billionaires and millionaires far eclipse the number in other cultures. *greed,* will give all peoples serious competition. *humanitarians,* first of the first in line worldwide. *technology,* one reason their influence far exceeds their numbers. *military,* recent experts. *sports,* as owners and promoters, uniquely understand the power of its draw. *entrepreneurship,* essential players in the initial public offerings of the last and future century. *environment,* key thinkers and theory makers. *internet, facebook, itunes, and twitter,* on the ground floor. *history,* writing theirs and everybody else's. *architecture,* lighting up cities the world over. *dreamers,* living peacefully and

productively with most peoples, notable exceptions are palestinians and other arabs. *culture,* game changers, human progressive values, great expectations, making bright tomorrows and finding new ways of life by studying the past, present and future, contributors to identity, language and the way you do what you do. *psychology,* foundational, made the first moves in the study of the mind. *justice,* a people who continually and publicly question the actions or non-actions of its own people and purposely move to correct that which is incorrect, wrong, or unjust, consumed by searching and following the right path, moral mentors. *union movement,* initiators and leadership, people and labor first, worldwide, worker's advocate, first in line for human rights. *law enforcement,* as lawyers, judges and proponents of legal aid, legal watchdogs, at the intersection of law and justice for the least of us, forever thinking about and questioning the entire legal profession. *nationalism,* serious to the core about the ongoing, continuous development and influence of their people on international stages worldwide, a people within a people with no apologies. *israel,* 1949 international border, the green line has little meaning today, the palestinians define the founding of israel as the nakbeh: the disaster, two state talks after over fifty years is in serious doubt; *the wall* is the latest transgression; internationally 24/7 fighting nazi-holocaust denials, good will, honest will by all needed immediately. *jerusalem,* muslim, jewish, christian? what about the *occupation,* another sixty years? *philosophy,* idea makers, reason walkers, original thinkers and questioners, most are not zionist. *aspiration,* to be better than the last generation in carving a better world out of difficulty. *scholarship,* honey on the book, reading is like eating, breathing new ideas to a world often stuck on stop, is food for the soul and intellect. *political science,* have helped to make presidents, closely studies the potential maps of the world, constantly. *talent,* would take on all challenges in all areas of creativity. *social science,* urban studies, city planning bringing clean water to the thirsty and much more. *fashion,* odds are you are wearing their designer shoes, clothes, hats, underwear and makeup, influential in dressing the west. f*act,* the closest and most supportive white people to black people in america. *fact,* by any honest and critical measurement for their number, truly a phenomenal people. let's see, there are approximately sixteen million jews in a world of seven billion plus people, making jews less than one percent of the worlds' population. the majority of jewish people hopefully and passionately are in love with justice, fairness and the investigation of ideas from all cultures. they are the quiet and loud engines driving key areas of
civilization.

remind me one more time why does anti-semitism exist?
what would the world do without jews?

Greed is Not Enough: Affinity Theft

you don't need a gun to rob the people.
being white, male, middle-aged with
salt and pepper or little hair opens the first door.
networking family and strangers, glad handing
at private clubs, banks, investment houses, law firms,
golf outings, poker games, real estate establishments and
political circles to familiarize your face
with the pay-to-play crowd gives unquestioned entry.

you don't need a gun to rob the public.
wear the right suits, ties and women,
nurture a kind and believable grandfatherly smile
that is perfected the more you lie about money.

you don't need violence.
you need hubris, politicians, judges, effective p.r.,
"master of the universe" insider information and
stone eyes, heart and a tradition of "show me the money."
an m.b.a. from a research-one university
signatured by "greed is not enough" culture cements
your "smartest guy in the room" credentials
who's rap can open pocketbooks, empty wallets,
wrestle direct deposits from the gilded rich,
bilk widows who think like five-year-olds and
charm pension fund managers as you display supreme confidence
while lobbying constantly for favorable legislation from
politicians not expected to read a triple-spaced three-page proposal.

you don't need a gun to rob the arrogant economically ignorant,
just official looking data, hyper inflated numbers, right connections,
location, location, location with stone eyes and heart
forever highlighting that killer-kind and believable smile
that will take your trust and rape it.

(for Bernard Madoff and others)

Art: A Comment

the summer & winter beauty
or a people's culture rides
heroically in their arts.
study human creation for the secrets to
killers & saints,
fools & wise speakers.
search their music for heartbeat,
their drama for recall and tomorrows,
their literature for will and vision,
their visualforms for uncluttered love and
mountains.
the art makers
those tenacious forgers of truth
are hungry for your smile,
they know in america that plastics & soaps are in,
that the cry is sameness in the skyscrapers and
the captive form is to defeat flowers
& strap concrete to ideas
while pursuing relationships that would
embarrass babies.
among the new and few
it is accepted that art exposes
rats in the crib,
clowns in the temple,
idiots in the congress,
rot in the wheat.
art provides the beat the tellin heat, the ellington
bounce
wright's anger, brooks' hook, dunham's glide, the
feelings' feel & field.
the rounded calling cards
washing change in the city,
fightin suffocation & money looking for investments
are
visionaries claiming elegant & ugly.

artist
do not seek immortality
seek ears & eyes minds & conformation
seek smiles in the young change in the motion
& are aware of harm in daylight and of nations
planning cross cultural trips to africa
while simultaneously implanting your image on
postage stamps.

(Remembering Murry DePillars and Jeff Donaldson
and for the continued work of Bing Davis, Jon Lockard,
Akili Anderson, Floyd Coleman
and the National Conference of Artists)

Too Late the Truth

who quieted the fourth estate,
took words, images and liberating ideas
from the recently blind and stole the nation?

why was there not a storm among us
confronting the wealth of ignorance?
what is the price of deceptive and enriched silence?

who compromised the music of truth,
the poetry of deep thought?
what of the carpentry of inner peace and community?

the people are not derivatives,
know little of hedge funds, credit default swaps
or greed passing as compassionate investing.

it is the cowards of all professions
who sell their children's and elders' futures
for the fairy tale of quick unearned money.

we have witnessed superior failure,
eight years of the lowest mediocre denominator,
passing as expertise, proving again

it's much easier to believe than think.

Recession Proof Sex

the unheard screams
in the missing uneasy lives of the
unprotected innocents imported from china, europe,
russia, africa, india, the americas and cracks in between,
ever growing numbers of not yet teenagers,
clean girls, smiling sisters and daughters with inadequate fathers and
brothers,
crippled mothers, families and hollow governments to nurture their
tomorrows.
they fuel the oldest recession proof profession in the world;
claiming the young and youngest with failed promises and
quick lies spoken, written, read and rewritten by men
in the service of men as history denies the victims their own
stories, memories or horror voices guaranteeing that
misogyny remains the language of commerce.
that keeps the enslaved ignorant, beautiful, drugged and submissive.
sold and traded on an under/over ground world market
to men demanding profit, pleasure and "immortality"
by way of the vaginas of virgins.
the muted cries, the waterfall screams disappear
under the weight and rape of youth being stolen, defiled and brain damaged.

most innocents do not have sex as an act of love or pleasure;
they sex to procreate,
they sex to survive,
they sex to eat,
they sex to protect their children,
they sex to pay their father's and husband's debts,
they sex to better their lives,
they sex for pennies or less,
they sex to join families and tribes together,
they sex as expression of love expecting love,
they sex as an act of work,
they sex to maintain families,
they sex to keep men,
they sex to satisfy the lust of men,
they sex to question and answer,
they sex for education, promotion, and for others,
they sex for passports, green cards and visas
they sex for protection,

they sex as an act of religious obligation in the service
   of the pathological patriarch.
girls becoming women learn liberation on the streets of brutality
snatching knowledge, information, running routes and
modern underground railroads from the mouths of
customers, johns, tricks, coworkers, new friends and husbands.
most seeking good dreams, love and personal selection
quietly and systematically many plan to steal away into the night to
painfully make a life as goes the songs of billie holiday
somewhere, one day, finding my own way.

The Secret of His Success

barack obama is the holder
of the keys to the white house
the one in washington on pennsylvania avenue
that represents the nation that his people built.
be they un-credited, relegated to back doors,
kitchens, wine cellars and after dark clean-up duty
performed in physical and mental chains carefully chanting
"yes sir, boss" with a grin and heads bowed, yet unbeaten.

today, there is a Black man with
keys to the front door of the white house.
living there with a Black woman who
stopped his young, searching heart,
helped to unlock his history, heritage and religion
gave him two daughters, a brother and
a live-in mother, all darker than he is.

barack obama
birthed by a free euro-american from kansas
and a liberated african from kenya
is teaching his daughters the first lessons
that earned him the keys to the white house:
he stretched and amplified his persistent mind, traveled
found his calling, voice and his people,
designed a path, purpose and excelled in claiming other cultures
and never, I say never,
learned the acts of niggerization
or accepted victimhood.

you know, you know: thoughts from the 47th street poet who never reads books for fear of being influenced by others

quiet as its kept, he/she is you know
a visionary. always thinking outside the box,
define box. it is what it is, 24/7.
what goes around comes around,
it goes without saying, its not over until the fat lady sings
what's going on? is you is or is you ain't my baby? you know
I could care less and more about the
foreseeable future, fixed with no brainers, you know
actually freaked out by the skin of your teeth
be they false. I feel your pain, can't teach an old dog new tricks,
that idea has legs, it must belong to someone else
you know
let's not reinvent the wheel or count your blessings or
chickens before they hatch, acknowledging that
Rome wasn't built in a day, yet we still create lies to
make a mountain out of a molehill and thus become
our own worst enemy without   you know
a skill set, unable to play hardball, never
on the same page

is the reason we had to
downsize, downtime looking at all times towards the
big picture to add value for the head office you know
to become more efficient in formulating
the bottom line and protecting the golden haired ceo you know
who is good at directing whose heads should roll
never his own unless the human resource department
grows some balls and states categorically that
we are going to have to let you go, where?
you know
so far so good.

just say no' to what?   you know
bad language that puts me
on the edge of my seat while
looking for a needle in a haystack,
understanding that it's not exactly rocket science
of epic proportions that you put your two cents
in attempting to become a team player   you know
not fully comprehending that poetry writing is not a group sport
it requires individual initiative

you know
icing on the cake
like in the serious study of the canon
the one that stops the shooting off of your mouth
it is a great investment, not in money to give back
back to the drawing board to add value
by rediscovering libraries and books
without pictures with lines, stanzas, similes and metaphors
that contain ideas and word magic

you know if it ain't broke, don't fix it
all things considered and times and also by morning edition
working and reading hard or hardly working at reading
hopefully with brains to understand about what good   you know
poetry is and can be or aid you in becoming the big picture and
extraordinary poet that you think you bees' that is?
remember, where there's smoke, there's fire
watch me now!   you know.

Gwendolyn Brooks: No Final Words

somewhere between brilliant and genius,
in the neighborhood of great and unforgettable,
as unique wordgiver and kind heart,
she emerged as our able witness and deep participant
in a time of unwellness and deep need.
refusing to tap dance with the garbage men of rulership,
corporate acceptance or literary sainthood,
she deciphered the multiple layers of accommodation
that often trap the best of us.
she refused first class passage and caviar.
she sidestepped isolation, re-enslavement and tell-lies culture.
she remained attached to her language, her people and all children.
she was our kindness.
there will be no final words.

Liberation Narratives

I.
it may be
a man's world   yet
it's women who write music
who navigate the harmony, who
grow children, drive learning,
prepare knives for the cutting of green beans & lies
while dodging genocide & rape
as men
who run the world
bathe in the power of extreme illusion
over-use collateral-damage &
deficit language to justify
it's a man's world.

II.
best advice to men
marry women smarter than you!
occasionally let them know it.

III.
my mother was
prettier than imagination soaked in
honey flavored with
hot water and lemon,
her heart was there too.

she was a short poem.

dead at 34, buried without flowers
notation or truthful stories.
she challenged men walking on her life like
she was a used treadmill years
before they were invented.
I have her eyes,
I see damage everywhere,
I have become a stop sign.

IV.
janet liked girls
and told them so,
robert liked boys
and kept it a secret.
both grew into teenagers
still liking girls,
still liking boys.
each kept their desires to themselves.
in the 21st century parts of the world
began to mature and finally
understood why
janet loved women
and
robert loved men.
they were born that way,
enough said.

V.
if poetry is to have meaning
it must mean something,
more than metaphor and simile,
more than tree-talk & looking for gigs,
more than competition in unrhymed free verse
serious to the bone of incomprehension
surely to land the poet
a guggenheim or mac arthur genius grant.
artists should not expect from readers,
listeners and observers fairness, objectivity or
deep knowledge of word-play or
interpreted ideas of paint or jumping notes.
often a smile will do, and yes
to buy and share books, visuals and music will help.
saying yes to children may get you into heaven,
saying no to war builds character and conscious,
giving ten percent of what you earn to the homeless
will aid in your sleeping a full night
hopefully to awake creating healthier
poems, prose, pictures &
critical perceptions of the
potential of the letter p beyond politics,
potholes, profiteers, poverty, pimp juice, patriots,
protestants and playboys of the western world.

VI.
if you don't know
who you are,
anybody can
name you.

VII.
if the world loses elephants,
dolphins, polar bears, frogs, trees,
the ability of the majority to do good,
clean water, prayer & meditation in all languages,
if the world loses love across borders,
honest vegans & vegetarians
a mother's love, a father's caring,
children dancing to knowledge & colors,
artists not lying for money, privilege or fame,
if the world loses books, newspapers,
clear thinkers, practical doers, poets,
promising futures for the great majority, rainforests,
a world vocabulary that accents yes & possibilities
rather than no and you can't do that,
if the world loses the great apes, schools,
giraffes, salmon, the coral reefs, insects,
worms, organic farmers, compost, green tea,
workers who use their hands
to build & repair stuff, north and south poles,
teachers, people of faith, engineers,
wheat-grass, carrot juice, oatmeal and seven grain bread.

if the world loses you and water,
yes, precious you and the daily taste of life
it finally means that
we've lost butterflies yesterday

and failed our children.

Think Black! (1966)

Introduction to *Think Black!*

I was born into slavery in February of 1942. In the spring of that same year, 110,000 persons of Japanese descent were placed in protective custody by the white people of the United States. Two out of every three of these were American citizens by birth; the other third were aliens forbidden by law to be citizens. No charges had been filed against these people nor had any hearing been held. The removal of these people was on racial or ancestral grounds only. World War II, the war against racism; yet no Germans or other enemy aliens were placed in protective custody. There should have been Japanese writers directing their writings toward Japanese audiences.

Black. Poet. Black poet am I. This should leave little doubt in the minds of anyone as to which is first. Black art is created from Black forces that live within the body. These forces can be lost at any time as in the case of Louis Lomax, Frank Yerby and Ralph Ellison. Direct and meaningful contact with black people will act as energizers for the Black forces. Black art will elevate and enlighten our people and lead them toward an awareness of self, i.e., their blackness. It will show them mirrors. Beautiful symbols. And will aid in the destruction of anything nasty and detrimental to our advancement as a people. Black art is a reciprocal art. The Black writer learns from his people and because of his insight and "know how" he is able to give back his knowledge to the people in a manner in which they can identify, learn and gain some type of mental satisfaction, e.g., rage or happiness. We must destroy Faulkner, dick, jane and other perpetuators of evil. It's time for Du Bois, Nat Turner and Kwame Nkrumah. As Frantz Fanon points out: destroy the culture and you destroy the people. This must not happen. Black artists are culture stabilizers; bringing back old values, and introducing new ones. Black art will talk to the people and with the will of the people stop the impending "protective custody."

America calling.
negroes.
can you dance?
play foot/baseball?
nanny?
cook?
needed now. negroes
who can entertain
ONLY.
others not
wanted.
(& are considered extremely dangerous.)

d.l.l.

Back Again, Home

(confessions of an ex-executive)

Pains of insecurity surround me;
shined shoes,
conservative suits,
button down shirts with silk ties.
bi-weekly payroll.

Ostracized, but not knowing why;
executive haircut,
clean shaved,
"yes" instead of "yeah" and "no" instead of "naw,"
hours, nine to five. (after five he's alone)

"Doing an excellent job, keep it up;"
promotion made—semi-monthly payroll,
very quiet—never talks,
budget balanced—saved the company money,
quality work—production tops.
He looks sick. (but there is a smile in his eyes)

He resigned, we wonder why;
let his hair grow—a mustache too,
out of a job—broke and hungry,
friends are coming back—bring food,
not quiet now—trying to speak,
what did he say?

"Back Again,

BLACK AGAIN,

Home."

"Stereo"

I can clear a beach or swimming pool without
touching water.

I can make a lunch counter become deserted
in less than an hour.

I can make property value drop by being seen
in a realtor's tower.

I ALONE can make the word of God have little
or no meaning to many
in Sunday morning's prayer hour.

I have Power,

BLACK POWER.

Wake-Up Niggers
(you ain't part Indian)

were
don eagle & gorgeous george
sisters
or did , they just
act that way—
in the ring,
in alleys,
in bedrooms of the future.
(continuing to take yr/money)

have you ever
heard tonto say
"I'm part negro?"
(in yr/moma's dreams)
the only time
tonto was hip
was when he said:
"what you mean WE,
gettum up scout"
& left
that mask man
burning on a stake
crying for satchal page
to throw his
balls
back.

&
you followed him niggers—
all of you—
yes you did,
I saw ya.

on yr/ tip toes
with
roller skates
on yr/ knees
                    following Him
down the road,
                       not up
following Him
that whi
te man with
that
cross on his back.

Re-Act for Action

(for brother H. Rap Brown)

re-act to animals:
cage them in zoos.
re act to inhumanism:
make them human.
re-act to nigger toms:
with spiritual acts of love & forgiveness
or with real acts of force.
re-act to yr/self:
or are u too busy tryen to be cool
like tony curtis & twiggy?
re-act to whi-te actors:
understand their actions;
maggot actions & actions against yr/dreams
re-act to yr/brothers & sisters:
love.
re-act to whi-te actions:
with real act of blk/action
BAM BAM BAM

re-act to act against actors
who act out pig-actions against
your acts & actions that keep
you re-acting against their act & actions
stop.
act in a way that will cause them
to act the way you want them to act
in accordance with yr/acts & actions:
human acts for human beings

re-act
NOW niggers
& you won't have to
act
false-actions
at
your/children's graves.

First Impressions on a Poet's Death

(for Conrad Kent Rivers)

blk/poets die
from
not being
read
& from, maybe,
too much
leg.
some drank
themselves
into
non-poets,
but most
poets who poet
seldom
die
from
overexposure.

Taxes

Income taxes,
every year—due,
Sales taxes,
I pay these too.
Luxury taxes,
Maybe—one or two
Black taxes,
on everything I do.

Awareness

BLACK	PEOPLE	THINK
PEOPLE	BLACK	PEOPLE
THINK	PEOPLE	THINK
BLACK	PEOPLE	THINK—
THINK	BLACK.	

Education

I had a good teacher,
He taught me everything I know:
how to lie
cheat
and how to strike the softest blow.

My teacher thought himself to be wise and right
He taught me things most people consider nice:
such as to pray,
smile,
and how not to fight.

My teacher taught me other things too,
Things that I will be forever looking at:
how to berate.
segregate,
and how to be inferior without hate.

My teacher's wisdom forever grows,
He taught me things every child will know:
how to steal,
appeal,
and accept most things against my will.

All these acts take as facts,
The mistake was made in teaching me
How not to be BLACK

Black Pride (1968)

The New Integrationist

I
seek
integration
of
negroes
with
black
people.

The Cure All

The summer is
coming.

CONGRESS HAS ACTED:

money into the
ghetto,

to keep the weather
cool.

Two Poems
(from "Sketches from a Black-Nappy-Headed Poet")

last week
my mother died/
& the most often asked question
at the funeral
was not of her death
or of her life before death
                                        but
why was i present
with/out
a
tie on.

i aint't seen no poems stop a .38,
i ain't seen no stanzas brake a honkie's head,
i ain't seen no metaphors stop a tank,
i ain't seen no words kill
& if the word was mightier than the sword
pushkin wouldn't be fertilizing russian soil/
& until my similes can protect me from a night stick
i guess i'll keep my razor
& buy me some more bullets.

Only a Few Left

(America's Pushkin sings no more
—to Langston Hughes)

The time has come
when bravery
is not he
who is abundant
with heroic deeds
for the state.
Bravery is that
little black man
over there
surrounded by people
he's talking—
bravery lies in his
words,
he's telling the
truth
they say he's
a
poet.

The Self-Hatred of Don L. Lee
(9/22/63)

i,
at one time,
loved
my
color—
it
opened sMall
doors of
tokenism &
acceptance.
    (doors called, "the only one" & "our negro")
after painfully
struggling
thru Du Bois,
Rogers, Locke,
Wright & others,
my blindness
was vanquished
by pitchblack
paragraphs of
"us, we, me, i"
awareness.

i
began
to love
only a
part of
me—
my inner
self which
is all
Black—
& developed a
vehement
hatred of
my light
brown
outer.

The Only One

i work days, (9 to 5)
in the front office
of a well known Chicago
company.
this company is,
"an Equal Opportunity Employer,"
you can look at Me
and tell——everybody does.
my job??
it's unclear, it's new,
created just for me,
last week.
(after a visit from some human righters)
i've been with the company
for 15 years—
at last they gave me my own desk,
(toilet, lunch area & speeches too)
they like me—
(i mind my own business)
i've had two years of college.
(it didn't matter until now)
They
call me an
EXECUTIVE—
but we,
you and i,
know the
Truth.

In the Interest of Black Salvation

Whom can I confess to?
The Catholics have some cat
They call father,
mine cutout a long time ago—
Like his did.
I tried confessing to my girl,
But she is not fast enough—except on hair styles,
clothes face care and television.
If ABC, CBS, and NBC were to become educational stations
She would probably lose her cool,
and learn to read
Comic Books.
My neighbor, 36—19—35 volunteered to listen but
I couldn't talk—
Her numbers kept getting in the way,
Choking me.
To a Buddhist friend I went,
Listened, he didn't—
Advise, he did,
"pray, pray, pray and keep one eye open."
I didn't pray—kept both eyes open.

Visited three comrades at Fort Hood,
There are no Cassandra cries here,
No one would hear you anyway. They didn't.
Three tried to speak, "don't want to make war." why???
When you could do countless other things like
Make life, this would be—
Useless too . . .
When I was 17,
I didn't have time to dream,
Dreams didn't exist—
Prayers did, as dreams.
I am now 17 & 8,
I still don't dream.
Father forgive us for we know what we do.
Jesus saves,
Jesus saves,
Jesus saves—S&H Green Stamps.

The Primitive

taken from the
shores of Mother Africa.
the savages they thought
we were—
they being the real savages.
to save us. (from what?)
our happiness, our love, each other?
their bible for
our land. (introduction to economics)
christianized us.
raped our minds with:
t.v. & straight hair,
reader's digest & bleaching creams,
tarzan & jungle jim,
used cars & used homes,
reefers & napalm,
european history & promises.
Those alien concepts
of whi-teness,
the being of what
is not.
against our nature,
this weapon called
civilization—
they brought us here—
to drive us mad.
(like them)

Message to a Black Soldier

The black brothers at home refuse
to go to war. They say:
"the Viet Cong never
called us nigger."

As the black soldier shot the Cong,
The Viet cried:
"we are both niggers—WHY?"

Contradiction in Essence

I
met
a
part
time
re
vo
lu
tion
ist
too—
day

(natural hair, african dressed,
always angry, in a hurry &c.)

talk
ing
black
&
sleep
ing
whi
te.

The Death Dance

(for Maxine)

my empty steps mashed
your face in a mad
rhythm of happiness.
as if i was just learning to
boo-ga-loo.

my mother took the
'b' train to the loop
to seek work & was laughed at by
some dumb, eye-less image maker as
she scored idiot on "your" i.q. test.

i watched mom;
an ebony mind
on a yellow frame.
"i got work son, go back to school."
(she was placed according to her
intelligence into some honkie's kitchen)

i thought & my steps
took on a hip be-bop beat
on your little brain
trying to reach any of
your senseless senses.

mom would come home late at night
& talk sadtalk
or funny sadtalk. she talked
about a pipe smoking sissy
who talked sissy-talk & had
sissy sons who were forever playing
sissy games with themselves
& then she would say,
"son you is a man, a black man."
i was now tapdancing on your
balls & you felt no pain.
my steps were beating a staccato
message that told of the past 400 years.

the next day mom cried &
sadtalked me. she talked about
the eggs of maggot colored,
gaunt creatures from europe
who came here/ put on pants, stopped eating with their hands,
stole land, massacred indians,
hid from sun, enslaved blacks &
thought that they were substitutes
for gods. she talked about a
faggot who grabbed her ass as
she tried to get out of the
backdoor of his kitchen & she said,
"son you is a man, a black man."

the African ballet
was now my guide; a teacher of self &
the dance of a people.
a dance of concept & essence.
i grew.

mom stayed home & the
ADC became my father/ in projects without
backdoors/ "old grand dad" over
the cries of bessie smith /
until pains didn't pain anymore.

i began to dance dangerous steps,
warrior's steps.
my steps took on a cadence with other blk/brothers
& you could hear the cracking of
gun shots in them & we said that,
"we were men, black men."
i took the 'b' train to the loop &
you SEE me coming,
you don't like it,
you can't hide &
you can't stop me.
you will not laugh this time.
you know,
that when i dance again
it will be the
Death Dance.

The Traitor

He
wore
a whit
te
shirt
&
bow tie,
a pretty
smile
&
the people called him
doctor.
        (honorary degrees from fisk,
        tenn. state a&i, morehouse &c.)

KA BOMMMM
KA BOMMMM

blood
splattered
his whi
te
shirt his face
dis-
figured
by shot
gun
pellets
&
his head
fell
against
his
black
cadillac
&

bent
his
"clergy"
sign
toward the
black earth
&
somebody said,
"deal baby———deal."

Don't Cry, Scream (1969)

Foreword: A Further Pioneer

Gwendolyn Brooks

At the hub of the new wordway is Don Lee.

Around a black audience he puts warm healing arms.

He knows that the black man today must ride full face into the whirlwind—with small regard for "correctness," with limited concern for the possibilities of "error." He knows that there are briefs even for the Big Mistake. The Big Mistake is at least a violent Change—and in the center of a violent Change are the seeds of creation.

Don Lee knows that nothing human is elegant. He is not interested in modes of writing that aspire to elegance. He is well-acquainted with "elegant" literature (what hasn't he read?) but, while certainly respecting the advantages and influence of good workmanship, he is *not* interested in supplying the needs of the English Departments at Harvard and Oxford nor the editors of Partisan Review, although he could mightily serve as fact factory for these. He speaks to black hungry for what they themselves refer to as "*real* poetry." These blacks find themselves and the stuff of their existence in his healthy, lithe, lusty reaches of free verse. The last thing these people crave is elegance. It is very hard to enchant, with elegant song, the ears of a fellow whose stomach is growling. He can't hear you. The more interesting noise is too loud.

Don Lee has no patience with black writers who do not direct their blackness toward black audiences. He keeps interesting facts alive in his mind. "I was born into slavery in February of 1942. In the spring of that same year 110,000 persons of Japanese descent were placed in protective custody by the white people of the United Stated.... No charges had been filed against these people nor had any hearing been held. The removal of these people was on racial or ancestral grounds only. World War II, the war against racism; yet no Germans or other enemy aliens were placed in protective custody. There should have been Japanese writers directing their writings toward Japanese audiences." (Think Black!)

Lee's poetry is—necessarily: imperatively—capable of an awful fang and of a massive beautifully awful supersedure.

From "Malcolm Spoke/who listened?":

> animals come in all colors.
> dark meat will roast as fast as whi-te meat
> especially in the
> unitedstatesofamerica's
> new
> self-cleaning ovens
>
> if we don't listen.

From "The Revolutionary Screw":

brothers,
i
under/overstand
the situation:......

From "blackmusic/a beginning":

pharaoh sanders
had
finished
playing
&
the whi-
to boy was to
go on next.

him didn't

him sd
that
his horn
was
broke.

And from "A Message All Blackpeople Can Dig":

we'll move together
hands on weapons & families
blending into the sun,
into each/other.
we'll love,
we've always loved.
just be cool & help one/another.
go ahead.
walk a righteous direction
under the moon,
in the night
bring new meanings to
the north star,
to blackness,
to US.

discover new stars:
street-light stars that will explode into evil-eyes,
light-bulb stars visible only to the realpeople,
clean stars, African & asian stars,
black aesthetic stars that will damage the whi-te mind;
killer stars that will move against
the unpeople.

And always, in the center of acid, beauties that are not eaten away! "The black writer learns from his people," says Don L. Lee. "...Black artists are culture stabilizers, bringing back old values, and introducing new ones."

Poetry should—"allatonce"—distill, interpret, and extend. Don Lee's poetry does.

Black poets are the authentic poets of today. Recently, one of the Critics* opined (of white poets): "it's hardly surprising to find a deep longing for death as the terrible sign of their self-respect and indeed the means by which they continue to live—if not as men, at least as poets." And on: "Although death may not be the resolution of everyone's problems, it is nevertheless the one poets wait and pray for."

Can you imagine Don Lee subscribing to any of this? Black poets do not subscribe to death. When choice is possible, they choose to die only in defense of life, in defense and in honor of life.

White poetry! Never has white technique-in-general been as scintillant and various. Never has less been said. Modern corruption and precise limpness, modern narcissism, nonsense, dry winter and chains have a grotesque but granular grip on the white verse of today.

Sometimes there is a quarrel, "Can poetry be 'black'? Isn't all poetry just POETRY?" The fact that a poet is black means that his life, his history and the histories of his ancestors have been different from the histories of Chinese and Japanese poets, Eskimo poets, Indian poets, Irish poets. The juice from tomatoes is not merely called juice. It is always TOMATO juice. If you go into a restaurant desiring tomato juice you do not order the waiter to bring you "juice": you request, distinctly, TOMATO juice. The juice from cranberries is called cranberry juice. The juice from oranges is called orange juice. The poetry from black poets is black poetry. Inside it are different nuances AND outrightnesses.

This is part of the decision of Don Lee—who is a further pioneer and a positive prophet, a prophet not afraid to be positive even though aware of a daily evolving, of his own sober and firm churning. He is a toughness. He is not a superficial toughness. He is the kind of toughness that doesn't just sass its mammy but goes right through to the bone.

(*Jascha Kessler: "The Caged Sybil." *Saturday Review,* December 14, 1968.)

Preface: Black Poetics/for the many to come

The most significant factor about the poems/poetry you will be reading is the *idea.* The *idea* is not the manner in which a poem is conceived but the conception itself. From the *idea* we move toward development & direction (direction: the focusing of yr/idea in a positive or negative manner; depending on the poet's orientation). Poetic form is synonymous with poetic structure and is the guide used in developing yr/idea.

What u will be reading is blackpoetry. Blackpoetry is written for/to/about & around the lives/spiritactions/humanism & total existence of blackpeople. Blackpoetry in form/sound/word usage/innotation/rhythm/repetitition/direction/definition & beauty is opposed to that which is now (& yesterday) considered poetry, i.e., whi-te poetry. Blackpoetry in its purest form is diametrically opposed to whi-te poetry. Whereas, blackpoets deal in concrete rather than abstract (concrete: art for people's sake; black language or Afro-American language in contrast to standard English, &c.). Blackpoetry moves to define & legitimize blackpeople's reality (*that* which is real to us). Those in power (the unpeople) control and legitimize the negroes' (the realpeople's) reality out of that which they, the unpeople, consider real. That is, to the unpeople the television programs *Julia* and *The Mod Squad* reflect their vision of what they feel the blackman *is* about or *should* be about. So, in effect, blackpoetry is out to negate the negative influences of the mass media; whether it be TV, newspapers, magazines or some whi-te boy standing on a stage saying he's a "blue eyed soul brother."

Blackpeople must move to where all confrontations with the unpeople are meaningful and constructive. That means that most, if not all, blackpoetry will be *political.* I've often come across black artists (poets, painters, actors, writers, &c.) who feel that they and their work should be apolitical; not realizing that to be apolitical is *to be* political in a negative way for blackfolks. There is *no* neutral blackart; either it is or it *isn't,* period. To say that one is not political is as dangerous as saying, "by any means necessary," it's an "intellectual" cop-out, & niggers are copping-out as regularly as blades of grass in a New England suburb. Being political is also why the black artist by defining and legitimizing his own reality becomes a positive force in the black community (just think of Le Roi Jones [Amiri Baraka] writing the lyrics for the music of James Brown). You see, *black* for the blackpoet is a way of life. And, his totalactions will reflect that blackness & he will be an example for his community rather than another contradictor.

Blackpoetry will continue to define what is and what *isn't.* Will tell what is *to be* & how to *be* (or bes it). Blackpoetry is and will continue to be an important factor in culture building. I believe Robert Hayden had culture building in mind when he wrote these lines in an early poem:

It is time to call the children
Into the evening quiet of the living-room
And teach them the legends of their blood.

Blackpoetry is excellence & truth and will continue to seek such. Blackpoetry will move to expose & wipeout that which is not necessary for our existence as a people. *As a people* is the only way we can endure and blacknation building must accelerate at top speed. Blackpoetry is Ornette Coleman teaching violin & the Supremes being black again. Blackpoetry is like a razor; it's sharp & will cut deep, not out to wound but to kill the inactive blackmind. Like, my oldman used to pickup numbers and he seldom got caught & I'm faster than him; this is a fight with well defined borders & I know the side I'm ON. See u. Go head, now.

Don L. Lee

Gwendolyn Brooks

she doesn't wear
costume jewelry
& she knew that walt disney
was/is making a fortune off
false eyelashes and that time magazine is the
authority on the knee/grow.
her makeup is total-real.

a negro english instructor called her:
"a fine negro poet."
a whi-te critic said:
"she's a credit to the negro race."
somebody else called her:
"a pure negro writer."
johnnie mae, who's a senior in high school, said:
"she & langston are the only negro poets we've
read in school and i understand her."
pee wee used to carry one of her poems around in his
back pocket;
the one about being cool. that was befo pee wee
was cooled by a cop's warning shot.

into the sixties
a word was born . . . . BLACK
& with black came poets
& from the poet's ball points came:
black doubleblack purpleblack blueblack been black was
black daybeforeyesterday blackerthan ultrablack super
black blackblack yellowblack niggerblack blackwhi-te man
blackerthanyoueverbes 1/4 black unblack coldblack clear
black my momma's blackerthanyourmomma pimpleblack fall
black so black we can't even see you black on black in
black by black technically black mantanblack winter
black coolblack 360degreesblack coalblack midnight
black black when it's convenient rustyblack moonblack
black starblack summerblack electronblack spaceman

black shoeshineblack jimshoeblack underwearblack ugly
black auntjimammablack uncleben'srice black williebest
black blackisbeautifulblack i justdiscoveredblack negro
black unsubstanceblack.

and everywhere the
lady "negro poet"
appeared the poets were there.
they listened & questioned
& went home feeling uncomfortable/unsound & so-
    untogether
they read/re-read/wrote & re-wrote
& came back the next time to tell the
lady "negro poet"
how beautiful she was/is & how she had helped them
& she came back with:
        how necessary they were and how they've helped her.
        the poets walked & as space filled the vacuum between
        them & the
lady
"negro poet"
u could hear one of the blackpoets say:
        "bro, they been callin that sister by the wrong name."

But He Was Cool
or: he even stopped for green lights

super-cool
ultrablack
a tan/purple
had a beautiful shade.

he had a double-natural
that wd put the sisters to shame.
his dashikis were tailor made
& his beads were imported sea shells
    (from some blk/country i never heard of)
he was triple-hip.

his tikis were hand carved
out of ivory
& came express from the motherland.
he would greet u in swahili
& say good-by in yoruba.
woooooooooooo-jim he bes so cool & ill tel li gent
                                        cool-cool is so cool he was un-cooled by
                                                other niggers' cool
                                        cool-cool ultracool was bop-cool/ice box
                                                cool so cool cold cool
                                        his wine didn't have to be cooled, him was
                                                air conditioned cool
                                        cool-cool/real cool made me cool-now
                                                ain't that cool
                                        cool-cool so cool him nicknamed refrigerator.

cool-cool so cool
he didn't know,
after detroit, newark, chicago &c.,
we had to hip
            cool-cool/super-cool/real cool
      that
to be black
is
to be
very-hot.

communication in white

dee dee dee dee dee wee weee eeeeee wee we
  deweeeeeeee ee ee ee nig
nig nig nig niggggggggggggggg cleek cleek cleek
  cleeeeee cleekcleek
rip rip rip rip rip/rip/rip/rip/rip/ripripripripripripripri
  pi pi pi pi pip
bom bom bom bom bom/bom/bom/bombombombom
  bombbombbombbombbombbomb
deathtocleekdeathtocleekdeathtocleekdeathtocleek
  deathtocleekdeathtodeathto
allllllllllallllllllllll allll lllllll deathtoalllllll l allllllllll
  alllllleeeeeeee
te te te te te te te/te/te/te/te/te/tetetetetetetetetetete
  tetetetetetetete:
the paris peace talks, 1968.

Don't Cry, Scream

(for John Coltrane/ from a black poet/
in a basement apt. crying dry tears
of "you ain't gone.")

into the sixties
a trane
came/out of the
fifties with a
golden boxcar
riding the rails
of novation.
blowing
a-melodics
screeching,
screaming,
blasting—
driving some away,
(those paper readers who thought
manhood was something innate)

bring others in,
(the few who didn't believe that the
world existed around established whi
teness & leonard bernstein)
music that ached.
murdered our minds (we reborn)
born into a neoteric aberration.
& suddenly
you envy the
BLIND man—
you know that he will
hear what you'll never
see.

your music is like
my head—nappy black/
a good nasty feel with
tangled songs of:

we-eeeeeeeeeee — sing
WE-EEEeeeeeeeee — loud &
WE-EEEEEEE EEEEEEEEE — high
with
feeling

a people playing
the sound of me when
i combed it. combed at
it.

i cried
for billie holiday.
the blues. we ain't blue
the blues exhibited illusions of manhood.
destroyed by you. Ascension into:

scream-eeeeeeeeeeeeee-i ng — sing
SCREAM-EEEeeeeeeeeeee-ing — loud &
SCREAM-EEEEEEEEEE EEE-ing — long with
feeling

we ain't blue, we are black.
we ain't blue, we are black.
(all the blues did was
make me cry)
soultrane gone on a trip
he left man images
he was a life-style of
man-makers & annihilator
of attache case carriers.

Trane done went.
(got his hat & left me one)

naw brother,
i didn't cry,
i just—

Scream-eeeeeeeeeeeeee e-ed sing loud
SCREAM-EEEEEEEEEEE EEEEEEE-ED & high with
we-eeeeeeeeeeeeeeeeeeeeeeee ee feeling
WE-E-EEEEEeeeeeeeee EEEEEEEE letting
WE-EEEEEEEEEEEEEEEEEEEEEEE yr/voice
WHERE YOU DONE GONE, BROTHER? Break

it hurts, grown babies
dying. born. done caught me
a trane. steel wheels broken
by popsicle sticks. i went out
& tried to buy a nickle bag
with my standard oil card.

blonds had more fun—
with snagga-tooth niggers
who saved pennies & pop bottles for week-ends
to play negro & other filthy inventions.
be-bop-en to james brown's
cold sweat—these niggers didn't sweat,
they perspired. & the blond's dye came out,
i ran. she did too, with his pennies, pop bottles
& his mind. tune in next week same time same station
for anti-self in one lesson.

to the negro cow-sissies
who did tchaikovsky &
the beatles & live
in split-level homes & had
split-level minds & babies.
who committed the act
of love with their clothes on.

(who hid in the bathroom to read
jet mag., who didn't read the chicago
defender, because of the misspelled
words & had shelves of books by
europeans on display. untouched. who
hid their little richard & lightnin'
slim records & asked: "John who?"

instant hate.)
they didn't know any better,
brother, they were too busy getting
into debt, expressing humanity &
taking off color.

SCREAMMM M/we-eeeee/screech/teee
aheeeeeeeee/screeeeeee/theeee/ee
ahHHHHHHH/WE EEEEEEE/scrEEE
EEEE
we-eeeeeeWE-EEEEEEEEWE-EE-EEEEE

improvise
with
feeling

the ofays heard you &
were wiped out. spaced.
one clown asked me during,
my favorite things, if
you were practicing.
i fired on the muthafucka & said,
"i'm practicing."

naw brother,
i didn't cry.
i got high off my thoughts
they kept coming back,
back to destroy me.

& that BLIND man
i don't envy him anymore
i can see his hear
& hear his heard through my pores.
i can see my me. it was truth you gave,
like a daily shit
it had to come.

can you scream-brother?
can you scream-brother?

very
soft

i hear you.
i hear you.

and the Gods will too.

Assassination

it was wild.
the
bullet hit high.
                (the throat-neck)
& from everywhere:
     the motel, from under bushes and cars,
     from around corners and across streets,
     out of the garbage cans and from rat holes
     in the earth
they came running.
with
guns
drawn
they came running
toward the King—
                all of them
                fast and sure—
as if
the King
was going to fire back.
they came running,
fast and sure,
in the
wrong
direction.

Blackrunners/blackmen
or run into blackness

(for brothers Tommie smith & john carlos—
super-sprinters—but most of all blackmen)

u beat them
brothers;
at their own game.
      (outran the world-runners)
whi-te boys
& others
had a dust-meal.

u beat them.
now
in this time and space
the rule-makers
are also
the vanquished.

anyhow/way
we can't eat gold medals
& sportsmanship is racism
in three syllables.

u beat them brothers
and u/we
will beat them again.
they
just don't know
that
u've/got friends
&
we know how to
fight dirty.

A Poem to Complement Other Poems

change.
like if u were a match i wd light u into something beautiful.
change.
change.
for the better into a realreal together thing. change, from
a make believe
nothing on cornmeal and water. change.
change. from the last drop to the first, maxwellhouse
did. change.
change was a programmer for ibm, thought him was a
brown computer. change.
colored is something written on southern outhouses.
change.
greyhound did, i mean they got restrooms on buses.
change.
change.
change nigger.
saw a nigger hippy, him wanted to be different.
changed.
saw a nigger liberal, him wanted to be different.
changed.
saw a nigger conservative, him wanted to be different.
changed.
niggers don't u know that niggers are different. change.
a doublechange. nigger wanted a double zero in front of
his name; a license to kill,
niggers are licensed to be killed. change. a negro: some
thing pigs eat.
change. i say change into a realblack righteous aim. Like
i don't play
saxophone but that doesn't mean i don't dig trane.
change.

change.
hear u coming but yr/steps are too loud. change. even a
lamppost changes nigger.
change, stop being an instant yes machine. change.
niggers don't change they just grow. that's a change;
bigger & better niggers.

change, into a necessary blackself.
change, like a gas meter gets higher.
change, like a blues song talking about a righteous to-
morrow.
change, like a tax bill getting higher.
change, like a good sister getting better.
change, like knowing wood will burn. change.
know the realenemy.
change,
change nigger: standing on the corner, thought him was
cool. him still
standing there. it's wintertime, him cool.
change,
know the realenemy.
change: him wanted to be a tv star. him is. ten o'clock
news.
wanted, wanted. nigger stole some lemon & lime
popsicles,
thought them were diamonds.
change nigger change.
know the realenemy.
change: is u is or is u aint. change. now now change. for
the better change.
read a change. live a change. read a blackpoem.
change. be the realpeople.
change. blackpoems
will change:

know the realenemy. change. know the realenemy. change
yr/enemy change know the real
change know the realenemy change, change, know the
realenemy, the realenemy, the real
realenemy change you're the enemies/change your change
your change your enemy change
your enemy. know the realenemy, the world's enemy.
know them know them know them the
realenemy change your enemy change your change
change change your enemy change change
change change your change change change.
your
mind nigger.

Hero

(a poem for brig. general frederic davison,
if he can dig it)

little willie
a hero in
the american tradition.
a blk/hero.
he
received the:
    bronze star: which read "meritorious action,"
            (his momma had to look the word up)
    good conduct medal,
    combat infantry badge,
    purple heart,
    national defense service medal,
    vietnam campaign ribbon,
    & some others i can't even spell.

little willie
a hero in
the american tradition.
a blk/hero.
he
received his medals

p
o
s
t
h
u
m
o
u
s
l
y
.
.
.

Black Sketches

1.
i
was five when
mom & dad got married
& i
didn't realize that
i
was illegitimate
until i started
school.

2.
i was at
the airport
& had
to use the
men's room
real bad
& didn't have a
dime.

3.
somebody
made a
mistake
(they said)
&
sent the
peace corps to
europe.

4.
went to cash
my
1968 tax refund
&
the check bounced;
insufficient funds.

5.
i
read the
newspapers today
&
thought that
everything
was
all right.

6.
nat turner
returned
&
killed
william styron
&
his momma too.

7.
ed brooke
sat at his
desk
crying & slashing
his wrist
because somebody
called him
black.

8.
general westmoreland
was transferred
to the
westside of chicago
&
he lost
there too.

9.
in 1959
my mom
was dead at the
age of
35
& nobody thought it unusual;
not even
me.

10.
in 1963
i
became black
& everyone thought it unusual;
even me.

11.
the american dream:
nigger bible
in every hotel;
iceberg slim (pimp) getting
next to julia;
& roy wilkins on
the mod squad.

Blackwoman:

will define herself. naturally. will
talk/walk/live/& love her images. her
beauty will be. the only way to be is
to be. blackman take her. u don't need
music to move; yr/movement toward her
is music. & she'll do more than dance.

The Third World Bond

(for my sisters & their sisters)

they were
blk/revolutionists.
& they often talked
of the third world
& especially of the power
of
china.
    (quoting mao every 3rd word)
they were
revolutionists
& the blk/sisters knew it
& looked,
& wondered
while the brothers/
the revolutionists,
made bonds
with the
3rd world
thru
chinese women.
the sisters waited.
(& wondered when the revolution would start)

The Revolutionary Screw

(for my blacksisters)

brothers,
i
under/overstand
the situation:

i mean—
    u bes hitten the man hard
    all day long.
a stone revolutionary, "a full time revolutionary."
    tellen the man how bad u is
    & what u goin ta do
    & how u goin ta do it.

it must be a bitch
to be able to do all that
talken. (& not one irregular breath fr/yr/mouth)
being so
forceful & all
to the man's face (the courage)
& u not even cracken a smile (real mean).

i know,
the sisters just don't
understand the
pressure u is under.

&
when u ask for a piece
of leg/
it's not for yr/self
but for
yr/people———it keeps u going
& anyway u is a revolutionary
& she wd be doin
a revolutionary thing.

that sister dug it
from the beginning,
had an early-eye.
i mean
she really had it together
when she said:
            go fuck yr/self nigger.

now
that was
revolutionary.

Reflections on a Lost Love

(for my brothers who think they are lovers
and my sisters who are the real-lovers)

back in chi/
all the blackwomen
are fine,
super fine.
even the ones who:
          dee bob/de bop/she-shoo-bop
          bop de-bop/dee dee bop/dee-she dee-she-bop
          we-We eeeeeeeee eeeee/ WEEEEEEE EEEEEEEE
they so fine/
that
when i slide up
to one & say: take it off   sing
                    take it off   slow
                      take it all off   with feeling

& she would say: "if i doos,
                      does us think u can groove dad-dy"
& i wd say: "can chitlins smell,
              is toejam black,
              can a poet, poet,
              can a musician, music?"

              weeeee/weeeeeee/de-bop-a -dee-bop
              whooo-bop/dee-bop a-she-bop
as she smiled
& unbuttoned that top button
i sd: take it off   sing
          take it off   slow
            take it all off   with feeling

first the skirt,
then the blouse
& next her wig (looked like she made it herself)

next the shoes & then
the eyelashes and jewelry
&
            dee-bop/bop-a-ree-bop/ WOW
the slip
& next the bra (they weren't big, but that didn't scare me
cause i was grooven now): dee/dee-bop-a-she-bop/
      weeeeeEEEEEEEEEE
as she moved to the most important part,
i got up & started to groove myself but my eyes stopped
      me.
first
her stockens down those shapely legs—
followed by black bikini panties, that just slid down
and
i just stood—
& looked with utter amazement as she said: in a deep
                  "hi baby—my name is   man-like
                  joe sam."   voice

A Poem Looking for a Reader

(to be read with a love consciousness)

black is not
all-inclusive,
there are other colors.
color her warm and womanly,
color her feeling and life,
color her a gibran poem & 4 women of simone.
children will give her color
paint her the color of her
man.

most of all color her
love
a remembrance of life
a truereflection
that we
will
move   u will move with
i want
u
a fifty-minute call to blackwomanworld:
    hi baby,
    how u doin?
need u.
listening to
young-holt's, *please sunrise, please.*

to give   i'll give
most personal.
what about the other
scenes: children playing in vacant lots,
    or like the first time u knowingly kissed a girl,
    was it joy or just beautifully beautiful.

i
remember at 13
reading chester himes'
cast the first stone and
the eyes of momma when she caught me: read on, son.

how will u come:
  like a soulful strut in a two-piece beige o-rig'i-nal,
  or afro-down with a beat in yr/walk?
how will love come:
  painless and deep like a razor cut
  or like some cheap 75¢ movie;
  i think not.

will she be the woman
other men will want
or
will her beauty be
accented with my name on it?

she will come as she would
want her man to come.
she'll come,
she'll come.
i
never wrote a love letter
but
that doesn't mean
i
don't love.

We Walk the Way of the New World (1970)

Introduction to *We Walk the Way of the New World*

Louder but Softer

Yesterday is not today. What was visible in the old books is *still* there, that's why new ones are written. Yesterday's light was bright and lived suspended within its own energy. Today the only time we see it is by traveling 35,000 feet above the earth at some ridiculous speed; our children will not know the sun as we knew it, but will appreciate it more.

We're talking about our children, a survival of a people. A people can't possibly survive if they become something else. The process of change, of reconditioning a people to be something other than themselves started centuries ago: we used to be blackmen/women (or Africans); now we're known as *negroes.* That movement toward becoming an adjective was not accidental; but carefully planned and immaculately executed to completely rape a people of their culture. Whereas, most of us have become another man's imagination, a reflection of another man's fantasy, a nonentity, a filthy invention. So, in effect we'll be talking about definitions & change. When we say definitions, we mean the present and the past with the proper perspective. Understand that *objectivity* is a *myth,* where "one makes judgments in terms of one's culture and in keeping with the cultural values which are a part of his personal and immediate heritage. These cultural values depend for their duration upon the survival of the classes which created them." Change is to be that, an on-going process aimed at an ultimate definition of our being. But when we talk about change, we don't mean from *Winston* to *Marlboro.* Actually, we mean from negative to positive, from the creative to the anti-cliche.

> What is meant is that we'll have to move from imitation to initiation; from number one to number first; from the *Tonight Show* to our own Lenox Avenue where brothers shadowbox with wind because the wind is the only element that will touch them. Check it out, if u ain't scared to venture back.

Can you believe in yourself? It's not enough to say *I'm Somebody*: we've always known that. The question *is* who/what? Are you a dead raindrop, reborn in a used coal mine now existing in an oblique closet of your closed mind, only to re-emerge singing "I'm black and I'm proud" while soft peddling before the jew into the new self-cleaning ovens. After all, it takes little or no work to be insignificant, but to leave our print, our image on the world, you'll find that 24 hours in a day is like seconds in a fast minute.

The rejection of that which was/is ours has been the basis for the acceptance of that which is someone else's. The most effective weapon used against us has been the educational system. We now understand that if white nationalism is our teacher, white nationalism will be our philosophy regardless of all its contradictory and anti-black implications. The educational process is set up largely to preserve that which is, not that which necessarily needs to be created, i.e., black nationalism or black consciousness. Thus we find ourselves trying to determine which are the correct answers for future development. Some of the answers will have to be a surprise, but at least we know a surprise is coming.

In the late sixties we existed in a state of *cultural nihilism*, and the destruction that came was mainly against our own in our own. Destruction and mis-direction became the overwhelming directives. Positive influences existed in the sixties and before, but their accessibility was limited to the few. So we moved, traveling speedily from one consciousness to another, hoping that our actions would not betray our movement. Blackness as we speak of it today is nothing new; other writers at other times wrote about themselves and their people as we do now. The main difference, if there has to be one, is the audience which the writers directed their voices toward. Black writers—from the first and up into the sixties—have largely (with few exceptions) followed the trend of being or becoming "American writers," not *negro* writers but writers who happened to be *negro*. All that is in the process of being erased. We discovered a new psychology. The sixties brought us the work of one Frantz Fanon and his powerful *The Wretched of the Earth* and other books: the Honorable Elijah Muhammad, the prophet of the Nation of Islam, ultimately produced the loudest and clearest voice for the young blacks through El Hajj Malik el Shabazz, better known as Malcolm X, who in turn moved us toward a national consciousness. He heavily influenced a writer who proved to be a consistent bullet in the side of white America—Imamu Amiri Baraka (LeRoi Jones).

> What does it take to reach you, into you? What is the stimulus that will force you to act; what motivates you in yr inability to conceive of yrself as something special? Will it take the death of a loved one? Will the values you consider valuable have to be destroyed? Is the knowledge of self so painful as to demand that you not accept it and continue to squalor in yr naiveté?

Culture is the sustaining force of any nation. An effective con game has been played on black people in this country. We've been taught to be anti-black, anti-self. No need in documenting that, for all one has to do is walk in any black neighborhood and if you possess only an ounce of perception, the examples will fly at you. We are the only people in a nation of many people who have consistently let other guide us. We've been so busy taking directions from others that our ability to conceive of ourselves as direction-givers has not had a chance to flourish. However, others—those that traditionally have led us—recognized our revolutionary potential. Harold Cruse puts it this way:

> They understood it *instinctively*, (the Negro's white radical allies) and revolutionary theory had little to do with it. What . . . the Negro's allies feared most of all was that this sleeping, dream-walking black giant might wake up and direct the revolution all by himself, relegating his white allies to a humiliating, second class status. The Negro's allies were not about to tell the Negro anything that might place him on the path to greater power and independence in the revolutionary movement than they themselves had. The rules of the power game meant that unless the American Negro taught himself the profound implications of his own revolutionary significance in America, it would never be taught to him by anyone else.

We black people in America are not culturally deprived, but "culturally different"; actually we're products of a dual culture, having the benefits and evils of the dominant WASPS and our own unique Afro-Americanism. Here we are, about 30 million voices (larger than some nations) coming into a new decade, still not fully cognizant of the ultimate reality of our power, if only in sheer numbers.

> Almost daily, small bands of Jewish arrivals tramp up the gangplank of the Saint Lawrence, the hotel ship acquired by the Danish Refugee Council to house them temporarily . . . 'You must understand,' a recently arrived 40-year-old female physician said. 'Our world has been shattered. My husband and I . . . had almost forgotten that we were Jews; we were simply Poles. But then someone denounced us.'. . . The doctor and her husband—who is also a physician were . . . accused of hiding their 'Jewishness.'
>
> —*Newsweek*, January 12,1970

The theater was Poland, the former homeland of more than three million Jews, reduced to 75,000 after Hitler's Aryan society came into power, and today Poland contains less than 15,000. The year is 1970 and the issues are the same, *race*. We can continue to cloud our direction with meaningless rhetoric and romantic illusions, but when it comes down to the deathwalk, no one will save a people but the people themselves. Let's look at the Jewish and black situations here, since Jews and blacks are among the largest "minority" groups.

How can less than six million American Jews be more effective than Afro-Americans that outnumber them almost five to one? The watchword is culture and a steady "survival motion." The Jewish people have a tradition of togetherness and peoplehood. They've developed a nationalist consciousness that's interwoven with their religious reality. They've developed life-giving and life-saving institutions. They've developed the sophistication for survival. If a Jew hates you, you'll never know it; if he plans to kill you, you know even less: Sophistication. They recognized years ago that *Mission Impossible* and *James Bond* are for real. So, how does one compete with such impossible odds without inviting suicide? Simple, yet difficult. You become a nation within a nation. You create and sustain your own identity. In effect, Jewish teachers teach Jewish children, especially in the primary levels; Jewish doctors administer aid to Jewish patients (and others); the Jewish business world services the Jewish community; and each sector continually draws on one another to build that community. Rabbi Zev Segal, head of the country's largest and most influential Jewish Orthodox rabbinical group, estimated that close to one hundred million dollars has been spent annually in the last few years on Jewish educational institutions; he also goes on to say that Jewish education is necessary for the survival of Judaism. Also, he and others rightly feel that they face "physical danger" if they as a people cannot remain as a people. Thus, Rabbi Segal feels that the Jewish schools are the "core institutions for Jewish survival and identity."

Elsewhere I've said that if all you are exposed to is Charlie Chan, you'll have a Charlie Chan mentality. A better example is Tarzan. Remember Tarzan grew out of one man's imagination, but because of prevailing anti-black conditions, he immediately became a nation's consciousness. What Tarzan did was not only to turn us away from Africa, but from ourselves. And that's where we are now, still unsure of ourselves, walking after somebody else's dreams, while the only fighting being waged is within the race. The killing of each other is not a test for manhood. But manhood has not been defined. And our survival will ultimately be determined by the will or non-will of black men—it will not be an overnight process and we see that our most important asset is the next/and present generation of black college students.

> Stop!
> Black student after winter vacation on his way back to school (University of America) a part of the Jet set. I wouldn't have noticed him, but he was dressed rather oddly; along with about a five-inch natural he had an Indian band around his forehead; with a gold earring in his left ear. A black tiki hung around his neck partially hid under a red and green scarf that loosely covered an orange dashiki that housed a black turtle neck sweater. His tailor made white bell-bottoms were accented by brown buckled cowboy boots while a black slick-haired fur coat rested on his right arm looking like it could bite. Now, here we have a brother that didn't know what he was, an international nigger—you name it, he'll be a part

of it. As I approached him, his first words after "What's happnin, baby," were "do you smoke, bro?"

Stop!
Time is not new; it must be on our side, we're still here. Send young black brothers and sisters to college and they come home Greeks, talking about they can't relate to the community anymore. So here we have black Alpha Phi Alpha, Delta Sigma Theta, etc., unable to speak Greek, with an obvious non-knowledge of Greek culture only supported by an ignorance of their own past (or present); only, after four years, to be graduated as some of the best whist players since the Cincinnati Kid who didn't finish high school.

Today's black college students fall into two categories: the serious and the unserious. By the unserious I mean the lesser but growing portion of black students who attend today's universities with the attitude that they are "students" and nothing else. Whereas being a "student" implies superficial intellectuality that borders on hipness—that is, being hip enough to be able to quote all the current writers to impress those who are impressed by that; very little study (that's for squares, u a brain anyhow); a lot of partying (with the 3 R's of reading, riting, and rithmetic being replaced with ripple, reefer, and rappin'); and a possession of the attitude that "I got mine, you get yours" or "every man for himself," so there exists no real commitment to themselves, or to their people. And lastly, we have the student who will say that all the courses are irrelevant—not realizing it's going to take some of that irrelevance to put us in a position for survival.

Finally, we have the serious student who is not only committed to himself, but to his people. Students who realize that they come to college as black men or women will come out as doctors, lawyers, teachers, historians, writers, etc.—who are black and not doctors, lawyers, teachers, historians, writers, etc., who happen to be black. No, you are black men and women who are black first and products of your vocation second—therefore understanding our priorities. These are New World students who are in the process of developing the necessary group consciousness, nationalistic consciousness or black consciousness that is absolutely necessary for real development.

You as black students will become the new heroes for our children; will move to replace the pimps, prostitutes and wineheads who are now viewed as heroes because of no meaningful alternative. A part of your responsibility will be to change a rather complex and growing situation in our communities. Think about it, be for real about realness; it's not for the community to relate to you, you relate to that which you left. The community is still there unchanged. You have changed; the question is how? Please, don't space on us just because you think you're educated now. Don't become the new pimps, educated pimps existing as a creation of your own mind, unwilling to share with anyone because you think you're too deep. Try us, you may not be as deep as you think you are. Stop romanticizing your existence, stop romanticizing the black revolution. Like Brother Malcolm said, "*if you really understood r*evolution, you wouldn't even use the term," or as a sister put it—all the revolutionaries she knew were either dead or off quietly planning somewhere. Need I say more?

So we say, move into yr own self, clean. If we were as together as our music and dancing, we'd be a trip in itself. Can you dig that, if we were as up tight as our dancing and music? we wouldn't have a worry except how to stay new and inventive. For an example, take our music. It is commonly accepted that it is the only cultural form that is uniquely American—that is, not an off-shoot of European culture. But still, we don't control our own contributions—the money makers have not been the black musicians but the producers and record companies. What is even worse is that our music is being stolen each and every day and passed off as another's creation—take Tom Jones and Janis Joplin, two white performers who try to sing black. They've not only become rich, while black musicians starve in their own creation, but those two whites, plus others—who are at best poor copies of what they consider black—will after a short period of time become the standard. It will get to the point where when you speak of soul and black music, you will find people automatically thinking of white imitators.

We now find ourselves in the seventies and cannot possibly use the tactics of the sixties. We need innovators and producers of positive change. The older generation's resistance to change is natural; so how do we change without alienating them? How can we reduce if not completely eliminate all the negativism, pettiness and cliquishness that exists and are so damaging? How can we enlarge the narrow choice factor—where in most cases our reality is controlled by Christianity, drugs, or alcohol? How can we create a common consciousness, based on a proven humanism—as we stop trying to prove our humanism to those who are unhuman? It's on us; nobody, nowhere will do it for us.

We Walk the Way of the New World. It's new. As indicated above, we are much louder, but softer, a logical progression, still screaming like a super-sonic wind tuned to a special frequency, but hip enough to realize that even some of those brothers and sisters tuned in will still not hear. The new book is in three parts: "Black Woman Poems," "African Poems," and "New World Poems." Each part is a part of the other: Blackwoman is African and Africa is Blackwoman and they both represent the New World.

Actually all three sections are reflections of one blackman—which is to say that the whole book is based upon the direction I feel blackmen should be traveling. When we talk about nationalism, we mean real nationalism—that which embodies culture, politics, defense, and economy. We talk about a nationalism that will draw brothers and sisters into self and not alienate them; will answer questions and not only present problems; will build people, not individuals, with leadership qualities. That is, each one of us must possess those qualities of good leadership—a community of leaders —not just followers—who can and will work together. Remember *a leader is not only one that leads but is the best example of that leadership.*

Blackman/ an unfinished history

the old musicman   beat into an alien image of nothingness
we
remember you & will not forget
the days, the nights, the weekends
the secret savings for the trip north
or up south. We entered the new cities—
they were not ready for us—
those on the great rivers, the lakes
they were clean then, somewhat pure,
u cd even drink fr/them
& the fish lived there in abundance.
we came by backseat greyhound & special trains
up south came us
to become a part of the pot that was supposed to melt
                    it did and we burned
and we burned into something different & unknown
we acquired a new ethic   a new morality   a new history
and we lost
we lost much   we lost that   that was
we became americans   the best   the real
and blindly adopted america's heroes as our own
our minds wouldn't *function.*
what was wrong?
it couldn't have been the air it was clean then.

today
from the clouds we look back
seat 16C in the bird with the golden wings.
we came & were different shades of darkness
& we brought our music & dance,
that which wasn't polluted.
we took on the language, manners, mores, dress & religion
of the people with the unusual color.
into the 20th century we wandered rubber-stamped
a poor copy!

but the music was ours, the dance was ours, was ours.
& then it was hip—it was hip
to walk, talk & act a certain neighborhoodway,
we wore 24 hr sunglasses & called our woman *baby*,
our woman,
we wished her something else,
& she became that wish.
she developed into what we wanted,
she not only reflected *her*, but reflected us,
was a mirror of our death-desires.
we failed to protect or respect her
& no one else would,
& we didn't understand, we didn't understand.
why,
she be doing the things she don't do.

the sixties brought us black
at different levels, at different colors we searched
while   some of us still pissed into the wind.
we tasted
& turned our heads into a greater vision.
greatness becomes our new values—OOOOOOOO
like   telling yr daughter she's beautiful
& meaning *it*. Vee. Boom Veeeee Boom
You going to do it jim! BOOOOOOOOM
You goin ta jump around & startle the world blackman.
goin ta space man, all u got ta do is think space thoughts.
You're *slick* jim, yes you is
slicker than a oil slick, yes you is
just been sliding in the wrong direction. click.
be a *New World* picture.   click,   click.
blackman click blackman click into tomorrow.
Spaced from the old thoughts into
the new. Zooomm. Zoooommmmm Zooommmmmm.
click.
design yr own neighborhoods,   Zoom   it can be,
teach yr own children,   Zoom   Zoom   it can be,
build yr own loop,   Zoom   Zoom   it can be,
feed yr own people.   Zoom   Zoom   it can be,

Watch out world greatness is coming.   click   click.
protect yr own communities,   Zoom   Zoom   it can be.

create *man* blackman....
walk thru the
world
as if You are world itself,   click.
be an extension of everything beautiful & powerful, click
click.
HEY   blackman look like
you'd be named something
like .... *earth, sun*
or mountain.
Go head, *universe*
Zoommmmmmmm. Zooommmmmmmmmm
Zoooommmmmmmmmmmmm   click   click.
be it,
blackman.

Soft, Hard, Warm, Sure

soft: the way her eyes view her children.
hard: her hands; a comment on her will.
warm: just the way she is, jim!
sure: as yesterday, she's tomorrow's tomorrow.

Judy-One

she's the camera's
subject:
the sun for colored film.

her smile is like
clear light bouncing off
the darkness of the
mediterranean at nighttime.

we all know it,
her smile.
when it's working,
moves like sea water—
always going somewhere

strongly.

Man Thinking About Woman

some thing is lost in me,
like
the way you lose old thoughts   that
somehow seemed unlost at the right time.

i've not known it or you many days;
we met as friends with an absence of strangeness.
it was the month
that my lines got longer & my metaphors softer.

it was the week   that
i felt the city's narrow breezes rush about
me
looking for a place to disappear
as   i walked the clearway,
sure footed in used sandals screaming to be replaced

your empty shoes (except for used stockings)
partially hidden beneath the dresser
looked at me,
as i sat thoughtlessly   waiting
for your touch.

that day,
as your body rested upon my chest
i saw the shadow of the
window blinds   beam
across the unpainted ceiling
going somewhere
like the somewhere i was going
when
the clearness of yr/teeth,
& the scars on yr/legs stopped me.

your beauty: un-noticed by regular eyes   is
like   a blackbird resting
on a telephone wire   that moves
quietly with the wind.

a southwind.

Marlayna

harlem's night upon the world
women there
are drops of algerian sand
with joy-eyes overworked to welcome.
beauty flows the curves of her natural,
hangs
on out like saturday night skipping sunday
she walks/moves the natureway.
to a hungry man
she's his watermelon.

Big Momma

finally retired   pensionless
from cleaning somebody else's house
she remained home to clean
the one she didn't own.

in her kitchen where we often talked
the *chicago tribune* served as a tablecloth
for the two cups of tomato soup that went
along with my weekly visit & talkingto.

she was in a seriously-funny mood
& from the get-go she was down, realdown:

roaches around here are like
letters on a newspaper
or
u gonta be a writer, hunh
when u gone write me some writen
or
the way niggers act around here
if talk cd kill we'd all be dead.

she's somewhat confused about all this *blackness*
but said that it's good when negroes start putting themselves
first and added: we've always shopped at the colored stores,
& the way niggers cut each other up round
here every weekend that whiteman don't
haveta
worry bout no revolution specially when he's
gonta haveta pay for it too, anyhow all he's
gotta do is drop a truck load of dope out
there on 43rd st. & all the niggers & yr
revolutionaries
be too busy getten high & then they'll turn
round
and fight each other over who got the mostest.

we finished our soup and i moved to excuse myself,
as we walked to the front door she made a last comment:
now *luther* i knows you done changed a lots but if
you can think back, we never did eat too much pork
round here anyways, it was bad for the belly.
i shared her smile and agreed.

touching the snow lightly i headed for 43rd st.
at the corner i saw a brother crying while
trying to hold up a lamp post,
thru his watery eyes i cd see big momma's words.

at sixty-eight
she moves freely, is often right
and when there is food
eats joyously with her own
real teeth.

Mixed Sketches

u feel that way sometimes
wondering:
as a nine-year-old sister
with burned out hair oddly
smiles at you and sweetly calls you
brother.

u feel that way sometimes
wondering:
as a blackwoman & her six children
are burned out of their apartment with no place
to go & a nappy-headed nigger comes running thru
our neighborhood with a match in his hand cryin
revolution.

u feel that way sometimes
wondering:
seeing sisters in two hundred dollar wigs & suits
fastmoving in black clubs in late surroundings   talking
about late thoughts in late language waiting for late men
that come in with, "i don't want to hear bout nothing black
    tonight."
u feel that way sometimes
wondering:
while eating on newspaper tablecloths
& sleeping on clean bedsheets that couldn't
stop bedbugs   as black children watch their
mothers leave the special buses returning from
special neighborhoods
to clean their "own" unspecial homes.
u feel that way sometimes
wondering:
wondering, how did we survive?

Man and Woman

(for earnie, 1964)

two baths in one day!
at first i thought that you
just wanted to be clean.
then, u pulled the lights off
& the darkness took me away from my book.
lightly,
i asked about your perfume
u answered,
& added that u splashed it in unknown & strange places
and again lightly,
i asked,
if the perfume was *black.*
at first
our backs touched & we both played sleep.
u turned toward me
& the warmth of yr/blood rushes over me   as
u throw yr/left leg over my left leg
& get dangerous, very dangerous with yr/left hand.
the soul-station comes on automatically
with the aid of yr/right hand.
ike & tina turner are singing "get back"
from yr/touch i flinch and say,
listen to the record, woman!
you don't and i don't   while
"get back" is in rhythm
with the shaking of the bed
that's
mixed with our soft voices
that undoubtedly are heard unconfused through
thin walls.

Blackgirl Learning

she couldn't quote french poetry
that doesn't mean that she ain't read any
probably not
tho gwendolyn brooks & margaret walker
lined her dresser.

she did tell me that
the bible was pure literature
& she showed me her own poetry.
far beyond love verse (& it didn't rhyme)
she wrote about her man.

she said that her man
worshiped her,
he wasn't there.
she told me that he had other things to do:

learning to walk straight.

On Seeing Diana Go Maddddddddd

(on the very special occasion of the death of her two dogs—
Tiffany & Li'l Bit—when she cried her eyelashes off)

a dog lover,
a lover of dogs   in a land where poodles
eat/live cleaner than their masters
& their masters use the colored people
to walk that   which they love, while they
wander in & out of our lives running the world.

(stop! in the name of love, before you break my heart)

u moved with childlike vision
deeper into lassieland to become
the new wonderwoman of the dirty-world
we remember the 3/the three young baaaaad detroiters
of younger years when i & other blacks moved with u
& all our thoughts dwelled on the limits of forget & forgive.

(stop! in the name of love, before you break my heart)

diana,
we left u (back in those un-thinking days)   there
on the dance floor teaching marlon brando the monkey
(the only dance you performed with authority)
we washed our faces anew
as the two of you dreamed a single mind.
diana,
yr/new vision worries me because i,
as once you, knew/know the hungry days   when
our fathers went to ford motor co.,
and our mothers
in the morning traffic to the residential sections of dearborn.
little supreme, only the well fed forget.

(stop! in the name of love, before you break . . .)

ladies & gents we proudly present
the swinging sur-premessssss .... correction, correction.
ladies & gents we proudly present
diana rossss and the supremes.
and there u stood,
a skinny earthling viewing herself as a mov
ing star. as a mov ing star u will travel
north by northwest deeper into the ugliness
of yr/bent ego. & for this i/we cannot forgive.

(stop! in the name of love,...............)

u, the gifted voice, a symphony, have now joined the
hippy generation to become unhipped,
to become the symbol of a new aberration,
the wearer of other people's hair.
to become one of the real animals of this earth.
we wish u luck & luckily u'll need it
in yr/new found image of a mov
ing star, a mov ing star, mov ing moving
moving on to play
a tooth-pick in a *rin tin tin* mov ie.

First

first.
a woman should be
a woman *first,*
if she's anything.
but
if she's *black,* really *black*
and a woman
that's special, that's
realspecial.

We're an Africanpeople

WE'RE an Africanpeople
hard-softness burning black.
the earth's magic color our veins.
an Africanpeople are we;
burning blacker softly, softer.

A Poem for a Poet

(for brother Mahmoud Darwish)

read yr/exile
i had a mother too,
& her death will not be
talked of around the world.
like you,
i live/walk a strange land.
my smiles are real but seldom.

our enemies eat the same bread
and their waste
(there is always waste)
is given to the pigs,
and then they consume the pigs.

Africa still has sun & moon,
has clean grass & water u can see thru;
Africa's people talk to u with their whole faces,
and their speech comes like drumbeats,
comes like drumbeats.

our enemies eat the same bread
and the waste from their greed
will darken your sun and hide your moon,
will dirty your grass and misuse your water.
your people will talk with unchanging eyes
and their speech will be slow & unsure & overquick.

Africa, be yr/own letters
or
all your people will want cars
and there are few roads.
you must eat yr/own food
and that which is left,
continue to share in earnest.

Keep your realmen; yr/sculptors
yr/poets, yr/fathers, yr/musicians, yr/sons, yr/warriors.
Keep your truemen of the darkskin,
a father guides his children,
keep them & they'll return your wisdom,
and
if you must send them,   send them
the way of the Sun
as to make them

blacker.

Change is Not Always Progress

(for Africa & Africans)

Africa.

don't let them
steal
your face   or
take your circles
and make them squares.

don't let them
steel
your body   as to put
100 stories of concrete on you
so that you
            arrogantly
scrape
the

sky.

Knocking Donkey Fleas off a Poet from the Southside of Chi
(for brother ted joans)

a worldman.
with the careful eye; the deep look, the newest look.
as recent & hip as the uncola being sipped by
thelonious monk
jackie-ing it down to little *rootie tootie's.*

he's a continent jumper,
a show-upper, a neo-be-bopper.
he's the first u see the last to flee,
the homeboy in African land;
with an inner compass of the rightway.
at times he's the overlooked like
a rhinoceros in a bird bath.

the sound of his trumpet is the true *off minor.*
to hear him tell it: *bird* is alive, blacks must colonize europe,
jazz is a woman & I did, I was, I am.
& I believe him.

he's younger than his poems
& old as his clothes,
he's badder than bad: him so bad he cd take a banana from a
gorilla, pull a pork chop out of a lion's
buttocks or debate the horrors of
war with spiro agnew with his mouth closed.

a worldman,
a man of his world.

ted joans is the tan of the sun; the sun's tan.
a violent/ peace
looking for a piece.
he'll find it (in the only place he hasn't been)
among the stars, that star.
the one that's missing.
last seen
walking slowly across Africa
bringing the rest of the world with it.

Change

change.
create a climate for
change.
yesterday's weather has been un-
changeable.
there is a young dark storm coming;
has   nappy-hair.

Sun House

(a living legend)

his fingers leaned
forcefully against the neck
of a broken gin bottle
that
rubbed gently on
the steel strings of a borrowed guitar.

the roughness of his voice
is only matched by his immediate
presence that is lifted into
life with lonely words: "is u is or is u ain't
my baby, i say,
is u is or is u ain't
my baby, if u ain't
don't confess it now."

to himself he knew the answers
& the answers were amplified
by the sharpness of the broken bottle
that gave accent
to the muddy music as it screamed
& scratched the unpure lines
of our many faces,
while our bodies jumped to the sounds of

mississippi.

One Sided Shoot-out

(for brothers fred hampton & mark clark, murdered 12/4/69
by chicago police at 4: 30 AM while they slept)

only a few will really understand:
it won't be yr/mommas or yr/brothers & sisters or even me,
we all think that we do   but we don't.
it's not *new*   and
under all the rhetoric the seriousness is still not serious.
the national rap deliberately continues, "wipe them niggers
    out."
(no talk do it, no talk do it, no talk do it, notalk notalknotalk do it)

& we.
running circleround getting caught in our own cobwebs,
in the same old clothes, same old words, just new adjectives.
we will order new buttons & posters with: "remember fred"
    & "rite on mark."
& yr/pictures will be beautiful & manly with the deeplook/
    the accusing look
to remind us
to remind us that suicide is not black.

the questions will be asked & the answers will be the new
    cliches.
but maybe,
just maybe we'll finally realize that "revolution" to the real
    world
is international 24 hours a day and that 4:30 AM is like
        12:00 noon,
it's just darker.
but the evil can be seen if u look in the right direction.
were the street lights out?
did they darken their faces in combat?
did they remove their shoes to creep softer?
could u not see the whi-te of their eyes,
the whi-te of their deathfaces?
didn't yr/look-out man see them coming, coming, coming?
or did they turn into ghostdust and join the night's fog?

it was mean.
& we continue to call them "pigs" and "muthafuckas"
forgetting what all
black children learn very early: "sticks & stones may break
my bones but names can
never hurt me."

it was murder.
& we meet to hear the speeches/the same, the duplicators.
they say that which is expected of them.
to be instructive or constructive is to be unpopular (like: the
leaders only
sleep when there is a watchingeye)
but they say the right things at the right time, it's like a
stageshow:
only the entertainers have changed.
we remember bobby hutton. the same, the duplicators.

the seeing eye should always see.
the night doesn't stop the stars
& our enemies scope the ways of blackness in three bad
shifts a day.
in the AM their music becomes deadlier.
this is a game of dirt.

only blackpeople play it fair.

For Black People

(& negroes too. a poetic statement on black existence in america with a view of tomorrow. all action takes place on the continent of north america. these words, imperfect as they may be, are from positive images received from gwendolyn brooks, hoyt w. fuller, imamu baraka & joe goncalves.)

I. IN THE BEGINNING

state street was dead, wiped out.
ghetto expressways were uplifted
and dropped on catholic churches.
all around us trees were being uprooted.
and flung into the entrances of bars, taverns & houses
of prostitution
lake meadows and prairie shores
passed out faces with human bodies of
black & whi-te mixed together, like salt & pepper,
—in concrete silence.
though deceased, some of the bodies still had smiles
—on their faces.
BONG BONG BONG BONG BONG BONG BONG BONG
IT STARTED LAST SUNDAY.
for some unknown reason all the baptist ministers—
          told the truth.
it was like committing mass suicide.
it was cold, mid-december, but the streets were hot.
the upward bound programs had failed that year.
the big bombs had been dropped, harlem &
          newark were annihilated.
another six million had perished and now
the two big men were fighting for universal survival.
the scene was blow for blow at the corner of 59th & racine,
right in front of the "Lead Me By the Hand"
          storefront church.

J.C, the blue eyed blond, had the upper hand for his
opponent, Allah, was weakening because of the strange—
climate.
ahhhhh, ohoooooo, ahhaaaaa, ahhhaaaeeEEEE
in a bedroom across the street a blk/woman tearlessly
cries as she spreads her legs, in hatred, for her landlord—
paul goldstein.
(her children will eat tonight)
her brothers, boy-men called negroes, were off hiding
in some known place biting their nails & dreaming of
whi-te virgins.
that year negroes continued to follow blind men whose
eye-vision was less than their own & each morning
negroes woke up a little deader.
the sun was less than bright, air pollution acted as a filter.
colored people were fighting each other knowingly
and little niggers were killing little niggers.
the "best" jobs were taken by colored college graduates
who had earned their degrees in a four-year course of
self-hatred with a minor in speech.
negroes religiously followed a blondhairedblueeyedman
and no one forced them
whi-te boys continued to laugh and take blk/women.
negroes were unable to smile & their tears were dry. They
had no eye-balls.
their sisters went to strangers' beds cursing them.
that year negroes read styron, mailer, joyce and rimbaud.
last year it was bellow, wallace, sartre & voznesensky
(yevtushenko was unpoetic).
somebody said that there was no such thing as black
literature & anyway we all knew that negroes didn't write,
except occasional letters to the editor.
niggers 3 steps from being shoeshine boys were dressing
and talking like william buckley jr.—minus the pencil.
their heroes danced unclothed out of greek mythology.
janis smyth & claude iforgethislastname often quoted passages
from antigone (pronounced anti-gone).

the pope, all perfumed down—smelling like a french sissy,
watched 59th and racine from st. peters with a rosary
    in his hand:
        hell mary full of grace the lord is with thee.
        hell mary full of grace the lord is with thee.
        hell mary full of grace the lord was with thee.
blk/poets were not citizens & were being imprisoned and put to death.
whi-te boys remained our teachers & taught the people of color
how to be negroes and homosexuals.
some invisible fiction writer continued to praise the poverty
    program & is now being considered for 'negro writer
    in residence" at johnson city, texas.
a blind negro poet compared himself with yeats
not knowing that he, himself, was a "savage side show."
all this happened in the beginning
and the beginning is almost the end.

II. TRANSITION AND MIDDLE PASSAGE

gas masks were worn as were side-arms.
the two nations indivisible & black people began to believe
in themselves.
muhammad ali remained the third world's champ &
taught the people self defense.
blk/poets were released from prison & acted as consultants
to the blk/nation.
there were regular napalm raids over the whi-te house.
college trained negroes finally realized that they weren't
educated and expressed sorrow for losing their
virginity in europe.
the urban progress centers were transformed into hospitals
& the records were used for toilet paper.
the room was whi-te & the blacks entered only to find
that the two colors wouldn't mix.
deee-bop a bop bop, dee dee abop, bop-o-bop dee dee,
wee, WEEEEEE.
willie johnson, all processed down, was noticeably driving
down cottage grove in a gold & black deuce & a quarter;
hitting the steering wheel at 60 degrees off center, with
his head almost touching the right window. willie, dressed
in a gold ban-lon that matched his ride, slowly moved his
left foot to his dual stereo that coolly gave out jerry
butler's: "never gone ta give you up."
while miss wilberforce, alias miss perm of 1967, tried
to pass him on his right side in her pine-yellow 287 mustang
with the gas tank always on full. dressed in a two-piece
beige marshall field's o-ri-ginal, miss perm with hair
flowing in the wind was nodding her head to the same tune:
"never gone ta give you up."
both, the stang & the deuce hit the corner of 39th & cottage
at the same time; and as if somebody said, "black is
beautiful," miss perm and processed-down looked at each
other with educated eyes that said:
i hate you.

that year even lovers didn't love.
whi-te boys continued to take blk/women to bed; but they
ceased to wake up alive.
this was the same year that the picture "guess who's
coming to dinner" killed spencer tracy.
negro pimps were perpetual victims of assassination
& nobody cried.
Amiri Baraka wrote the words to the blk/national anthem &
pharoah sanders composed the music. tauhid became
our war song.
an alive wise man will speak to us, he will quote du bois,
nkrumah, coltrane, fanon, muhammad, trotter and himself.
we will listen.
chicago became known as negro-butcher to the world &
no one believed it would happen, except the jews—
the ones who helped plan it.
forgetting their own past—they were americans now.
eartha kitt talked to nbc about blk/survival; receiving
her instructions from the bedroom at night.
blk/people stopped viewing TV & received the new
messages from the talking drum.
dope pushers were given overdoses of their own junk
& they died. no one cried.
united fruit co. & standard oil were wiped out & whi-te
people cried.
at last, the president could not control our dreams
and the only weapon he could threaten us with
was death.

III. THE END IS THE REAL WORLD

it is a new day and the sun is not dead.
Allah won the fight at 59th & racine and his sons are not
dead.
blk/poets are playing & we can hear. marvin x & askia
muhammad toure walk the streets with smiles on their
faces. i join them. we talk & listen to our own words.
we set aside one day a year in remembrance of whi-tness.
(anglo-saxon american history day)
the air is clean. men & women are able to love.
legal holidays still fall in february: the 14th and 23rd*
all the pigs were put to death, the ones with men-like
minds too.
men stopped eating each other and hunger existed only in
history books.
money was abolished and everybody was rich.
every home became a house of worship & pure water runs
again.
young blk/poets take direction from older blk/poets &
everybody listens.
those who speak have something to say & people seldom
talk about themselves.
those who have something to say wait their turn & listen to
their own message.
the hip thing is not to be cool & get high but to be cool &
help yr/brother.
the pope retired & returned the land & valuables his
organization had stolen under the guise of religion.
Allah became a part of the people & the people knew &
loved him as they knew and loved themselves.
the world was quiet and gentle and beauty came back.
people were able to breathe.

**Birth dates of Frederick Douglass and W. E. B. Du Bois*

blk/women were respected and protected & their actions
proved deserving of such respect & protection.
each home had a library that was overused.
the blackman had survived.
he was truly the "desert people."
there were black communities, red communities, yellow
    communities and a few whi-te communities that were
    closely watched.
there was not a need for gun control.
there was no need for the word peace for its
    antonym had been removed from the vocabulary
like i sd befo
the end is the real world.

July, 1968

See Sammy Run in the Wrong Direction

(for the ten *negro* editors representing n.n.p.a. who visited occupied *Palestine* [known as Israel] on a fact finding trip, but upon their return—reported few facts, if any.)

we know others.
are u others, or are u inbetweens?
imitation imitations. like junior sammy davises
kissing the wailing wall
in the forgotten occupied country.
his top lip stuck
& in a strange land he hollered for his momma
not being jewish
naturally
she was off some place   being herself.

with his bottom lip free
he talked to himself as his bad eye
saw the wall coming
even at the deathmoment he tried to steal
the newsong.
afterall
he was just a jewish boy
who happened to be negro.

the deathmoment coming, the wall.
& the jewishnegro tried his infamous impersonations:
        cagney, sullivan, bogart, martin,
        lewis, durante, lawford, sinatra,
        with tom jones & janis joplin both
        singing, "i wish i was black."

but the good eye saw
the realdeath   the certaindeath
while the brainmessages charged the body
for the impression of impressions

& sammy tried but his blood was   gone
                                        his inner self was   gone
                                        his hair turned   back

and
he began to really see
as the wall came,
it failed and   he failed   to do
an impression of a

blackman.

We Walk the Way of the New World

1.
we run the dangercourse.
the way of the stocking caps & murray's grease.
(if u is modern u used duke greaseless hair pomade)
jo jo was modern/an international nigger
        born: jan. 1, 1863 in new york, mississippi.
his momma was mo militant than he was/is
jo jo bes no instant negro
his development took all of 106 years
& he was the first to be stamped "made in USA"
where he arrived bow-legged a curve ahead of the 20th
    century's new weapon: television.
which invented, "how to win and influence people"
& gave jo jo his how/ever look: however u want me.

we discovered that with the right brand of cigarettes
that one, with his best girl,
cd skip thru grassy fields in living color
& in slow-motion: Caution: niggers, cigarette smoking
        will kill u & yr/health.
& that the breakfast of champions is: blackeyed peas & rice.
& that God is dead & Jesus is black and last seen on 63rd
    street in a gold & black dashiki, sitting in a pink
    hog speaking swahili with a piglatin accent.
& that integration and coalition are synonymous,
& that the only thing that really mattered was:
  who could get the highest on the least or how to expand
  & break one's mind.

in the coming world
new prizes are
to be given
we *ran* the dangercourse.
now, it's a silent walk/a careful eye
jo jo is there
to his mother he is unknown
(she accepted with a newlook: what wd u do if someone
    loved u?)

jo jo is back
& he will catch all the new jo jo's as they wander in & out
and with a fan-like whisper say: you ain't no
                tourist
                and Harlem ain't for
                sight-seeing, brother.

2.
Start with the itch and there will be no scratch. Study
    yourself.
Watch yr/every movement as u skip thru-out the southside of
    chicago.
be hip to yr/ actions.

our dreams are realities
traveling the nature-way.
we meet them
at the apex of their utmost
meanings/means;
we walk in cleanliness
down state st/or Fifth Ave.
& wicked apartment buildings shake
as their windows announce our presence
as we jump into the interior
& cut the day's evil away.

We walk in cleanliness
the newness of it all
becomes us
our women listen to us
and learn.
We teach our children thru
our actions.

We'll become owners of the   New World
the New World.
will run it as unowners
for
we will live in it too
& will want to be remembered
as   realpeople.

Move Un-noticed to be Noticed: A Nationhood Poem

move, into our own, not theirs
into ours.
they own it (for the moment): the unclean world, the
polluted space, the un-censored
air, yr/ foot steps as they run
wildly in the wrong direction.
move, into our own, not theirs
into ours.
move, you can't buy own.
own is like yr/hair (if u let it live); a natural extension of
ownself.
own is yr/reflection, yr/total-being; the way u walk, talk,
dress and relate to each other is own.
own is you,
cannot be bought or sold: can u buy yr/ writing hand
yr/dancing feet, yr/ speech,
yr/woman (if she's real),
yr/manhood?
own is ours.
all we have to do is *take it,*
take it the way u take from one another,
the way u take artur rubenstein over thelonious monk,
the way u take eugene genovese over lerone bennett,
the way u take robert bly over imamu baraka,
the way u take picasso over charles white,
the way u take marianne moore over gwendolyn
brooks,
the way u take *inaction* over *action.*

move. move to act. act.
act into thinking and think into action.
try to think. think. try to think think think.
try to think. think (like i said, into yr/own)
think. try to think. don't hurt yourself, i know it's new.

try to act,
act into thinking and think into action.
can u do it, hunh? i say hunh, can u stop moving like a drunk
 gorilla?
 ha ha che che
 ha ha che che
 ha ha che che
 ha ha che che

move
what is u anyhow: a professional car watcher, a billboard for
 nothingness, a sane madman, a reincarnated clark
 gable?
either you is or you ain't!

the deadliving
are the worldmakers,
the image breakers,
the rule takers: blackman can you stop a hurricane?

"I remember back in 1954 or '55, in Chicago, when we had
13 days without a murder, that was before them colored
people started calling themselves *black*."
move.
move,
move to be moved,
move into yr/ownself, Clean.
Clean, u is the first black hippy i've ever met.
why u bes dressen so funny, anyhow, hunh?
i mean, is that u Clean?
why u bes dressen like an airplane, can u fly,
i mean,
will yr/blue jim-shoes fly u,
& what about yr/tailor made bell bottoms, Clean?
can they lift u above madness,
turn u into the right direction,
& that red & pink scarf around yr/neck what's that for Clean,
hunh? will it help u fly, yeah, swing, swing ing swing
 swinging high above telephone wires with dreams
 of this & that and illusions of trying to take bar-b-q
 ice cream away from lion minded niggers who
 didn't even know that *polish* is more than a sausage.

"clean as a tack,
rusty as a nail,
haven't had a bath
since columbus sail."

when u goin be something real, Clean?
like yr/own, yeah, when u goin be yr/ownself?

the deadliving
are the worldmakers,
the image breakers,
the rule takers: blackman can u stop a hurricane, mississippi
        couldn't.
blackman if u can't stop what mississippi couldn't, be it. be it.
blackman be the wind, be the win, the win, the win, win win:

        wooooooooooowe boom boom wooooooooooowe bah
        wooooooooooowe boom boom wooooooooooowe bah
if u can't stop a hurricane, be one.
        wooooooooooowe boom boom wooooooooooowe bah
        wooooooooooowe boom boom wooooooooooowe bah

be the baddddest hurricane that ever came, a black
hurricane.
        wooooooooooowe boom boom wooooooooooowe bah
        wooooooooooowe boom boom wooooooooooowe bah
the badddest black hurricane that ever came, a black
        hurricane named Beulah,
go head Beulah, do the hurricane.
        wooooooooooowe boom boom wooooooooooowe bah
        wooooooooooowe boom boom wooooooooooowe bah
move
move to be moved from the un-moveable,
into our own, yr/self is own, yrself is own, own yourself.
go where you/ we go, hear the unheard and do,
do the undone, do it, do it, do it *now,* Clean
and tomorrow your sons will
be alive to praise
you.

Change-up

change-up,
let's go for ourselves
both cheeks are broken now.
change-up,
move past the corner bar,
let yr/spirit lift u above that quick high.
change-up,
that toothpick you're sucking on was
once a log.
change-up,
and yr/children will look at us differently
than we looked at our parents.

Directionscore (1971)

Positives: for Sterling Plumpp

can u walk away from ugly,
will u sample the visions of yr self,
is ugly u? it ain't yr momma, yr woman,
    the brother who stepped on yr alligator shoes,
    yr wig wearen believen in Jesus grandmomma, or
    the honda ridden see-thru jumpsuit wearen brother.

yeah,
caught u upsidedown jay-walking across europe
to catch badness running against yr self.
didn't u know u were lost brother?
confused hair with blackness
thought u knew it before the knower did,
didn't u know u lost brother?
thought u were bad until u ran up against BAD:
Du Pont, Ford, General Motors   even the latest
Paris fashions: & u goin ta get rich off dashikis before Sears.
didn't u know u were lost brother?

beat laziness back into the outside,
run the mirror of ugliness into its inventors,
will u sample the visions of yr self?
quiet   like the way u do it soft spoken   quiet
quiet   more dangerous than danger a new   quiet
quiet   no name quiet no number quiet pure   quiet
quiet   to pure to purer.

a full back clean-up man   a black earthmover
my main man
change yr name like the wind
blow in any direction catch righteousness,
u may have ta smile at the big preacher in town,
thats alright organize in the church washroom,
trick the brother into learning—
be as together as a 360 computer:
    can u think as well as u talk,
    can u read as well as u drink,
    can u teach as well as u dress?

sample the new visions of yr work brother & smile
we'll push DuBois like they push the racing form.
yr woman goin ta look up to u,
yr children goin ta call u hero,
u my main nigger
the somethin like the somethin
u ain't suppose   *to be.*

With All Deliberate Speed

(for the children of our world)

in july of 19 somethin
the year of the "love it or leave it" stickers,
a pink sharecropper former KKK now
a wallacite pro-bircher
undercover minuteman
living in n.y. city as
a used hardhat flag waving,
beer belly torn undershirt wearen
hawk

is also
an unread bible carrying preacher
& secret draft dodger from WW 2
who
went to washington d.c.
at government's expense for
the 1970 honor america day and
support our boys in viet nam
also
took time out to find
& wildly slap slap slap slap
one
B.A., M.A., LLD., N.E.G.R.O.,
supreme court justice in the mouth and
with all deliberate speed
went home to alabama
to brag about
it.

To be Quicker
for Black Political Prisoners
on the inside & outside—real

(to my brothers & sisters of OBAC)

climb ape mountain backwards
better than the better u thought u had to be better than
jump clean.   cleaner.
jump past lightning into field-motion, feel-motion, feel mo
feel mo than the world thought u capable of feelin.
cd do it even fool yr momma, jim! fool yrself, hunh—

goin ta be cleaner,   hunh.
goin ta be stronger, hunh.
goin ta be wiser,   hunh.
goin ta be quick to be quicker   *to be.*

quick to be whats needed to be   whats needed:
quicker than enemies of the livingworld,
quicker than cheap smiles of a cadillac salesman,
quicker than a dead junky talkin to the wind,
quicker than super-slick niggers sliding in the opposite,
quicker than whi-te-titty-new-left-what's-left suckin niggers,
quicker to be quick, to be quick.

u wise brother.
u wiser than my father was   when he
talked the talk   he wasn't suppose to talk.

quicker to be quick, to be:

a black-African-fist slapping a wop-dope pusher's momma,
a hospital a school anything workin to save us to pull us
closer to Tanzania to Guinea to Harlem to the West Indies to
closer to momma to sister to brother closer to closer to
FRELIMO to Rastafory to us to power to running run to build
to controllifelines to Ashanti to music to life to Allah closer
to Kenya to the black world to the rays of anti-evil.

climb ape mountain backwards   brother
feel better than the better u thought was better
its yr walk brother,
lean a little, cut the smell of nasty.
jump forward into the past
to bring back

goodness.

An Afterword: for Gwen Brooks

(the search for the new-song begins with the old)

knowing her is not knowing her.

is not
autograph lines or souvenir signatures & shared smiles,
is not
pulitzers, poet laureates or honorary degrees
you see   we ordinary people
just know
ordinary people

to read gwen is to be,
to experience her in the *real*
is the same, she is her words,   more
like a fixed part of the world   is there
quietly penetrating   slow
reminds us of a willie kgositsile love poem   or
issac hayes singing *one woman.*

still
she suggests more;
have u ever seen her home?
it's an idea of her: a brown wooden frame
trimmed in dark gray with a new screen door.
inside: looks like the lady owes everybody on the southside
            nothing but books momma's books.
her home like her person is under-fed and small.

gwen:
pours smiles of african-rain
a pleasure well received among uncollected garbage cans
and heatless basement apartments.
her voice the needle for new-songs
plays unsolicited messages: poets, we've all seen
poets. minor poets ruined by
minor fame.

Mwilu/or Poem for the Living

(for Charles & Latanya)

jump bigness upward
like u jump clean   make everyday the weekend
& work like u party.

u justice brother, in the world of the un
just be there when wanted when needed when
yr woman calls yr name Musyoka* when yr son
wants direction strength give it, suh. suh
we call u strength suh, call u whatever.

be other than the common   build the sky
work;
study the bringers of anti-good,
question Jesus in the real,
& walk knowledge like you walk unowned streets, brother.
read like u eat   only betta   betta Musomi,
Musomi be yr name run emptiness into its givers
& collect the rays of wisdom.
there's goodness in yr eyes giver, give.
yr wind is chicago-big, Kitheka: Afrikan forest right-wind
running waking dullness of the night-thinkers in the wrong.

why we rather be evil, momma?
why we ain't togatha, Rev. Cleopelius?
why we slide under with tight smiles of forgiveness, Judas?
why our women want to be men, Amana?
why our men want to be somethin other, Muthusi?
what's goin ta make us   us, Kimanthi?
why we don't control our school, Mr. Farmer?
why we don't have any land, big negro?
why we against love, pimps?

FRELIMO* in chicago talking to the *stones*
hear what the real rocks have ta say.
be strange in the righteous
move away dumbjunkies leaning into death
    never Muslim eating pig sandwiches never
    never listerine breath even cuss proper never
    never u ignorant because *smart* was yr teacher never
    never wander under wonder fan-like avenues never
    never *will be never* as long as never teaches never.
snatching answers from the blue while
giving lip service   before imitating yr
executers

jump bigness upward
Impressions putting Fanon to music & sing like
black-rubbermen over smoked garbage cans with
music of a newer year among stolen nights in
basement corners meet u in the show, baby
just below the health food sign by sam's with
clean water over oiled fish as miniskirted sisters
wear peace symbols supporting the Israelis as
unfeeling as the *east india company*. wdn't dance
to the words of Garvey on pill hill eatin cornbread
with a fork in a see-thru walking suit while running
the fields of crazy while teaching the whi-te boy
the hand-shake. Would sell yr momma if somebody wd buy
    her
hunh. roach-back challenge space after un-eaten spit
goin ta still call u brother
goin ta still call u sister too, hunh.
brother, sister
young lovers of current doo-wops
rake cleanliness brother:

& study unwritten words of manhood.
young lovers of current doo-wops
what's yr new name sister:
reflect the goodness of yr man.
like the way u talk to each other,   like it.
the way yr voices pull smiles
u+u=2 over 2 which is 1.

raised higher than surprised quietness
kiss each other   and
touch the feel of secret words
while we all walk the
shadows of greatness.

---

* The African names used are from the Swahili language
of central & east Africa Mwilu (Mwi-lu)—of black; likes black
Musyoka (Mu-syo-ka)—one who always returns
Musomi (Mu-so-mi)—scholarly; reads; studies
Kitheka (Ki-the-ka)—wanderer of the forest
Amana (A-ma-na)—peacefulness; serenity; feminine
Kimanthi (Ki-ma-nthi)—one who searches for freedom, wealth, love
FRELIMO—Freedom fighters from Mozambique (Southeast Africa)

Book of Life (1973)

Introduction: Discovering the Traitors

This work comes at a difficult time in our lives. Comes at a period when we, as a race, are under much weight and can smell and feel the call of death in our very midst. This is odd. It is odd to be so concerned about death when we know deep inside that life is for living, is for developing, is for building, is for creating, is for loving. Yet today, August 27, 1973, our smiles are still few—yet we do smile because we know too that we must not, if possible, convey the death to our children. We know that we must *seem* and *be* the promise of tomorrow. We know that we must be the music of days coming. We know that we must dance while we prepare to fight.

Time moves and passes many of us by, leaving both the closed and open eyed, leaving the hangers-on and the pimps of the race. And, the question remains: how do we, as a *people,* regain our rightful place in the world? Good question, difficult question, and there are other good and difficult questions that must be asked if we are to get answers and begin to prepare. We came as lovers worldwide not understanding *what it ain't.* We *attack the anti* rather than *be the pro.* We seek answers in the enemy's den and dare to lie to our mothers about our secret associations. The time for honesty has passed—it was about sixty years ago that negroes betrayed each other for recognition from the enemies of the world. It didn't get us anything then and it will not get us anything now. Except—certain defeat and disrespect. Yes, we came as lovers and left as killers. Enemies to ourselves. We have become our own worst enemy—a cliché, yes, but oh so true. We revolve around each other like aged boxers going for a last TKO. Our exercise now is leaning out third floor windows observing our part of the world speed by us; our exercise now is the daily ritual of putting on false eyelashes. Tell me, talk to me—why are we so immobile in a world of mobility? *We must question our powerlessness.* We must recognize the necessity for collective movement among so many *individuals.* It may be that the most individual of the world's individuals is the *negro.* This speaks to our defenselessness, speaks to our ignorance, our stupidity.

Any act of giving is an act of receiving. We are not a weak people: we're just weakened at this moment. We'll find strength in each other—we'll reinforce each other, thus giving and receiving simultaneously. Togetherness at a revolutionary *level.* We are a world people. We black people exist in abundance worldwide and must begin to forge a *black world unity.* Black world unity is the only vehicle that will enable us to survive *white world unity.* However, we fall into many traps and unknowingly play games with our children's lives and mistakenly call these games jobs, positions, status, security, etc. The only job that is mandatory is working for the race. The only security we *have* is each other, working for the race together. And as long as a people do not know these basic facts, they will not function as a people and will remain enslaved as a people, not as individuals.

This is obvious to some. The poets know it. But the poets have become the traitors. The poets have become comfortable and published. The poets now talk of "private lives" and "my business." The poets make best-seller records and sip coffee with the editors of America's leading publishing houses. They talk of the best for "my child" and about going to the Bahamas to write the next book. They too now talk of making it and getting over. The poets have become traitors. And

when you can't trust the poets, who is left?
After the fact comes the expected,
After the act come the poets and poems,
After the killing come the singer and songs,
After the funeral come the pimps in disguise.
What does U.N.I.T.A.* do with the poets who betray them?
What does P.A.I.G.C.** do with the poets and artists who
betray the people?
What did the Vietnamese do about them?
What type of re-education do the poets receive in China and Guinea?

Yes, we know, but we are not prepared for that here in the land of the "artists." And really are the poets worth such attention? Probably not. But when you're so close to the air, you must breathe it. Life comes in many forms and leaves in many forms also. They die. They live. We must forget them and build.

This book speaks to the void that developed in me after discovering traitors in our midst. But it also speaks more forcefully to the strengths gained in discovering in our people a new critical judgment that will not just forgive and forget those that do us harm-regardless of who they are. We all must face the coming test and it will not be an easy one. But, most will not recognize that they are being tested and they will undoubtedly fail. The few who pass will start the re-building. They will begin the final movement for Kawaida (Afrikan Tradition and Reason), peoplehood and land. We continue to work and await them and leave with you this, the *Book of Life.*

Haki R. Madhubuti (Don L. Lee)
Poet-in-Residence, Howard University

**National Union for the Total Independence of Angola*

*** African Party for Independence of Guinea (Bissau) and Cape Verde Islands*

Worldview

fact is stranger than fiction
here in america in the year of 1973
many black people don't even know how
we came to this land

some black people believe that
we were the first people
to fly
and that we came first class.

Positive Movement Will be Difficult but Necessary

(for John O. Killens)

remember past ugly to memories of the *once*
to memories of the used to be
lost days of glory, the forgotten-forgiven history of the race:
when sun mattered and the night was for sleeping
and not for planning the
death of enemies.

beautiful
realpretty like morning vegetation beautiful
like Afrikanwomen bathing in Tanzanian sun
beautiful a word now used exclusively to describe the
 ungettable
 a word used to describe roaches disguised as
 people that viciously misrule the world.
times is hard rufus & they gointa be harda
come on champ chop chop
hit hard hit harda catch up chop chop
sleep less eat right rise earlier
whip dust into the eyes of excuse makers
talk to yr children about meaning,
talk to yr children about working for the race.
chop chop hit hard hit harda
beat it beat it beat it now

in this world
we face our comings as hip slaves unknown to ourselves
unknown to the actual challenges of the race
do you know yr real name?
do you know the real reasons you are here?
check the smiles on yr enemies' faces
if you can identify yr enemies
they crawl from the earth in many faces: negroes,
militants, revolutionary integrationists, soul-brother
number 15, black capitalists, colored politicians

and pig-eaters lying about their diets.
listen now listen
open yr ears we got a number for you
listen, somebody is trying to tell us something,
listen, somebody is trying to pull our minds.
it ain't magic we be better if it will   listen
let the words seek greater levels of meaning
split in there   words be   beat it beat it words
beat it now
it ain't gypsy tales or trails
or false eyes frontin for the devil
it ain't about the happy ending of the west
unless you are reading the future wrong.

We are Some Funny "Black Artists"
And Everybody Laughs at Us

random house and double day publish the
"militant black writers"
who write real-bad about the
"money-hungry jew" and the "power-crazed irishman."
random house and double day will continue to publish the
"militant black writers"
while sending much of the profits received from the books
by the
"militant black writers"
to Israel and Ireland to build a nation for the
"money-hungry jew" and the "power-crazed irishman"
while the
"militant black writers"
who write real-bad about white people
can't even get a current accounting of their
royalties from random house or double day
and black nation-building never crossed their minds.

Rise Vision Comin
May 27, 1972
(for Osagyefo Kwame Nkrumah 1909-1972)

there is quietness   hear
time to regroup time to rethink   time to reassess
the world we think belongs to somebody else.

there is quietness   hear
time to create an Afrikan-mind
time to create an Afrikan-mind in a european setting had his Chaka
(if we had called the blood Afrikan 4 years ago he wd a
had his whole family out for the kill lookin for a crazy negro, an unamerican,
a communist, a no nothin tree swingin jungle waker-er) but

there is quietness   hear
shootin for the 21st century with 19th century weapons
while the whi-te boy is walkin on the moon
& negroes are runnin down to moonlounge on hot-pants
    night
we some BAD diamond wearers, you Bad brother:
badly taught
badly situated &
badly organized   but

there is a quietness   hear
time to re-educate time to redirect our limits super
time to stop being the *buts* in the undefined, unfinished
sentences of the flesh-eaters: he's a first class doctor *but*
he's colored, she's one of the best teachers ever *but* she's
negro, he's a fine worker *but* he's black.   but
there is quietness   hear

we are what we are
we are what we are not
we are what we are going to be
we are what we are
the reflection the image the backward word world of what
the substance of that we must become the positive side of
    comin

send roy wilkins to Afrika if he don't act AFRIKAN
think him have mo wisdom than the OAU
a real credit to his race: bad credit a piece of 15th century
science fiction talkin bout his momma as if she was
    the enemy
a for real beatin down negro unsure of the space he occupies
if he occupies any him show not invisible we see rat
    through him
feel his opposite a walkin back steppin X-rated movie with
blocked vision   but
we comin

we are what we are not
think him Gulf Oil, IBM or GM the way he talk about
    industrializing
Afrika
if they took the water faucet from him he'd die of
    water-freeze

think him Dow Chemical or the Pentagon the way he talk
about arming
Afrika
but we goin a need mo than wine bottles, promises & ray
    gun dreamin

think him Harvard or MIT the way he talk about educating
Afrika couldn't even teach a day care center if it was already
    taught

we are what we are going to be
comin sam   comin willie   comin mable   comin jesus malinda
    pepper
now u different
comin rise risin comin   talkin about doin it yoself   hunh
about institutionalizing yr thoughts yr actions comin risin

to
claim the tradition & collective culture of your world
comin *rise*
rise junebug beat evil back into the cold Zimbabwe
expose the enemy FRELIMO u goin a do it Angola rise
now u different blood new stronger
stronger than storm bigger betta betta than a bad footed
negro
in fifty dollar shoes comin runnin call u swift call u fast fasta
fasta than stolen Bar-B-Q in a baptist meetin on last sunday
comin
live the land the purity of the first humans is in you comin *rise*
dash-on flash dodgin skyscrapers vacant lots & evil highs
with a conscious feel for earth for land for yrself comin rise
transformin reborn renurtured in purpose in goodness in
direction new
u dynamite Musi where did u arrive from Kikuyu
where u been hidin Rastafarian which way SWAPO
what universe did u crash thru NewArk call u speed speeda
make yr own gas create yr own energy dig an escape hatch
into us rise
redirectin our focus callin ourselves AFRIKANS
callin ourselves AFRIKAN men & women callin ourselves
builders of the
FIRST callin ourselves stylers of tomorrow: the shape to
come shaper
comin 21st century fly golden antelope a black lion is u simba
and the world is still here still evolving even the devil can't
stop that gave us the worse Enemy EVER: *aint never seen*
nothin like the europeans lost they taste fo life-living. but
they can't stop higher vision can't stop newrisin right talkin
good doin it gettin it done Afrikans can't stop organized
builders of righteousness
pull the fight together Guinea-Bissau
we with u southern Sudan fight on runnin wise Mozambique
jump quick lightin FROLIZI teach Nyerere watch our backs
Osagyefo
guide our future Lumumba describe our enemies Garvey
we're comin Toure comin PAIGC goin to surprise the world

surprise
our father's Malcolm   we have mo than mouth mo than fast-
talk
mo than Harvard rhetoric   we are comin

we are what we are
we are what we are not
we are what we are going to be
comin comin risin risin to a higher beat of Afrikan movement
comin fast
dancin hard makin sense remembering Sharpeville
remembering Orangeburg
comin remembering yesterday's plant risin out of the earth
fast
challenging new thoughts challenging concepts of false gods
comin *rise*
elevator up juju blackworld vibrations beatin us into eachother
rise comin risin thru visions of Afrikanlove rise comin feet
get back negative we comin shine fightin thru spacesun
son is
slidin closer to the expected comin nationalists
comin christians comin muslims comin pan-afrikanists ancient
black spirits
comin comin
rise buba rise brothers rise sisters rise people of the summer
comin
comin comin come in come in come in
we are here quick

gathered gathered gathered

to save the future for our children.

Hooked

the only time
the brother is sober is
when he tryin to
find another
high.

Afrikan Men

(for Hoyt W. Fuller & Lerone Bennett Jr.)

there is a certain steel-ness about you
the way u set the vision & keep it
the way u view the world & warn us.
the coming tomorrows the limited memory of what was
the image the reflection the realness of what is to be.

our pace is faster but without wisdom
our "advances" are louder yet without movement
our mistakes are many & often deadly
yet we seek examples seek the quality of substance
while the lies drop around us
making the actors into the reactors
and even though we don't wear for sale signs
we've been bought rather cheaply, yet

we
with the limited memories have learned
not to trust the easy music
not to trust the processed food
not to trust the comfortable compromise,
have learned
that love will not stop the enemies of the world
their nature will not allow them
to submit to the beautiful
& our minds quicken knowing that
if a rat is chewing at yr baby's skull
you don't negotiate you
kill it.

there is a certain stillness about you
unwilling to be pushed by the opportunities of the world,
your insight into the holocaust will not permit
fastness, non-movement or mistakes
you understand that these are the luxuries of the young
& the young have limited memories.

we've now passed the dangers of youth because
there is a certain steel-ness about you
the way u set the vision & keep it
the way u view the world & warn us.

Spirit Flight into the Coming

For Amilcar Cabral (1925–1973), Imamu Amiri Baraka
and Congress of Afrikan People)

Ever get tired of people playing with yr life, playing with
yr children's lives, playing with blackness, playing with Afrika?
Ever get tired of other people telling you what you shd be
doing for yr self? Ever get tired of people posturing,
posing and profiling?
We all know niggers look good   but
We don't own nothing
We don't have no land
We don't have no army
We don't control no major institutions
We don't
We don't even teach our children how to be themselves
We don't influence black domestic policy
We don't influence foreign policy toward Afrika
We are a powerless, defenseless people   but we're
looking good, looking very good   step now   step
step now yo step now get in step brother lookin very good
The white boy make the clothes and put em on the store
          dummy
and we, lookin good—out dress the dummy
Hey   step now   get in step brother   let's get a strong
line lookin good step on in
We are a powerless, defenseless people lookin very good
and don't even make the make-up we whiten our faces with
we don't do nothin except talk about what others need to be
doing for ourselves, while ourselves are too busy being
like others we talk about we don't want to be like
as ourselves wear their clothes better than they do, drive their
cars faster than they do, talk their language as well as they
     do
while it all spells out to be theirs as ourselves illusionize
about doin our thang and don't understand the world our
     selves
live in but ourselves are down there just below
nixon's toilet eatin pig meat and lying to our
children about blackness.
Witness the negro asst. asst. to the president's asst.
going thru his post black period talkin about what

the administration is doing for the race   maybe
him talkin about the Indianapolis 500.

We sick because we don't know *who we are.*
We sick because we don't have a *purpose* in life.
We sick because we don't have *direction* for ourselves.

Step in CAP: Congress of Afrikan People step in
refix the world clear the rust from our eyes
navigate the wind, expose the enemy, inform the mind
connect the black organs. Work a wonder:
make the negro black and Afrikan again—even if
we don't wanta be. We don't wanta be here, but we are!

Everything else is Jive! negro congressmen
can't even pass a bill to save they people. Colored general
too busy welcoming home war criminals, probably kill his
momma
for another star star him in a John Wayne movie
one eyed negro Jewish dancer sleeping in the white house
hope him sleep there forever
dance sammy dance, dance sammy dance,
as our people gaze blankly at garbage men passing thru our
communities
at midnight while
negro pimps fight their people for recognition from Agnew's
momma.

Reflect the image CAP—step in somebody
shine brightness for a dead people.
show us that there is value in ourselves
prove to us that we are worth saving—heal the forgotten mind
the forgotten bodies of the east.
prove to us that we are worth saving
cure the negativism in us
provide the example   teach the doctrine

display identity: we were builders of the first.
display purpose: our children, our parents, our
ancestors *great* as *we be*

display direction: sharing land, raising our children,
building a world the way a world is
supposed to be built.

Everything else is Jive: Ph.D.'s in french, can't eat no french
can't farm no land with french. wake up showboat, wakeup
showboat
Dr. Clearhead Knowitall Ph.D., summa cum laude U of
Chicago 1973
now teaching the *psychology of blackness* in the suburbs
proving to the enemy—that taught him—how smart him is
what have you done for your people lately Dr. Knowitall?
what have you done for the race except, race away
waving flags about it's a human and class problem
ask your great, great, great grandmomma, fool,
was she raped from a continent due to the human/class
problem?

Step in Imamu:
plant the seed and regulate the growth you are the
vegetation of life. bloods are getting up earlier now
catching the sun on the second mile run getting ready
for the day's work getting ready for the heavy load
cleaning up. washing down. disciplining ourselves consistent
with nature now. getting ready to re-make the life in us,
telling ourselves how we back stepped into what we
now be. tomorrow is our coming.

Everything else is Jive: we got negroes arguing the necessity
of Marx and Engels to empty-bellied children,
we got negroes married to white people speaking for the race.
don't no Arabs speak for Jews.
we slaves because we wanta be. we slaves because we
wanta be.
unbelievable
but being a slave is hip
being a slave in america is *really* hip
slaves think they can buy their freedom

slaves drive big cars
slaves take dope
slaves love big houses
slaves teach blackness at big universities
slaves love their enemy
slaves love death in any form
slaves love paper money
slaves live for pleasure only
if we slaves be let free we'd buy ourselves back into slavery.
it is hip being a slave in America cause we got everything
   slaves need,
we're the richest slaves in the world.

Step in Imamu:
all that is good and accomplished in the world takes work
work is what we need an abundance of
work for a better value system   work
work for ourselves like we work for general motors,
like we work for integration, like we work for the
son of mary   work
teach one   reach one   work and study
study the math, the physics, the chemistry   that is
   revolutionary
study the science of building   that is revolutionary
study the inner workings of yr self   that is revolutionary
think about building a livable world   that's revolutionary
meditate on a new way of life   that's revolutionary
Juba Juba Juba du
move Juba into agriculture like we move in fashions
work Juba work Juba work
Juba Juba Juba du now work Juba
write some work songs Juba work
paint some work pictures Juba work
play some work music Juba work
Juba Juba Juba du
work raw honey for the brain
work exercise for the dead blood cells
work life serum for the tired muscles
work chakula for the body

work the land into food
work to keep yr woman by yr side
work the evil into good
work the enemy into submission
work and organize organize and work work
and develop develop the work work
and study study the work
work energizes Afrika and Afrikan people
work energizes Afrika and Afrikan people
All that is good and accomplished in the world takes work
Everything else is Jive

17 june 1973

Life Poems

1.
the best way to
effectively fight an
alien culture
is to live your own.

2.
pride in one's people is desirable
pride in black people is necessary for black people
but
pride must be properly cultivated and
displayed in moderation
too much pride alienates brother from brother
alienates sister from sister
alienates us from community and nation
too little pride
confuses the natural direction we must take
and hinders the building of nations
pride in abundance is bad
too little pride is bad
strike a balance.

3.
is a sign of life in your face?
is the sign of life in your thoughts?
is the sign of life in your actions?
if not there can be no life in you.
if so you are life.

4.
there is life in men
men are life but
when men put themselves above others
life becomes disproportionate and loses clarity
when a man puts material and worldly goods above humanity
our understanding of and value for real life ceases
his wife becomes something he sleeps with
his children become objects to order about
his friends become competition
the land becomes property to fence in
his aim in life is toward making it and getting over
his tradition ceases to have meaning
and is not passed on to his children
his tomorrows are now measured in material production
   & acquisition
and his future is that which he puts in the bank today.

5.
those who know
both ways
and proceed to take the incorrect one
may not be able to reverse themselves later.

6.
to know is to be
to be and not know is not to be
to know and not know that you know is not to know
to know and not be is not to know
to know is to be

7.
to seek all the answers of life
into yourself is to misunderstand life.
we are only a minute portion of all
that makes up life and our relationship
to other forms of life gives meaning to
our life.
we are all in the cycle of return and give.
understand yourself first but also go
outside of yourself so as to understand the
cycle of life.
seek answers of the world in the world
while understanding that the world
is part of you.

8.
it is true that nature in time will
solve the world's problems and
resolve the world's disputes
however, nature and time are unpredictable
and may not act in our lifetime.
our understanding of life
demands that we respect nature & time
but our children's future
demands that we help nature solve our problems
today with the little time we have on earth.

9.
if we are not for ourselves
who is for us?
if we are men and women
why are other people giving us orders?

10.
there is much to be learned
there is much to be unlearned
to do both
takes an open mind and a mind that questions.
we can get correct answers only
if we ask the correct questions.

11.
we have people in our midst
who can quote
every body from *can* to *can't*
but do nothing else.
theory without practice is like
a car without gas is like
land without cultivation is like
poetry without content.
men and women *act*
others re-act and talk about acting.
which are we?

12.
there are those who
have never left
home
but understand the universe.

13.
those who think nothing of themselves
are not full and cannot appreciate others
because they cannot appreciate themselves.
those who think only of themselves
have no room for others
and cannot appreciate others.
those who are secure in themselves
will not fear security in others
and
will be motivated toward the most secure of relationships
that of friendship
and friendship reinforces security.

14.
weak people hide
behind titles
and status to aid their egos.
weak people
attack from the rear.
watch your back
as you move forward.

15.
know yourself first
that which is good
that which is bad
correctly assess yourself
and you will not mistakenly assess your neighbors.

16.
we are not a tribe
we are a nation.
we are not wandering groups
we are a people.
we are not without land
there is Afrika.
if we let others define us
our existence, our definition will be dependent upon
the eyes, ears, and minds of others.
other people's definitions of us cannot be accurate for us
because their hurt is not our hurt,
their laughter is not our laughter,
their view of the world is not our view of the world.
other's definition of the world
is necessary for their survival and control of the world
and for us to adopt their view of the world is a necessary
step toward their continued control over us
therefore to let others define us is to assure
we *will* be a tribe,
we *will* be wandering groups,
we *will* be
landless
self-definition is the first step toward
self-control.

17.
if you know who you are
the identity of others
will be respected, appreciated
understood.

18.
talk little and listen with care
those who talk much
cannot hear the silences around them
cannot hear the noises around them
they hear only their own voice
and will mainly talk of themselves.
talk little and listen with care
there is more to the world than your own voice.

19.
if you are silent
no one can hear you coming
if you make much noise
your enemies can prepare for you.

20.
knowledge of self starts at home
understand that which is
closest to you first.
understanding that which is nearest
brings meaning to that
which is far.

21.
many people fear knowledge
knowledge stimulates change and most people fear change
to acquire knowledge is to grow
to grow is to change
growth without knowledge is not growth
growth with knowledge leads toward wisdom
there are few wise people in our time
and change is what we need

22.
if the people
think that they can buy everything or
that everything is for sale
then there is little left in life of real value.
they will spend their days making money
spend their evenings thinking about what to buy
and spend their weekends buying.
this is not normal and is in conflict with
the natural way of life,
if a people feel that they can buy everything
their values are corrupt and they too
can be bought and are not to be trusted.

23.
the need of expensive clothes, cars and homes
to impress others and yourself
only means
that you have no meaning without them
which also means
that you have no meaning with them.

24.
to
betray a trust
is to
cut yourself off from being
trusted.

25.
to be ignorant of the world around you
is slavery
to not want to know of the world around you
is death.

26.
we must be able to function within ourselves
we must build and develop our inner spirit and force.
this gives autonomy to our outer movements
as we seek to forcefully interact with the larger world.
if this interaction is to be successful
it must be a force with spirit behind it that
no one will doubt. such a spirit
and force can only come from a people who
have faith in themselves and the path they
have chosen for themselves.
we are an Afrikan people.

27.
to know nothing is a statement of negative being
to know nothing speaks to a condition of uselessness
to know nothing puts one at the mercy
of those who know.

28.
if you are confused
you'll bring confusion to
everything you touch.

29.
people who eat
everything that is placed before them
by anybody, anywhere
cannot be healthy
choose your food as you choose friends
with care and knowledge of its ultimate value.

30.
to go without food
brings an understanding
of the people who are foodless
but
to go without food
and know that none is forthcoming
brings an appreciation and understanding
of food and the foodless
that is unlearnable any other way.

31.
those who eat and need
many meals in a day
cannot be eating the food that gives and maintains life.
life-giving foods such as vegetables and fruits
are the basis for good health and long life
and should be consumed modestly.
processed food from processed sources
produce a processed body with a processed mind;
produce men and women whose first love is to eat
and only aim in life is to
make it to the next meal.

32.
many of the modern day diseases
that hurt us did not exist many years ago.
however many years ago our diets didn't consist of:
powdered this and instant that,
frozen now and eaten later,
canned everything and contaminated water,
pour and mix and open and stir   all
preceded by any flesh of the world,
from fried monkey to boiled pig bellies,
you cannot sustain life with "foods"
out of boxes, cans, plastic and resealable jars.
you need live food for live bodies.
stay close to the earth
consume that which the earth naturally gives us.

33.
there is meaning here
in us under the weight of hours today
under the weight of misunderstanding of their world.
we clench our teeth, lie to our children and make it.
but the feared breaks through
the air is dirty and kills much,
the streets are trafficful and nothing moves,
the water is impure and slowly damages the drinker.
life cannot endure this way.
there is meaning here
if we seek it.

34.
the family is the basic unit of all nations.
the family structure has endured since recorded history
the family structure will continue to survive the sickness
of the day:
let the singles come,
let the bi-sexuals come,
let the homosexuals come,
let the non-family advocates come,
let the extreme individualists come,
let the unisexuals come,
let the transvestites come.
these are brief additions to our diversity
and if the nation is to live and prosper
the family will live and endure because
the nation is families united.

35.
there is much special
about black women,
the way they endure,
the way they grow,
the way they build,
the way they love,
it is traditionally thought that black women
are the reflection of black men.
and black men the reflection of black women.

36.
only fools limit women.
the full potential of a nation
cannot be realized unless the
full potential of its women
is realized.
only fools limit women.

37.
a nation cannot grow without its women
the intelligence of a nation
is reflected in its women
who bear the children for the nation
and are charged with the early education of the nation.
a nation cannot have intelligent women
unless the women are treated intelligently
and given much love.

38.
the substance and mental attitude of a nation
can be seen in its women, in the way they act
and move throughout the nation being productive.
if the women have nothing to do it reflects
what the nation is not doing.
if the women have substance and responsible positions
the nation has substance and is responsible.

39.
if a woman covers herself with paints
of blues, reds, grays and yellows
she unknowingly kills her skin,
she unknowingly smothers life from the first layer covering.
to paint a flower white that is naturally red is to
close its breathing pores and interrupt its natural skin growth
the flower will soon die.
to paint black skin green, orange and other colors
is to display black skin as something that
should be hidden from the actual world
and slowly suffocated from life.

40.
it is normal
for man to look at woman
but
it is abnormal to look
at woman the way we
have been taught to
look at her in the western world.

41.
we have been given
only one standard of beauty which
is the exact opposite of our own self-image.
due to this we see beauty in others
and fail to see it in ourselves.
this leads to destructive self-concepts that
will not only affect our relationship
with ourselves but will affect our
relationship with the world for the worst.

42.
nothing is created
without a mind
that is creative.

43.
institutions that reflect and guide a people
are important and necessary.
nations are made up of people who
create institutions that give substance
to the nation and its people.
where are the black institutions that
give substance to black people?
most of us would have difficulty identifying
more than one of them.
we must have new institutions in order
to institutionalize new thoughts and actions.
we must make current black institutions more
accountable to the needs of black people whom they
say they serve.

44.
we sit in our used cars
talking bad about others who don't own used cars and
we think that we are better off.
wonder who is running the world
while we talk about used cars?

45.
if you are silent
few will know
your ignorance.

46.
we must work to make life,
we must study to understand life,
we must create in order to support & stimulate life,
we must build to maintain life.

47.
the more complex life becomes
the more confused are the people.
we live in a world where we
pay to be born,
pay to live and
pay to die.
when the people seek work
they are computerized and given numbers,
when the people speak of hunger
they are photographed and made to feel less than people,
when the people seek medical care
they are filed into lines and experimented with,
when the people ask for education
they are scorned and laughed at,
when the people seek truth to be truth
they are lied to and ridiculed.
for those who need to know
you mistake the people's smiles for thank yous
and their sincerity for stupidity.
the people are not so soft and naïve
as not to be able to remove complexity
and wipe out confusion
when they bring the hour.

48.
you do not save people
by putting water on their foreheads
or by immersing them in the deep.
save people
by being and by telling them the truth.

49.
beware of quick smiles
and fast words.
one who smiles overmuch
mis-uses the face.
one who talks too fast
seldom says anything worth listening to.
quick smiles and fast words
fool the weak,
confuse the strong,
do damage to the face   and
mis-use the language.

50.
best teachers
seldom teach
they be and do.

51.
you
are nothing
as long as
nothing is on your
mind.

52.
let us not seek to impress our people
with the eloquence of our words.
words cannot feed the hungry,
words cannot clothe or house the needy,
words cannot heal the sick,
words cannot plant the food.
words take us away from the doing.
speak carefully and with substance
and
you will not have to speak much about nothing
if this is done
your presence will be welcomed,
the people will speak highly of you at family gatherings
and you will be sought after by many.

53.
how many of our children have
seen the ocean's ripple
or have felt the morning wetness of
country vegetation
or picked the just ripened fruit from trees or vines
or enjoyed the afternoon sun bathing
their bodies as they played in the green.
there is little that is green in the cities
other than the broken stop lights and
artificial grass.
our children's dreams are lost among the
concrete of too many promises
waiting for elevators to take them
to the top floors of public housing.

54.
corruption comes because we disrupt
and confuse the meaning of life.
we reorder natural and human
values to those of:
making money,
gaining power,
searching for sex,
pursuing fame,
seeking status
and lying to our children about life.
we need a new system of values speaking
to the real meaning of humanity.
corruption breeds corruption
the non-corrupt cannot live among
the corrupt and not become corrupt also,
one either leaves and exposes
or one becomes corrupt
there is no compromise,
there is no in between.

55.
when you work for yourself
you must *work* for yourself.
either we use the time we have wisely
or we do not use our time wisely.
if we say that our day starts at 6:30 a.m.
then it must. if we start at 7:30 a.m.
we are already an hour behind an hour that
cannot be made up.
our enemies work 24 hours a day and
do not have hours to make up.
there
is no substitute for work.
but
there is a substitute for talking about work.

work!

56.
we do not equate
poverty with blackness
nor do we equate the lavish
use of wealth with blackness.
we now live in a time
where the many go without
while for the few we have entrusted to lead us
luxuries have become needs.

57.
the cities kill the will,
dull the senses,
make white the eyes and
stop the future in us
before it starts.
if we survive the west
we survive the worst,
but let us not become
worse in our survival.

58.
a people without their culture
are a people without meaning.
a people without their culture
are a people without substance.
a people without their culture
are a people without identity, purpose and direction.
a people without their culture
are a dead people.

59.
the old of our people
are the elders of the race
and must be listened to,
must be looked after,
must be given meaningful work,
must be loved and cared for,
must be treated with the highest respect.
the elders of the race
are the reason we are here.

60.
to hate one's self and one's people
is not normal
to perpetually wish to be like other people
is not normal
to act against one's self and one's community
is not normal
that which is normal for us
will never be normal for us
as long as the abnormal
defines what normality is.

61.
we now have in our midst
people who *only* read and write and talk or argue.
they play with concepts and ideas,
can quote you the theory of the world,
can discourse for days on the meaning of life,
have usually an answer for everything and if they don't
have the answer they consult each other until
they come up with an answer.
they are powerless,
they are defenseless,
they have no land and mainly live in the cities.
they do not control major institutions
they do not control production,
they do not control distribution,
they do not make decisions on major policy for the nation,

they do not control the armed forces.
they would starve to death if somebody else didn't
bring them their food.
these are defenseless and powerless people.
they play with concepts and ideas and
divorce themselves from implementation.
they are not to be feared, they are to be re-educated.

62.
a man becomes the best runner in the country
because that is what he has been taught to be
and he wishes it and works hard for it.
a woman becomes the best doctor in the country
because that is what she has been taught to be
and she wishes it and works hard for it.
a man becomes the best hustler in the country
because that is what he has been taught to be
and he wishes it and works hard for it.
the major reason we don't work for our people
like we work at being runners, doctors and hustlers
is because no one has taught us to be and act as a people
or what the value and importance of being a people means.
therefore, we are busy being the best runners, doctors,
and hustlers in the country.

63.
our belief in our people
can only be measured by the
belief we have in ourselves
if we do not believe in ourselves
our belief in our people will not be real
because   we are the people.

64.
afrikan holidays
are holy days:
teach the history,
legitimize the nation,
reinforce the traditions
and
reunite the families.

65.
look beyond tomorrow
it will help you
accomplish that which is needed
today.

66.
a son needs direction if he is to be strong & work for the race
he does not need harsh words
about the way he should be
or words about how he should do this or that.
Fathers
study your own ways
so that your actions may guide him past the pitfalls of life
the best teacher is you being the example
of what others talk about.

67.
don't talk about
organizing the city or the world for self-reliance
when you can't organize
your own house or community.
start with self
and move to those closest to you
and each in turn do the same.
it is a slow but effective process
and it is better to be
slow and effective than to be
fast, ineffective and seen in all parts
of the city talking
nonsense.

68.
we know more about
how to kill than we know about
how to save.
our medicine is curative rather than preventive.
the weapons of war are more numerous
than schools, hospitals or places of worship.
we destroy small nations to save them from ideology.
we teach our children the ways of life
as we act out the ways of destruction.
our contradictions are catching up with us
and we will fall very fast in our lies and acts
because we are ill-prepared for saving.
we know more about how to kill.

69.
nations are like people
they need each other
no nation is truly independent
all nations are interdependent
however some nations are more dependent
on other nations than on themselves
so as
to put them at the mercy of other nations.
strengthen yourself internally before you seek
strength from the outside.

70.
the need to impress the world
shows little understanding of the world.
the need to make good impressions
means you have false impressions
the need to be The Best
is to misunderstand what best is.
the major reason for competition
is to take us away from cooperation and collective actions
and allows the many to be subtly controlled by the few.
put faith in the ability of each other
while strengthening the weaknesses of each other.
this is the natural order of things
and you will stand out
like vegetation in the desert
and will attract much water.

71.
it is said that,
"death is no threat to a people
who are not afraid to die."
yet
life today in part is controlled
by those who are afraid
to live.
a reordering of the world is due.

72.
there are no vacations
when a people are enslaved
there are just more sophisticated
forms of slavery disguised as
three weeks off with pay.

73.
understand the enemy within
and
the enemy without
will
be easier to deal with.

74.
we love our dogs
more than we love ourselves.
we feed our dogs three times a day.
we clothe our dogs in dog clothes.
we walk and talk with our dogs every day.
we call our dogs "man's best friend."
we play with our dogs and buy them dog toys.
when our dogs get sick we see that they get the
best of care.
if we dealt with each other one fourth as well
as we deal with our dogs this would be
more of a people world than a world
livable for dogs.

75.
if i make mistakes
tell me about them while i live
don't wait until i have left the earth
and then accuse me of contradictions
i may not have been aware of.

76.
in seeking answers
don't go too far on too little
you may not make it back

77.
black people
are all musicians
even though
they don't all
play instruments.

78.
move around wishes
and begin to control reality.
you can't wish good life upon a people,
you can't wish the best education upon a people,
you can't wish shelter and clothing upon a people,
you can't wish self determination upon a people,
you can't wish self respect upon a people.
you can't wish self defense upon a people.
replace most of your wishes with work
and you will not have time to wish often
you'll be too busy harvesting your crop.

79.
knowledge is like water
it is nourishment for those who seek it
and wasted on those who misuse it
but for all whom it touches
it does some good   so like water
let's spread knowledge worldwide.

80.
if you need to learn nuclear physics
you go to a nuclear physicist.
if you need to know how to work the land
you go to a farmer.
if you need to know how to build a house
you go to a carpenter.
if you need to know mathematics
you go to a mathematician.
if you need to know medicine
you go to medical school.
when all is learned that is needed to be learned
you return to your people and set up your own
schools for your own people.
this is one way
to fight and win wars.

81.
your world is in your eyes.
if you believe you have a future it will be in your eyes.
if you are well physically and mentally
it will be seen in your eyes.
if one is good and is to be trusted look into their eyes.
if one is evil their eyes will not hide it.
if one is afraid, their fear will look at you.
if one has strength, the part of the body
to show it first will be the eyes.
with the eyes you cannot deceive
nor can you make them up as to hide
their real meaning.
most people will not look you directly
in the eye.
some hide behind sunglasses,
some hide behind just not looking at you.
the eyes tell too much.
if you seek answers
do not look at one's possessions or non-possessions
to tell the way of a person
look into their eyes.

82.
why do most of our leaders who
start out as a part of their people
and genuinely work for their people
end up
living away from their people and
telling their people what *they* should
be doing while getting upset because
their people question their credibility?

83.
you can't define
tomorrow if you don't
know where you are
today.
if you do not read,
read!
if you do not think,
think!
add to reading and thinking
meditation.
meditate at a minimum of 1 hour a day
evenly divided.
1/2 at sunrise and 1/2 at sunset.
this will balance the internal
with the external and
bring knowledge of a *force*
greater than self.

84.
pimps and prostitutes
are the sickness of a nation.
are the sickness of a people.
but if a people are not able
to offer pimps and prostitutes
a tomorrow or a future that is believable
sickness will remain
and worsen
until death sets in.

85.
few things of value in life
are accomplished individually.
nations are built collectively,
schools are built collectively,
farms are farmed collectively,
holidays are observed collectively,
this is natural for those who have
direction and respect each other.
those who work share in the goods
produced and profits made.
those who are unable to work
are taken care of.
When the people of a nation begin
to use "I" more than "we"
the nation is dispersed and is in trouble.

86.
a negative act is a lesson,
a contradiction can be learned from and there
is meaning in evil
for those who are seeking good.

87.
if one
can be bought for $50.00
he/she can be bought twice for $100.00
if one will sell their self to you
he/she will sell their self to others, also.

88.
we wound each other
with false words,
evil eyes,
often lies
and pettiness disguised as criticism.
watch those who are closest to you
some of them carry the knives
that cut the deepest as they
agree with you while you die bleeding.
yet still,
even among the closest of enemies
the best defense
for your position
is your practicing
it.

89.
how many of us can
run a mile without tiring,
touch our toes without
bending our knees,
do pushups and pull ups
without damaging our bodies for life?
the body needs exercise
just as the mind needs exercise,
the mind cannot function at its peak
unless the body is physically
at its peak.
reading, studying and doing practical research and work
develops the mind.
morning exercise, physical work
and practical eating
develop the body
the mind and the body must work as one,
for you to be one.

90.
your name
tells us who you are,
where you come from,
where you are going,
how you may get there
and who is going with you.
your name
is legitimization of the past
confirmation of the present
and direction for the future.

91.
people play with the spirit
and at being "spiritual."
they cut themselves off from the real world
while meditating on rocks and water
and turning the sun into the moon.
the reality of life is confused abstractions
and the people do not understand them
and dismiss them as being crazy.
the people are correct.
meditation is needed and necessary
but must move the higher levels of the mind
into the people and not away from the people.
we meditate to maintain a balance in ourselves
while seeking greater wisdom of the outside.
it is not wise to seem abstract
when that which is practical is needed.
the most spiritual of acts
is
how positively you relate to and
work with your people.

You Will Recognize Your Brothers

You will recognize your brothers
by the way they act and move throughout the world.
there will be a strange force about them,
there will be unspoken answers in them.
this will be obvious not only to you but to many.
the confidence they have in themselves and in
their people will be evident in their quiet saneness.
the way they relate to women will be
clean, complimentary, responsible, with honesty and as
partners.
the way they relate to children will be
strong and soft full of positive direction and as example.
the way they relate to men
will be that of questioning our position in this world,
will be one of planning for movement and change,
will be one of working for their people,
will be one of gaining and maintaining trust within the culture.
these men at first will seem strange and unusual but
this will not be the case for long.
they will train others and the discipline they display
will be a way of life for many.
they know that this is difficult
but this is the life that they have chosen
for themselves, for us, for life:
they will be the examples,
they will be the answers, they will be the first line builders,
they will be the creators,
they will be the first to give up the weakening pleasures,
they will be the first to share a black value system,
they will be the workers,
they will be the scholars,
they will be the providers,
they will be the historians,
they will be the doctors, lawyers, farmers, priests
and all that is needed for development and growth.
you will recognize these brothers
and
they will not betray you.

Earthquakes and Sunrise Missions (1984)

Poetry

Poetry will not stop or delay wars, will not erase rape
from the landscape,
will not cease murder or eliminate poverty, hunger or
excruciating fear. Poems do not command armies, run
school systems or manage money. Poetry is not
intimately involved in the education of psychologists,
physicians or smiling politicians.

in this universe
the magic the beauty the willful art of explaining
the world & you;
the timeless the unread the unstoppable fixation
with language & ideas;
the visionary the satisfiable equalizer screaming for
the vitality of dreams interrupting false calm
demanding fairness and a new new world are the
poets and their poems.

Poetry is the wellspring of tradition, the bleeding
connector to yesterdays and the free passport to
futures.
Poems bind people to language, link generations to
each other and introduce cultures to cultures.
Poetry, if given the eye and ear, can bring memories,
issue in laughter, rain in beauty and cure ignorance.
Language in the context of the working poem can
raise the mindset of entire civilizations, speak to
two-year-olds and render some of us wise.

To be touched by living poetry can only make us
better people.
The determined force of any age is the poem, old as
ideas and as lifegiving as active lovers. A part of any
answer is in the rhythm of the people; their heartbeat
comes urgently in two universal forms, music and poetry.

for the reader for the quiet seeker
for the many willing to sacrifice one syllable
mumblings and easy conclusions
poetry
can be that gigantic river
that allows one to recognize
in the circle of fire
the center of life.

The Petty Shell Game

with raped memories and clenched fists. with small
thoughts and needless time we indulge in destruction
bathing ourselves in comedy and fraudulent posture:
 willa mae is going with big daddy t and lula is
 pregnant and don't know who the father is,
 cleavon said that the father is "we the people."

quite a profound statement among losers and people
beaten into the gutter and like desperate rats continue
to destroy with:
 richard g. is a faggot and pretty johnny is bald
 under that rag on his head, rev. jones is going
 with sister mary & sister emma & sister sara
 &   but
the important issue here always, especially among the
young is
where is the party this weekend &
where you get that boss smoke, man?
yet, as the hipped whipped often say, "only fools
work" not daring to take into consideration that
"fools" built the western world and raped the rest of it.
yes, "only fools work" as we non-fools every early
monday morn fight each other for position outside
the state welfare department.

Message

& if there is time
wait
measure stillness and quiet.
redo moments of kindness
& if there is misunderstanding
change yr words & come again.

We can do what we work to do.
slaves have children,
drive tanks,
visit playboy clubs, buy
$60 ashtrays and get extremely
angry at children leaning against their
cars.

Wait.
yes, there is time for love   but
equal & often more moments must be given to
war.
& even within this madness
special seriousness must be
got to be allocated for the
children.

We can do what we work to do
measure stillness and quiet
noise is ever present.
if we are not careful we will not
hear the message
when it
arrives.

Expectations

people Black and stone
be careful of that which is designated beautiful
most of us have been taught from the basements
of other people's minds.
often we mistake strip mining for farming
and that that truly glows is swept under
the rug of group production.
it is accepted in america that beauty is
thin, long & the color of bubble gum.
few articles generated by the millions are beautiful
except people.

trust people
one by one
the darker they come
the more you can give your heart,
their experiences most likely are yours
or will be yours.
even within the hue & hueless
among them are those
who have recently lost their
ability to recall.

they can hurt you
drop you to your knees with words
much of that which blasts from their mouths
is not them the offense is
they do not know that it is not them
as they rip your heart open
and reduce you to the
enemy.

The Writer

in america the major reward for
originality
in words, songs and visual melody
is to have dull people
call you weird
while asking what
you do for a living.

Everything's Cool:
Black America in the Early Eighties

in middle, rural, urban & combative america
it is a laborious challenge to explain racism and
    oppression
to a people that have among their members a
materially comfortable leadership and a complacent &
ignorant middle class that eats regularly, wears designer
socks, ventures into debt at will, loses themselves
in artificial stimuli, are extraordinarily mobile &
largely expect the serious rewards of life in the next world.

freedom is often confused with owning cars & bars
and being able to cross state lines without passports.
functional knowledge (e.g., computer technology,
producing food, governing self) is measured in one's
ability to quote the evening news & pontificate for
days on the merits of astrology or star power as it
relates to Black struggle. to many the haitian crisis
is a new dance, el salvador is mexican food, south
afrikan apartheid is a media creation and the only
foreign policy that is crucial to their lives is the paris
contribution to the yearly *ebony* fashion fair.
liberation on the real side is possessing the capacity
to swim in self pleasure & mundane acquisitions
without negative comment or challenge.

this cool crowd
believes that the majority of Black people suffer
because they are either lazy, unskilled, not motivated
or unlucky and that color & previous condition of
slavery is not germane to their current living status.
to quietly suggest to them that most of our people
exist in a state of dispirited boredom & wrecking
poverty only confirms their "lazy or unlucky" theory &
is accepted as a comment on the deficiencies of the
Black poor & have little to do with other people
and their economic & political systems. this
mindset is widespread among all cultures in america
& for poets or anyone non-white to issue reminders

is considered rude and "sixtyish" & is to be
construed as a note on one's own inability to "make
it" in the mainstream of the melted dreams.
the conscientious doer is labeled disrupter & is
perceived as an economic failure (the only kind that
counts) and one's words fall on blown out ears
& pac-man mentalities. the prevailing beliefs in the
land encourage individuals, families, corporations
and police departments to pursue their most
outlandish desires; representing an understatement of
acute confusion, where cultural and traditional values
are lost to the latest fads & electronic games.
it is clear and crystal
that the one
undeniable freedom
that *all* agree exist
for Black people in america
is the freedom
to
self-destruct.

The Secrets of the Victors

(the only fair fight is the one that is won
—Anglo-Saxon Proverb)

forever define the enemy as less than garbage,
his women as whores & gutter scum,
their children as thieves & beggars,
the men as rapists, child molesters & cannibals,
their civilization as savage and
beautifully primitive.

as you confiscate the pagan's land, riches & women
curse them to your god for not being productive,
for not inventing barbed wire and DDT,
perpetually portray the *natives*
as innocent & simple-minded while eagerly
preparing to convert them to *your way.*

dispatch your merchants with
tins & sweets, rot gut & cheap wines.
dispatch your priest armed with
words of fear, conditional love and
fairy tales about strangers dying for you.
dispatch your military
to protect your new labor pool.

if there is resistance
or any show of defiance
act swiftly & ugly & memorable.
when you kill a man
leave debilitating fear in the hearts of his
father, brothers, uncles, friends & unborn sons.
if doubt exists as to your determination
wipe the earth with his
women, girl children & all that's sacred;
drunken them in bodacious horror.

upon quiet, summon the ministers to
bless the guilty as you publicly
break their necks.
after their memories fade intensify the teaching.

instruct your holy men
to curse violence   while
proclaiming the Land Safe
introducing
the thousand year Reign of the Victors
as your Scholars
re-write the history.

Is Truth Liberating?

if it is truth that binds
why are there
so many lies   between
lovers?

if truth is liberating
why
are people told:
they look good when they don't
they are loved when they aren't
everything is fine when it ain't
glad you're back when you're not.

Black people in america
may not be made for the truth
we wrap our lives in disco and
sunday morning sermons
while
selling false dreams to our children.

lies
are refundable,
can be bought on our revolving
charge cards   as
we all catch truth
on the next go round
if
it doesn't hurt.

The Shape Of Things To Come

(December, 1980—what some people do to themselves is only the first chapter in what they will do to others)

in naples, italy
the earth
quaked and three hundred thousand are
without beds, toilets and knowledge
of loved ones.
hourly revisions enlarge the dead & injured.
normal shortages exist adding
burial coverings
for the young
(evidently falling into the earth by the thousands is
not punishment enough)
the word goes out
to the makers and shapers of sordid destinies
that
"this is the time to make the money"
immediately
quicker than one can pronounce
free enterprise
like well-oiled rumors   or
elastic lawyers smelling money
plastic coffins appear
& are sold at dusk behind the vatican
on the white market.
in italy in the christian month of eighty
in the bottom of unimaginable catastrophe
the profit motive endures
as
children replenish the earth in
wretched abundance.

Negro Leaderships

our leaders are manufactured
in upstate new york in nobackbone field
just outside the catskills
on the yes plantation.
most are conceived with fools gold
in their teeth & jelly beans in their
thinking units & slide out of the incubator
dancin doin the rump the charlie charlie bump
the rump the knee bends the crawl but but up
their palms are greased with pig's oil &
automatically turn upward when near money.
they define their interest identical to that
of the major diamond & gold producers in the world.
negro leaderships share more than a need for greed
most have rusty knees, purple tongues & dry lips.
sport pot bellies, sore buttocks & manicured toenails
& excrete waste frontal.
get it leroi step willie do the rump rump shuffle
now tongue out eyes big spread yo *butt now*
they are trained at the best divinity schools,
do not split verbs, read secular materials or
ponder too deeply about the negro problem.
black theology is blasphemous
& they view the world's enemy as
atheistic communism, scientific humanism &
thinking black women.

taught from birth 101 ways to say
no
to the realities of their people
the only value that
lights their fire
is
women bearing gifts,
an upward turn in the money market and
invitations from the mayor to march
in the annual st. patrick's day parade.

Women Black: Why These Poems

to see her is to realize why man was made different. is to realize why men were cut rough & unready & unfinished. the contrast would be like a magnet. and we fell into each other like wind with storm, like water into waiting earth. this woman black, this unbelievable wonder, would test the authenticity of a man's rough. a rap of beautifully rhymed words would not work with her. a well-rehearsed smile on the good side of your face or that special gleam from under your tanned shades could not penetrate this woman black. even the whole of you, in your pants tight with life, did not cause undo motion in her.

woman means more than woman
more than brown thighs
black lips, quick hips &
unfounded rumors
more than the common, more than the rational & irrational,
more than music, more than rough stones & unread books,
more than keepers of the kitchen, more than berry black,
mellow yellow & town brown, more than quick pussy, more than european names followed by degrees, more than nine to five order takers, more than fine, more than fox evil eyes big legs tight hips or women of the summer.

this is why i write about you. i want to know you better. closer. so this is my message to you. not a study. not a judgment or verdict. just observations and experiences. a lifestory, specifically the last sixteen years. above all poems of *love* going against that which is mistakenly passed off as *love.* this is a collection of intense feeling and complete touch. these are poems that were not ripe or ready for earlier books. these are poems that had to come to you in their own time, their own color & meaning. i have tried to do you justice in all of my works, but this Woman of the Sun, is the real test of my seriousness & dedication to you. my mother & her mother are here. my father's mother is here. my sister is here. the women black that i have loved & loved & loved & still love are here. my wife, quietly, as is her way, travels throughout these pages. this is the work that i slept, ate and travelled with. this is the beginning & middle the overtouched, with memories from arkansas to michigan. this is an inadequate gift to the other half of me, and to the whole of you. the you that often goes unnoticed, unheard & unthanked. the you that is lost is in the power plays of men and life.

woman black
i have tried to write about you
words
in a language strange & not of our making
words
refreshingly new
clean, lively, honest & uncomplicatedly indepth
words
forging & fighting their way into meaning
knowing too that
words
are like people are like you
woman black
& if left to simple interpretation
could be twisted, misused & misunderstood.
i will write about you with loving care
my woman
this is my pledge to you for already
there is too much confusion surrounding
someone as wordless as
you.

loved one this is a tribute to the beauty and strength of you, a comment on the good & bad of you, a commitment to the inside & out of you, a confession to the limited understanding of you, an appreciating love note to the intricate you. lady love sixteen years of you are here. over a decade of joy, struggle, hurt & growth. you have brought meaning & purpose to my life, have connected me to the tangibles & moved me beyond the rhetoric of ideas to the necessity of deeds. this is my testimony to you who have taught me & my comeback to those of you i have failed. please know that i have tried & will continue to go against *whatever* for & with you. finally, these poems; these words say as much about me as they do about you. there are no real spaces separating us. *we are one. believe it.* believe in it. women. *women of the sun.*

Maturity

emma jean aged one night
back in september of '63
it was after them girls
had received death in alabama
on their knees
praying
to the same god,
in the same church,
in the same space,
she prayed.

she aged that night
after the day had gone
and left her with her thoughts.
left her with the
history of her people in
america.
emma jean matured that night
and knew that in a country
that killed the children
under
the eyes of *their* god   that
she nor her people
were safe.

emma jean
decided back in september of '63
that she would let her people
know that they were not safe in
america
this is what she has done
and is doing   if she has not found you
look for her   kiss & hug her
thank her and then help her
to help us
mature.

Abortion

she,
walla (queen) anderson
miss booker t. washington jr. high of 1957,
miss chicago bar maid of 1961
had her first abortion at 32
after giving birth to
john (pee wee) jackson at 14,
mary smith at 15 and a half,
janice wilson at 17,
dion jones at 19,
sara jones at 21,
and
richard (cream) johnson at 27.

on a sun-filled day
during her 32nd year
after
as many years of aborting
weak men who would not stand
behind their own creations
she
walla (queen) anderson
by herself alone without consultation
went under the western butchers
to get her insides
out.

Safisha

1.
our joining into one proceeded like
sand through a needle's eye.
slow, bursting for enlargement & uncertainty.
a smoothing of passion and ideas
into spirited permanence and love.

there are decades of caring in you,
children loving that makes the father
in me active and responsible.
you forecasted the decline of marble shooting
& yo yo tricks, knowing too that hopscotch
& double dutch could retard early minds if
not balanced with challenges and language.

you are what brothers talk about
when serious & committed to loving life.
when examples are used to capture dreams
you are that woman.
for me you are summer at midlife,
daring spirit and middlenoon love
and the reason i return.

2.
dark women are music
some complicated well-worked
rhythms
others   simple melodies.
you are like soft piano
black keys dancing between
& not becoming the white.
you bring dance & vision into our lives.
it is good & good
to be your
man.

Winterman

janice was winter
she had been made cold by
years of maltreatment rough years
of loneliness and false companionship
and now in the middle of her time
she refused to ever take another chance with a
blackman.

janice cursed the race. didn't see no good that black
people ever done. raised on a plantation where her father was a sharecropper
she watched her mother, in her twilight years, steal away to jesus. the bible
was more than solution, more than heaven after earth, it was food and water.
it was ideas and values steeped in fear and peaceful salvation.

janice ran north at twenty and between her twenty-first and twenty-seventh
year visited every store front church on the west and south sides of chicago.
she now fashions herself a true missionary of the living gospel. her mission
was to save black men from the evil ways. she wanted black men to be like mr.
golding, the husband of the white woman she did day work for. mr. golding
took care of his family, had a big house and ate dinner with his family every
night that he didn't have to work late (he worked late at least twice-a-week).

most black men thought janice was fine but foolish. after loving her many
would brakelight fast. disappear, most leaving without an explanation. it
came out later that some of them didn't like being preached at at the point
of sexual climax. others felt that she prayed too much and were
uncomfortable with being compared to judas. after as many men as churches
janice in her thirty-fifth year decided to close her legs and like her mother
give her life, completely and unshared, to the only man in her life she
declared had never failed her. jesus would now be the only man in her heart.
it is not known exactly when during that year she was called but rumor has it
that the *ultimate light* touched her the day after billy william, her last lover,
started seeing her best and only friend minnie lou turner.

janice cursed the race. didn't see no good in black people. she turned slavishly and slowly toward her employers and began to live in. arlington heights, illinois was clean, peaceful and few black people lived there.

it was winter and windy
it was cold and white   and
jesus,
sweet, sweet jesus
was her man.

Lovepoems

1.
lately
your words are drugged passages
with razor edges
that draw blood & tears
    and
memories of less difficult moments
when love
that beautiful overused emotion-packed commitment
charged the body.
love
momentarily existed
actually transformed us defying the odds
flourishing enlarging us
if only for seconds
seconds that were urgently expected
and
overneeded.

2.
there are rumors afloat that love
is ill.
intimacy at best is overnight
clashes
and morning regrets.
are
bodies underwashed in strange bathrooms
as lovers
& others bang the door
softly running.
steppin cautiously in cracked silence
to spread rumors that
love
is a diseased bitch
deserving death and quick
cremation.

3.
do not wait to be loved
seek it,
the unexplainable.
fight for love
not knowing whether you have
lost or accomplished
poetic possibilities.
dig deep for love
search while acknowledging
the complexity of the heart & fading standards.
in seeking love use care.
to let strangers come into you
too quickly
may make you a stranger to yourself.

4.
from dawn to dusk in cities
that sunrises often fail to visit

we imprisoned light
& generated heat.

you are seedless grapes and
bright stars at winter & wind.
there are voices in your smiles
and confirmation in the parting of your lips.

The Changing Seasons of lfe

she is quality and light
a face of carob and ivory
of broad smiles and eyes that work.
she dresses in purples
& touches of aquablue.
plants grow profusely in her earthpots.
she seeks standards,
will not accept questionable roses or tapped water.
her taste is antique and bountiful heritage,
her music often void of melody
is firetone and harsh truths.
it is known that
dark rhythms played in & out of her early years
leaving temporary scars that lined her future
as beauty has it
wine is shared with shadows on prolonged trips
her smile broad & brandy
makes small miracles
emerge.

Lady Day

hearing from you are smiles in winter
you as you are
you warm and illuminating spaces
bring
blooming fruit in ice age times
with heated heated voices

believe me when i say
men will listen to you
most
will try to please you

there will be sun & thunder & mudslides
in your life
you will satisfy your days with work & laughter
and sunday songs.
your nights like most nights will
conjure up memories of easier seasons
happier suntimes and coming years

earthcolors and rainbows will enter your heart
when least expected
often
in small enduring ways like this
lovesong.

Some of the Women are Brave

her strength may have come from
not having the good things early in life
like
her own bed, unused clothes,
"good looks," uncritical friends
or
from the knee of her great grandmother.
whatever path she took
she was learning to become small danger.

organizer of mothers,
overseer of broken contracts,
a doer of large deeds,
unafraid of sky scrapers & monotone
bureaucrats.
monotones labeled her demands crippling & unusual.
she urged drinkable water, working elevators,
clean playgrounds, heat, garbage collection
and the consolation of tenant's dreams.

many damned her,
others thought her professional agitator & provocateur
dismissing her as a
man hating bulldagger
that was communist inspired.

she was quick burn against the enemy
a stand up boxer unattached to niceties
and the place of women.
she was waterfalls in the brain
her potency as it comes
needs to be packaged & overnight expressed
to Black homes; to be
served with morning meals.

Search Void of Fear

bronzed fire among the cold of cold,
she was happy moments & clear fields.
she was touch & yellow
soft rose with eyes that begged of sleep,
eyes that penetrated the cold of cold.

g.c. was lover & giver
searcher void of fear.
distances would be her metaphor
from cleveland to afrika over ocean & desert
travel expressed the search in her,
highlighting the afrikan in her.

just around her 28th season
g.c. passed through devastating hurt,
resulting in early burial of her man.
this is not talked of. her ancestors
demanded that she not be imprisoned with
dead thoughts or warm memories.

she was destined to be
searcher void of fear and
cold seconds should not detour
a soft rose with eyes that begged of sleep.
often
she was happy moments & clear fields,
she was sun-riped and ready for war
indeed
ready for love.

Womenblack: We Begin with You

(for Safisha)

our women we begin with you
black, beige, brown, yellowblack and
darkearth we dropped from your womb
in joyscreams lifegiver
you're worlds apart from the rest.

our women
imagine a warm breeze in any city
in the west that will not choke you,
be wife, be mother, a worker or professional
maker you still my lady.
our women
of fruits & vegetables
of greens & color   of sounds & potholes
of mountains & earth clearing danger   from
doorways who did not ruin their teeth & bodies
with the blood of pigs & cattle or fried chicken
after stumppin at bob's place til five in the daylight.
partyin was almost like a job
in motion on the run we are the rhythm people.

womenblack
unusual maker you say,
fine as all getout you say,
finer than lemonade in the shade,
we are a part of you maker, woman of
the autumn earth mother of sunlight
& i seldom say "i love you"
love is not our word. love belongs to
soap operas & comic books, is the
true confessions of the pale people from
the winter's cold.
we are the people of motion, move on motion
dance on, summer, summer lady.

womenblack we care about you
a deep & uncontrollable penetrative
care   as we listen to our own hearts,
whatever the weather.
you don't have to build a pyramid
in order to be one & you are still my
maker rhythm, rhythm lady.

our women we begin with you
black, beige, brown, yellowblack and
darkearth we dropped from your womb
in joyscreams lifegiver
you're worlds apart from the best.
you are in me & i in you
deep
deep and endless forever
touch to touch,
end to beginning
until the stars kiss the earth
and
our music will be songs of liberation.

Struggle

some called her
sunshine others berryblack
she was woman twice
laid way way back
her smile was winning-wide
her teeth glowed and captured light
she was woman twice
men thought her mighty nice

deep black off brown and mississippi grown lula mae was careful. she had experienced the heartaches, heard the stories and often hid the tears. lula mae was more watcher and listener now. yes, her emotions were still there, real & womanly strong but they had failed her too often in the past, her lovers had left memories that distorted her forehead and scars that even she didn't want to acknowledge.

(pretty willie g left his fist print under her left ear, larry the pimp provided her with a dislocated hip and baby frank left her $3000 in debt with promises of short life if she mentioned his whereabouts.)

lula mae now sought other signs of caring. she wanted relationships that were not so one-sided, short-termed or physically risky, she looked for verbal confirmation, evening phone calls, unexpected love notes and deep back and foot massages at the day's end. lula mae, not yet 30, knew that she was special, knew that her capacity for love was unusual and also knew that the next man in her life would understand and appreciate this specialness before he got any of it.

what will it be?
when will Blackmen learn that
fist & feet against the teeth
is like removing the heart of a people.
who will teach us
that slaps & kicks & verbal lashings
detour sharing, stop bonding,
destroy unifiers, retard respect & eliminate
connecting vision.
what will it be?
what messenger, what unmuted voice
will clarify touching

detail body contact without blackeyes?
what caller will articulate
disagreements without boxing,
love
without force.
where are the bold & rejuvenated men
and women that will head this most needed of
revolutionary struggles?

A Mother's Poem

(for G.B.)

not often do we talk.
    destruction was to be mine at 28
    a bullet in the head   or
    wrong-handed lies that would lock
    me in pale cells that are designed to
    cut breathing and will.
you gave me maturity at daybreak
slashed my heart
and slowed the sprint toward extinction,
delayed my taking on the world alone,
you made living a laborious & loving commitment.

you shared new blood,
challenged mistaken vision,
suggested frequent smiles,
while enlarging life to more than
daily confrontations and lost battles
fought by unprepared poets.

not often did we talk.
your large acts of kindness shaped memory,
your caring penetrated bone & blood
and permanently sculptured a descendant.
i speak of you in smiles
and seldom miss a moment
to thank you for
saving a son.

Rainforest

you are forest   rain
dense with life green colors
forever pulling the blue of life into you
see you walk and
i would like to burst rainwater into you
swim in & out of you
opening you like anxious earthquakes
uncontrollable but beautiful & dangerous.

get with this woman   come
fire frozen beauty,
men cannot sleep around you
your presence demands attention
demands notice
demands touch & motion & communication.

you are runner
swift like warm wind hurricanes
fast like stolen firebirds
& you disrupt the silence in me
make me speak memories long forgotten & unshared.
secrets uttered in strange storms,
deep full sounds reserved for magical,
magical lovers.

listen runner
i have shared pain with you,
i have commented on future worlds to you,
i have let you touch the weak & strong of me,
i have tasted the tip of your ripeness &
kissed sweat from your middle.
i have bit into your mouth &
sucked the lifeforces from yr insides   and
i know you. understand you.
i have shared books & travel & music & growth with you.

sweet knows honey & i know you.
under salted water tides
& running against polluted earth
i've tried to be good to you woman
tried to care beyond words
        care beyond distant spaces
sensitive phases & quiet lies
care
beyond cruel music & false images.

you are original high & dream maker
& true men do not try to limit you.

listen woman black
i do not wish to dominate your dreams
or obstruct your vision.
trust my motion   feel
know that i am near and with you
& will cut the cold of winter winds to reach you.
you
are delicate bronze
in spring-summers and special autumns
you are   forest rain
dark & runner & hurricane-black
frequently
i say frequently i bring you
midnight   *rain.*

In the Gut or Give Me Five

How many of you without doubt or hesitation can point out five Black men, locally or nationally, whose first priority is the liberation of Black people? How many of you can name five Black men right now, from the top of your head, who you believe under any circumstances, would not betray or sell out Black people for personal or political gain? Can you identify five true Black leaders who have not been compromised by money, white women, white privilege, oversized egos and media fame? Herein lies the legacy of our hurt. Serious and unbought Black men are few and fewer.

The century is not over. Let me issue this warning. Music comes in strange tones. The notes of our melodies are fast, slow and complexingly rhythmic. The songs of struggle must be unpredictable. The music players must constantly practice and continuously train body and mind. To become accomplished music makers there is but one method for serious preparation: study, train, practice, strive to tone the physical with the mental and the spiritual so that they function as one. Be reliable and proactive.

Study your strengths and weaknesses. Know your body like sweet knows honey. Keep yourself lean, hard and ready for war. Deeply examine the way of life. We must erase the landscapes of fear and inaction. Atlanta and Buffalo are still with us. Black life in America is cheap and according to the world-runners, highly dispensable. Hear me well. There are white men (and women) in this country (and the world) who see as their God-given task the effective neutralization of the Black movement, which at its base means the systematic destruction of Black boys and men. Violent aggression against Black men is nothing new; however, what is most revealing is that the current aggression against Blacks is taking place after two decades of "so-called" Black advancement. Only the critically weak-minded can fail to see the picture on the screen.

Active, consistent and effective Black struggle is our only *oasis.* As we travel the desert of our time, take a few minutes during the day to listen to the heartbeat of our children, stop often and look into their eyes, survey their smiles (if they are there) and ask yourself this question: *Do I want my children to be crippled zombies, incapable of decision or movement, totally dependent on the chief criminals of the world for their survival and development?* If the answer is *yes,* simply go back to sleep. If your answer is *NO,* quietly yet quickly start to transform your life. Critically assess the Word (study), don't give quarter or comfort to the enemy, learn to hide tears and anger with smiles and planning. Above all, believe, in the gut, that we can—Black men and women—create a better, better world.

The Destruction of Fathers

at the beginning he felt that it gave him
time
to do the acts of importance that somehow
he was unable to do before
the vacating of rooms before
the clearing of bookshelves & dresser drawers
before the
greed of lawyers
tears of children and
draining sleeplessness of fathers.

divorce generated an abundance of
time
to hear,
to contemplate the missing the mistakes
time
to seek pure noise,
for self-inflicted wounds,
planned interruptions,
& suicidal waiting moments for
wishing & rushing of weekend visits

at thirty-eight it was a devastating time
to have lost wife, children and familiar spaces
to "irreconcilable differences,"
obsolete definitions & a rapid-firing mouth.

again
it was a devastating time with only
quiet to debate at whether men should
share in garbage-emptying, floor-mopping,
dish-washing, laundry-doing, shopping, &c.
when one is alone there are no questions
only time
and clarity arriving
too late.

Poet: for Larry Neal

in time and time
in evening nights
in quiet search and final answer
they took the poets away

they promised them gifts of gifts and portable and
  lasting fame
they promised them beautiful life, hungerless days,
  rising riches
and lasting lust. they promised gold & university chairs
  & unlimited
publication.

they promised promises
and
in return
they suggested that the poets
sing a
falsesong.

this world is full of
missing,
and dying
& unpublished
poets.

My Brothers

my brothers i will not tell you
who to love or not love
i will only say to you
that
Black women have not been
loved enough.

i will say to you
that
we are at war & that
Black men in america are
being removed from the
earth
like loose sand in a windstorm
and that the women Black are
three to each of us.

no
my brothers i will not tell you
who to love or not love
but
i will make you aware of our
self-hating and hurting ways.
make you aware of whose bellies
you dropped from.
i will glue your ears to those images
you reflect which are not being
loved.

The Damage We Do

he loved his women
weak & small
so that he would not tire
of
beating them.
he sought the weakest & the smallest
so that they couldn't challenge
his rage of boxing
their heads up against refrigerators,
slamming their hands in doors,
stepping on them like roaches,
kicking them in their centers of life.
all of his women
were
weak and small and sick
& he an
embarrassment to the human form
was not an exception in america.

Rape: the male crime

there are mobs & strangers
in us
who scream of the women
wanted and
will get
as if the women are ours for the
taking.

our mothers, sisters, wives and
daughters ceased to be the
women men want   we think of them as
loving family   music & soul   bright wondermints.
they are not locker room talk
not the hunted lust or   dirty
cunt burnin hoes.
bright wondermints are excluded   by association as
blood & heart   bone & memory
& we will destroy a rapist's knee caps,
& write early grave on his thoughts
to protect them.

it will do us large to recall
when the animal in us rises
that all women are someone's
mother, sister, wife or daughter
and are not fruit to be stolen when hungry.

a significant few of their
fathers, brothers, husbands, sons
and growing strangers
are willing to unleash harm on the earth
and spill blood in the eyes
of
maggots in running shoes
who do not know the sounds of birth
or respect the privacy of the human form.

White on Black Crime

lately and not by choice
milton washington is self employed.
workin hard
he collects aluminum cans,
pop bottles, papers & cardboard
and sells them to the
local recycling center.

milton washington is an unemployed
master welder who has constantly sought
work in & out of his trade.
he is now seen on beaches, in parks,
in garbage cans, leaving well-lit alleys
in the evenings pushing one cart
& pulling the other, head to the side
eyes glued southward long-steppin homeward.

milton's unemployment ran out 14 months ago.
first the car went & he questioned his manhood.
next the medical insurance, savings & family
nights out ceased & he questioned his god.
finally his home was snatched & he disappeared
for 2 days & questioned his dreams
and all he believed in.

milton works a 15-hour day &
recently redefined his life for
the 6th time selecting as his only goal
the housing, feeding & keeping of his family
together.

yesterday the payout per pound
on aluminum was reduced by 1/4 cent
as the stock market hit an all-time high
& the president smiled through a speech
on economic recovery, welfare cheats & the
availability of jobs for those who want to work.

milton washington has suffered
the humiliation of being denied food stamps,
the laughter and cat calls of children,
the misunderstanding in the eyes of his family
and friends.
milton believed in the american way
even hung flags on the 4th & special days
and demanded the respect of god & country in
his home.

at 1/4 cent reduction in pay per pound
milton washington will have to add
an hour and a half to his 15-hour day.
milton washington, more american than black,
quiet and resourceful, a collector of dreams
cannot close his eyes anymore,
cannot excuse the failure in his heart,
cannot expect miracles in daylight,
is real close, very, very close to hurtin somebody
real bad.

A Poem for Quincy Jones, Sidney Poitier, Harry Belafonte, Kareem Abdul-Jabbar, James Earl Jones, Wilt Chamberlain, Richard Pryor, Redd Foxx, Lou Rawls, &c., &c., &c. for Days

it is actual and prophetic   that
when the money comes
when the fame and autograph seekers arrive,
when there is something to share & wear,
that the *root* is forced into basements,
backrooms and aching embarrassment.

acts toward the indigenous become frigid clichés
(after children wrecking & torturous, rise to the pinnacle)
the *root* is now tolerated baggage & excessive worry,
a for real style cramper & potential court warrior.
for him the current revelation is that
"people are just people"
converting the universe into one gigantic lovefest.
exempting
the berrycolored   nappyheaded   rustykneed
exempting
the widehipped   biglipped   cherrybrown women.

his eyes have gone pink sucking
venom from the people
who less than a word ago
less than a few missed meals ago
used his ass as a shoe shiner.
tap tap dance do the bounce now
do the white boy richard 357 *magnum yr car*
shoot death in yr toe freebase raw brilliance
fire up tap tap tap dance run out da pain in da
brain.

stardom is the ultimate drug,
fame fogs tradition dismembers values
& elevates egos to cocaine highs.
idol status
is volcanic to the insides evaporates memory
& neutralizes kindness.
the *root*
the unbought memory of the culture
flows red in the women.
when the women are traded and reduced to
matrilineal burning bitches
bleeding sets in families decay
rendering generational destruction
producing final stop orders.

ask your momma.

Comin Strong

and where are the men Black and ready?
some say,
they've lost their way
beneath pig's litter & fool's gold.
others say,
they are hid under political deception
& three dollar bills returning in numbers
as colored traitors clothed in abundance.

the real word is that the men have become
pregnant with spoiled food
& thoughts of false grandeur.
they drive boat-cars,
smoke strange weeds,
destroy their noses with crippling dust,
manicure their nails
& talk wrong about their women.
some say,
it is best that these men stay lost.

the new men Black
do not measure themselves in
the way of the elusive streets
do not look toward the west as the test.
the new men Black with dust & dirt
are clear thinkers and city learned
are not tied to garbage cans & whiskey breath.
these men take their sons seriously &
listen closely to their daughters.
they do not come as beggars or buyers
they are teachers and doers returning in
a force that's unimaginable.

the new men Black are
tongue silent, hawkeyed and dangerous.
many who should know say
that these men do not play,
do not pass blank checks.
they say that these men cannot be
bought.

Message to our Sons

son,
do not forget the women killed
by the whites & men negro made white.
do not disregard the women Black
killed for closing their legs to
bodies foreign to their insides,
for preserving the culture of their foreparents,
for daring to be the just.
son, let your memory not erase
or betray the sacred teachings of
these women. mothers, sisters, lovers and wives
whom the world has transgressed against.
record their tracks in code and memory.
my son do not neglect our women nor
forgive those who have *violated*
a precious part of you.

For Blackmen with Integrity and Convictions

there are people beyond clout and distance
who have orders
from above   on high   to do you
debilitating harm
worse than broken knee caps and twisted face
worse than ruining your good name or destroying your
    marriage
worse than turning your friends and people against
    you.

they have final stop orders
these people have cleaned weapons,
sharpened skills,
have mapped your every movement,
booked your weaknesses & dissected your strengths
you are a considerable foe
& many are preparing to exterminate you with
"extreme prejudice"

their design
is to close the history books on your name,
crown you traitor & child molester.
anything
to erase the people's positive memory of you.

it will be difficult to brace
against this storm.

continue as you must
intensify and insulate
let them know that
they're in for a fight.

Get Fired Up

get fired up
get excited about hue and dark colors
ignite truth in the temple
there will be many who will try to take you out
watch the light shadows
exemplify & scream cleanliness into the world
leave yr mark
the children must know that you
& you   & you
carried the message.

Hanging Hard in America

one does not want to hurt the word is that
bodies break easily in the west the word is that
the important articles are made of plastic & glue
put together by people whose major aim is
profit:

made in japan is no longer laughable
enter hong kong, taiwan, singapore, &c.,
to buy american is not quality it's patriotic,
the way is buy now pay if you catch me,
get it now tomorrow may be never,
pay for what you want beg for the needs.

families are disappearing.
children & vegetation are back seated
& automobiles and canned foods are the
measurements of normalcy. family bonding
or preparing for the long hike is what the crazy do.
lips thunder everywhere talking in tongues praising
"my god" & intellectual pursuits like reading & thinking
are left to fools, bureaucrats, compromising scholars
& a few starving & unlettered poets.

the urgent quests are for new money markets,
i. magnum & neiman marcus accounts.
it is taught that light shines on those who can
afford electricity & new definitions depend on your
politics and cash flow:
right means don't do it,
integrity translates as square,
honesty is lonely,
the rich are correct,
the poor are lazy,
loyalty is rewards in suitcases after dark &
the world is never too small for liars,
only for amateurs. were you not told that
professionals do not fabricate the truth they become
historians and anthropologists & reinterpret reality?

so we hurt,
we learn to hate as we dig in
for the long track.
as should be, our ancestors speak wisdom:
do not send your children to be taught by
those who do not love them;
raise strong, loving and sane children and
we will not have to repair broken adults.
above all the final call is:
do not forgive violation of people & loss of language,
do not forget dirt in the eye & the middle passage.

America: the future

in a country

where pride is measured
in body counts

a black
school aged boy
pledged
allegiance to the flag

as the words came
he
thought about today's
ball game
& about the
home runs he would hit
& his special willie mays catch

he didn't remember the flag
until after
he noticed the
canceled sign on the ball park's gate

that night he asked
his momma:
    "momma why the flag got holes in it?"
her reply:
    "daddy's back."

Biko

water dripping   drop by drop
into the ears of the broederbond*
leaving them waterlogged and senseless
desperately appreciating pain.
knowing the displacement of dreams
knowing what slavery is and raw smiles of Black
    mommas
following husbands to shanty towns to squat in
    squalor & mud

is to be born among apologists
in a land taken from one's ancestors
is a profound comment on how far
we have lost our way.

to be born among weaker apologies
from colored men in white collars
who constantly preach "a better day a comin,"
tomorrow

expect tennis and cricket,
jogging, handball & polo played on manicured greens.
better days of beer and evening playgrounds
and admission to divinity schools.
but never   never
the retrieval of one's land.

as the young   young men & women
steal away into the heat of the heart
seeking the uncompromising past in search of
clear sight inciting the alerting question,
"why did they kill Steve Biko?"
their message to Black america,
"don't send us no ribbons to wear."

**The white brotherhood that once held exclusive power in South Afrika.*

Sun and Storm

beyond weep and whisper,
beyond clown and show,
beyond why & where & not now
clear the voices

there is *storm* on the horizon.
beneath calm & cold & killer death
there is *vision* approaching.
beneath filth & fear & running asses
there is planning & hope & connecting trust.
beneath traffic stops and sex crazed negroes
there are new people arising
clothed in love & work & a will to advance.

newpeople
bold and sure   tested tough   fever wise
these are womenblack with brain and womb &
smiles that regenerate.
these are menblack with mind and seed &
strength of strength.
they are children-conscious and elder-wise
sweet lovers of life.
newpeople
known in afrika,
known in asia,
known in europe & the americas
with their rainbow smiles, willing minds,
and bridge-building backs as the
people of the sun.

End Notes

if parting is necessary
part as lovers.
part as two people
who can still
smile & talk & share
the good & important
with each other.
part
wishing the other
happy
happy life
in a world
fighting against the
beautiful,
fighting against the
men & women,
sisters and brothers
Black as
we.

Future

first
it is between the black and the black
come
not as empty earth,
not as wasted energy,
not as apologetic color consciousness,
not as fool blinded to light,
not as imitation cardboard.

come
as gifted lovers
eyes bright & daring life.
come
as ripening fruit
quick smiles and joyous words.
come
woman to man
man to woman
pursuing the way of life
within the colors of vision
between the
black and the black.

Earthquakes

(for Frances Cress Welsing)

in the hot of the eye
at the insertion of cayenne
what really matters is:
children catching breath,
children experiencing love and continuation,
children understanding the good and emerging evil,
children expecting a future,
children smiling quickly and uninhibited
in this world.
    as the smiles cease conflict beckons
    hearts hurt blood rushes hands sweat
    pain ensues and comes like pins in the spine
understand this:
conscious men do not make excuses
do not expect their women to carry their water,
harvest the food and prepare it too.
world over it is known that
breast sucking is only guaranteed to babies.
    sisters if the men do not fight,
    if the men are not responsible
cover the breast close the legs stop the love
cancel good times erase privileges question manhood.

if the men engage the enemy
get ready for rumor & divisive headaches
everyone will want to know their price,
traitors will try & confirm that the men can be
    bought,
enemies will pass gold to family & lovers to buy his
    dreams.
if the engaged men are of the wise kind
they will appreciate the greater needs and
without doubt or hesitation tell them our pay back is:
georgia, the states of florida & alabama, we want
texas.

when the smiles quit when the laughter quiets
conflict beckons   hearts hurt   blood rushes
     hands sweat
spines strengthen   & brothers comprehend.
catch the sun & get on up
rise on the run. open eyed
ready & expecting danger

expecting earthquakes.

Sun Rise Missions

(for Hoyt W. Fuller)

He will be missed, not lost among papers,
remembered in midnight study cells
and early morning runs.
remembered as an originator of
wisdom
from a vision that was sound & sane
steadfast and tempered
Tempo between song and dance   between
fist and articulation   call him
screamingly dangerous

Sang beauty first
notice the eyes of children
locate their living & eating space
try & smile now.
run with & against the common wind
do damage for damage be
unpredictable with map and compass
& weapons pressed against the cheek

Catch fire & fire
notice
there is an uneasiness among us
window shades are drawn,
people talk in nods and whispers
babies are again born in homes,
people are picking up books and nails
and anxiously listening to grandparents.
there is sunrise on the horizon
Pass this word quickly and quietly
there are rats in the streets.

Poison is needed. Now.

Destiny

under volcanoes & timeless years within watch
and low tones. around corners, in deep caves among
misunderstood and sometimes meaningless sounds.
cut beggars, outlaw pimps & whores. resurrect work.
check your distance blue
come
earthrise men deepblack and ready
come
sunbaked women rootculture on the move.

just do what you're suppose to do
just do what you say you gonta do
not the impossible,
not the unimaginative,
not copy clothed as original and surely
not bitter songs in european melodies.

take hold
do the necessary, the possible, the correctly simple
take hold
talk of missions & interpret destiny
put land and selfhood on the minds of our people
do the expected,
do what all people do

reverse destruction.
capture tomorrows.

Afterword to *Earthquakes and Sunrise Missions*

Darwin T. Turner

Earthquakes and Sun Rise Missions is Haki R. Madhubuti's first volume of poetry since *Book of life* (1973). Although he has continued to write poerty during this decade, the effort to publish it has submitted to other priorities—arduous work as the director of the Institute of Positive Education and of Third World Press, three books of essays, continuing his work as educator and nation builder, and the responsibilities of a husband and a father. Now the poet has reappeared in a volume of rich love of Black women, mature, compassionate observation, and cold contempt of the enemies of Black people.

Under the name "Don L. Lee," Madhubuti published his first books of poetry in the late 1960s as part of a generation of young Black writers using their skills to educate Black people to a heightened Black consciousness. Introducing his first collection of poems, *Think Black,* (1967), he wrote:

> Black art will elevate and enlighten our people and lead them toward an awareness of self, i.e., their blackness. It will show them mirrors. Beautiful symbols. And will aid in the destruction of anything nasty and detrimental to our advancement as a people.

But, as Dudley Randall asserted in an introduction to Madhubuti's second collection, *Black Pride* (1968):

> It is not his recital of received pieties which makes him a poet. Don Lee is a poet because of his resourcefulness with language. He writes for the man in the streeet, and uses the language of the street...with, inventiveness, and surprise...(He) joins words together or splits syllables into fractions for greater expressiveness. His shorter lyrics have a sting and his longer poems a force that make him one of the most interesting of the revolutionary young black poets.

In an essay published in *A Capsule Course In Black Poetry Writing* (1975), Madhubuti wrote:

> Originality for the Black poet essentially means you must either have something new and insightful to say...or you must find a new way of saying something that has already been said...Such

> themes as the *fact* that Europeans are bent on destroying Afrikan peoples, that the black middle class often copies the styles and values of Europeans and that Afrikan peoples' need to get together, are not original...Thus, if you choose to deal with such themes (and they must be dealt with), you must create a form/style which is original, which is not a copy of other poets.

Don't Cry, Scream (1970), his third collection of poems, brilliantly illustrates his advice. Improving as rapidly as Randall had predicted and growing beyond the introspection of his early poems, Madhubuti focused on themes and subjects that characterize his thought but are not new: satiric denunciations of games-players who do not comprehend Blackness ("But he was Cool/or: he even stopped for green lights," "Malcolm Spoke/who listened?"); impassioned exhortations for heightened Black consciousness (" A Poem to Complement Other Poems"); reverence for Blacks who commit their lives and work to Black people ("Gwendolyn Brooks," "Don't Cry, Scream—for John Coltrane/from a black poet/in a basement apt. crying dry tears of 'you ain't gone.'"); and love for Black women and Black children ("A Poem Looking for a Reader/to be read with a love consciousness," "A Message All Black people can Dig/& a few negroes too.")

What gave originality to these important but familiar subjects and themes was only partly Madhubuti's startling metaphors ("his wine didn't have to be cooled, him was air conditioned cool...so cool him nick-named refrigerator") and his unexpected twists of thought ("him wanted to be a TV star. him is. ten o'clock news./wanted, wanted. nigger stole some lemon & lime popsicles, thought them were diamonds.") Even more originally, however, he used word sound and staccato repetition with a skill that justifies Gwendolyn Brooks' praise in her introduction to *Don't Cry, Scream*: "At the hub of the new wordway is Don Lee." At times, he strained to overcome the limitations of the printed words by creating sound that artistically would evoke emotion. Demanding to be read aloud, his poetry in his third volume sometimes suggests the virtuoso efforts of jazz singers who use their human voices to replicate the sounds of musical instruments. For example, consider a passage from the title poem of *Don't Cry Scream*:

> Trane done went.
> (got his hat & left me one)
> naw brother,
> i didn't cry,
> i just—
> Scream-eeeeeeeeeeeeeeee-ed — sing loud
> SCREAM-EEEEEEEEEEEEEEEEE-ED — & high with
> we-eeeeeeeeeeeeeeeeeeeeeeeee — feeling
> WE-EEEEEEeeeeeeeeeEEEEEEE — letting

WE-EEEEEEEEEEEEEEEEEEEEEEE yr/voice
WHERE YOU DONE GONE, BROTHER?
break

Equally powerful is his use of repetition. In his essay in *A Capsule Course in Black Poetry Writing,* Madhubuti praised Amiri Baraka's artistic creation of black music rhythms through the repetition of "stressed sounds at intervals that are dictated by his feel for black life rhythms and blackmusic." Perhaps this is equally valid as an explanation of Madhubuti's style, but I do not believe that it is the complete explanation. Madhubuti's artistry conceals itself. In contrast to Baraka who, in such a poem as "Beautiful Black Women," seems to be manipulating metaphor and sound consciously as he leads a reader from an image of Black women weeping to am image of rain to a thought that Black women should not be weeping but should be queens who reign, Madhubuti seems at first merely to be repeating words. Unexpectedly, however, the repetition develops its own rhythm; and often the reader becomes conscious of a new message just as, when one is lazily listening to stereo, one may suddenly become aware of hearing a different theme from a second speaker. Consider the following examples, from "A Poem to Complement Other Poems":

change nigger change.
know the realenemy.
change: is u is or is u aint. change. now now change. for
the better change.
read a change. live a change. read a blackpoem.
change. be the realpeople.
change. blackpoems
will change:

know the realenemy. change. know the realenemy. change
yr/enemy change know the real
change know the realenemy change, change, know the
realenemy, the realenemy, the real
realenemy change you're the enemies/change your change
your change your enemy change
your enemy. know the realenemy, the world's enemy.
know them know them know them the
realenemy change your enemy change your change
change change your enemy change change
change change your change change change.
your
mind nigger.

and from "Gwendolyn Brooks"

> into the sixties
> a word was born ..... BLACK
> & with black came poets
> & from the poet's ball points came:
> black doubleblack purpleblack blueblack beenblack was
> black daybeforeyesterday blackerthan ultrablack super
> black blackblack yellowblack niggerblack blackwhi-teman
> blackerthanyoueverbes 1/4 black unblack coldblack clear
> black my momma's blackerthanyour momma pimpleblack fall
> black so black we can't even see you black on black in
> black by black technically black mantanblack winter
> black coolblack 360degreesblack coalblack midnight
> black black when it's convenient rustyblack moonblack
> black starblack summerblack electronbiack spaceman
> black shoeshineblack jimshoeblack underwearblack ugly
> black auntjimammablack, uncleben's rice black williebest
> black blackisbeautifulblack i justdiscoveredblack negro
> black unsubstanceblack.

We Walk the Way of the New World (1970) and *Directionscore* (1971) resonate and expand earlier themes: the unity of Blacks throughout the world, the love of Black women, and the vision of a new world. Three years later, *Book of Life* suggests a change in poetic concept and style. In Part I, Madhubuti continued to use the familiar style to assail "traitors" —Blacks who, having profited individually, jumped from the train of revolution or even tried to impede further progress—and to exhort Blacks to continue to move toward a new day. In Part II, however, the poet's voice no less determined than before—is quieter, more contemplative, more restrained. Abandoning slashing satire (which on occasion perhaps dissipated some of the seriousness of its criticism by provoking laughter), Madhubuti criticized through thoughtful aphorisms:

> We do not equate
> poverty with blackness
> nor do we equate the lavish
> use of wealth with blackness.
> we now live in a time
> where the many go without
> while for the few we have entrusted to lead us
> luxuries have become needs

Instead of dramatically proclaiming the need for a new world, he quietly urged people to think about life:

How many of our children
have seen the ocean's ripple
or have felt the morning wetness
of country
vegetation
or picked the just ripened fruit from trees
or enjoyed the afternoon sun bathing
their bodies as they played in the green.
there is little that is green in the cities
other than the broken stop lights and
artificial grass.
our children's dreams are lost among the
concrete of too many promises
waiting for elevators to take them
to the top floors of public housing.

Perhaps, in a sense, the change reflected his effort to follow his own observation:

best teachers
seldom teach
they be and do.

Now, a decade later, an older, quieter voice seems to control the poetry of *Earthquakes and Sun Rise Missions.* It is as though Madhubuti has chosen to move from the role of virtuoso performer and to assume more often the role of artistic, prophetic educator. Madhubuti has not abandoned the earlier style, which he continues to display in such poems as "Negro Leaderships," "Rainforest," "We Struggle for the People," or "destiny"; but now he often seeks to fuse poetry and prose, as in "Woman Black" or "Winterman," for example. He has not forsaken his stern criticism of Blacks who pursue false values, but he now also writes compassionately of the reasons some do ("Winterman"). There is an increased emphasis on a message of love for Black women, but there is continuing evidence of love for and commitment to Black people. As Gwendolyn Brooks wrote in the introduction to *Don't Cry, Scream,* "Around a black audience he puts warm hands."

More than a decade ago, while teachers in schools were complaining about students' lack of interest in poetry, Madhubuti was proving that people will listen to and buy poetry that speaks to them, that entertains and educates them. Now, concerned that some poets have lost their vision and that other poets' voices have been drowned by the sounds from the ever-present television sets, he is reaching out poetically once more to urge people to listen,

> We can do what we work to do.
> measure stillness and quiet
> noise is ever present.
> if we are not careful we will not
> hear the message
> when it
> arrives.

Madhubuti's powerful message will shut off some television sets, redirect some minds and may invite book burning in some quarters.

Killing Memory, Seeking Ancestors (1987)

Introduction: Getting to this Place

I have had the privilege to travel far and deep into other cultures. Any kind of travel to the imaginative mind is both rewarding and challenging. Travel can also be painful to the culturally sensitive; for example, it is extremely difficult to enjoy oneself in Haiti and in certain parts of Afrika. Afrika entered my consciousness in 1960 and there has not been a day that I have not considered my relationship to that vast and complex continent.

I first went to Afrika in 1969 to attend the first PanAfrikan Festival in Algeria. After a decade of serious struggle in the United States for Black self-determination, my visit to Afrika was crucial to my cultural development. I went looking for answers. The past ten years in the U.S. had been an intense period of struggle and study during which my generation fought to rid itself of a colonial-slave-centered mindset. My first trip to Afrika was instructive, but after seven visits to North, East, and West Afrika, I am still fighting with my questions. My searchings have also taken me to the West Indies, Europe, Asia, and South America. However, as a man of Afrikan foreparents, the land of the sun has a special meaning for me.

Youth has its own naivety. I long ago lost my innocence in the concrete of Detroit and the mud of Arkansas. Yet, I was still not prepared for the land that gave birth to civilization.

My personal journals eat into my poetry. It is in poetry that I have learned to communicate best. After fourteen books published in a twenty-one year period, I have become a poet. I now feel comfortable with the description *poet* or *writer.* America has a way of forcing even the strongest into denying reality. Afrika demanded reentry.

In all of my work I've tried to give the readers melodies and songs that foster growth and questions. I wanted my readers to become a more informed and better people. I think that, my experiences have made me a better person; I would like to think that I am a good and productive one also. That is partially what I am working for. Study, work, travel, and struggle have taught me not to take myself too seriously, but to be serious enough so that others, especially my enemies, do not mistake love and caring for weakness.

Moving culturally from negro to Black to Afrikan to Afrikan American has been quite a trip. I *never* had to get "high" because my quest for knowledge (i.e., truth) carried with it a multiplicity of altitudes and attitudes. Progressive thinking and acting in most of the world can get one killed. This is what Afrika and Afrikan American struggle, in a highly abbreviated form, has taught me:

1. Before doing what I say, see what I do.
2. Good words are healthy, but deeds are what bring the
   food, clothes and house the children, and build tomorrows.
3. When one is full, it is easy to criticize the hungry.
4. It is easier to believe than to think.
5. What is increasingly rare among Western people is friendship and caring.
6. Honesty and moral consciousness practiced among the
   people has a greater impact than sharp-witted demagoguery.
7. Ideas run the world.
8. Force is both an idea and a reality.
9. Children first, which means that family is pre-children.
10. That which is truly valuable cannot be bought.
11. Freedom is only given to people who do not understand it.
12. Greed disguised as need is a great enemy.
13. Do not surround yourself with people who always say yes.
14. Knowledge is non-decaying food, and study brings a vast harvest to those
    who partake of it.
15. A people that run from the truth will never know beauty and
    will sleep with lies.
16. The only ignorant question is the one not asked.
17. One's culture is one's life.
18. Values based upon tradition, reason, and practice are not negotiable
    and memory is knowledge.
19. Listening is to learning as water is to life.
20. Seeking beauty in relationships is as life-giving as the juice of carrots
    and the morning sun.

(There is much more, but let me stop here; brevity is respected.)

I have acquired a healthy skepticism; however, as many can attest, it is still easy to get to my heart. What is missing among Afrikan American people is vision. Many of our people think and act in a way that is embarrassing to the normal mind. However, in much of the world, the abnormal still defines normality.

It is a 24-hour-a-day job to be a conscious Afrikan in America (or the world) where the mass media hourly project anti-Black images. This is why a people's culture is critical to its development. It was Long and Collier who stated in their book, *Afro-American Writing,* that:

> Definitions are increasingly important. The survival of culture—any culture—depends in large measure on the nature of its definitions of itself and of those aspects of life on which its survival depends: for example, what the past implies, what freedom means, who the enemy is.

> The literature of a culture is a totality of the definitions, a self-portrait of that culture. Knowledge of a literature, then, yields valuable insight into the culture that produced it.

We are summertime people; therefore, it is not so odd that we act funny in this environment. However, the world is changing rapidly and we must ride with the tide as we try to humanize it. Question everything, study, study, and study some more. Smile often, stay clean, and seek beauty. Try not to be judgmental and petty in your actions. As the brothers say, "Stay up," and I will add: Keep struggling; stay strong and aware, too. To kill the people's memory is to remove them from history and future, but when the people believe in and act positively and passionately on such beliefs, only their children and the land will live longer.

H.R.M.
September, 1986

Killing Memory

(For Nelson and Winnie Mandela)

the soul and fire of windsongs must not be neutral
cannot be void of birth and dying
wasted life
locked
in the path of vicious horrors
masquerading
as progress and spheres of influence

what of mothers
without milk of willing love,
of fathers
whose eyes and vision
have been separated from feelings of earth and growth,
of children
whose thoughts dwell
on rest and food
and human kindness?

Tomorrow's future rains in
atrocious mediocrity and suffering deaths.

in america's america the excitement is over
a rock singer's glove and burning hair
as serious combat rages over
prayer in schools,
the best diet plan,
and women
learning how to lift weights
to the rhythms of
"what's love got to do with it?"

ask the children,
always the children caught in the
absent spaces of adult juvenility
all
breakdancing and singing to
"everything is everything" while
noise occupies the mind as
garbage feeds the brain.

in el salvador mothers search for their sons
and teach their daughters the way of the knife.

in south afrika mothers bury hearts without bodies
while pursuing the secrets of forgotten foreparents.

in afghanistan mothers claim bones and teeth from
mass graves and curse the silent world.

in lebanon the sons and daughters receive horror hourly
sacrificing childhood for the promise of land.

in ethiopia mothers separate wheat from the desert's dust
while the bones of their children cut through dried skin.

tomorrow's future
may not belong to the people,
may not belong to dance or music
where
getting physical is not an exercise but
simply translates into people working,
people fighting,
people enduring insults and smiles,
enduring crippling histories and black pocket politics
wrapped in diseased blankets
bearing AIDS markings in white,
destined for victims that do not question
gifts from strangers
do not question
love of enemy.

who owns the earth?
most certainly not the people,
not the hands that work the waterways,
nor the backs bending in the sun,
nor the boned fingers soldering transistors,
not the legs walking the massive fields,
nor the knees glued to pews of storefront or granite churches
nor the eyes blinded by computer terminals,
not the bloated bellies on toothpick legs
all victims of decisions
made at the washington monument and lenin's tomb
by aged actors viewing
red dawn and the *return of rambo part IX.*

tomorrow
may not belong to the
women and men laboring,
hustling,
determined to avoid contributing
to the wealth
of gravediggers from foreign soil
& soul.
determined to stop the erosion
of indigenous music
of building values
of traditions.

memory is only precious if
you have it.

memory is only functional
if it works for you.
people
of colors and voices
are locked in multi basement state buildings
stealing memories
more efficient
than vultures tearing flesh
from
decaying bodies.

the order is that the people are to
believe and believe
questioning or contemplating
the direction of the weather
is unpatriotic.

it is not that we distrust poets and politicians.

we fear the disintegration of thought,
we fear the cheapening of language,
we fear the history of victims and the loss of vision,
we fear writers whose answer to
maggots drinking from the open
wounds of babies
is
to cry genocide while demanding
ten cents per word and
university chairs.
we fear politicians
that sell coffins at a discount
and consider ideas blasphemy
as young people world over bleed from the teeth while
aligning themselves with whoever
brings the food.
whoever brings love.

who speaks the language of
bright memory?

who speaks the language of
necessary memory?

the face of poetry must be fire erupting volcanoes,
hot silk forging new histories,
poetry delivering light greater than barricades of silence,
poetry dancing, preparing seers, warriors, healers
and parents beyond the age of babies,
poetry delivering melodies that cure dumbness & stupidity
yes, poets uttering to the intellect and spirit,
screaming to the genes and environments
revitalizing the primacy of the word and world.
poets must speak the language of the rain,

decipher the message of the sun,
play the rhythms of the earth,
demand the cleaning of the atmosphere,
carry the will and way of the word,
feel the heart and questions of the people
and be conditioned and ready
to move.

to come
at midnight or noon

to run
against the monied hurricane in this
the hour of forgotten selves,
forgiven promises
and
frightening whispers
of rulers in heat.

The Union of Two
(For Ife and Jake)

What matters is the renewing and long running kinship
seeking common mission, willing work, memory, melody, song.

marriage is an art,
created by the serious, enjoyed by the mature,
watered with morning and evening promises.

those who grow into love
remain anchored
like egyptian architecture and seasonal flowers.

it is afrikan that woman and man join in smile, tears, future.
it is traditional that men and women share expectations,
        celebrations, struggles.
it is legend that the nations start in the family.
it is afrikan that our circle expands.
it is wise that we believe in tomorrows, children, quality.
it is written that our vision will equal the promise.

so that your nation will live and tell your stories accurately,
you must be endless in your loving touch of each other,
your unification is the message,
continuance the answer.

August 7, 1986

Possibilities: Remembering Malcolm X

it was not that you were pure.
your contradictions were small wheels,
returning to the critical questions:
what is good?
what does it mean to be black?
what is wise?
what is beautiful?
where are the women and men of honor?
what is a moral-ethical consciousness?
where will our tomorrows be?
what does a people need to mature?

it was your search and doings
that separated you from puppets.
"a man lives as a man does"

if you lived among the committed
this day how would you lead us?

what would be your strength,
the word, the example, both?

would you style in thousand
dollar suits and false eye glasses?

would you kneel at the feet of arabs
that raped your grandmother?

would you surround yourself with
zombies in bow ties, zombies with parrot tongues?

it was not that you were pure.
the integrity of your vision and pain,
the quality of your heart and decision
confirmed your caring for local people, and your
refusal to assassinate progressive thought
has carved your imprint on the serious.

Aberrations

(hair, color and quiet desperation in the last quarter of the
20th century post-1986 and it is still political to, consciously or
unconsciously,
desire hair that is straight or curly in the fashion of europe
and to seek the lightest and "fairest" of people to love while
proclaiming one's deepest and undying commitment to
all that is black, and on paper, beautiful.)

the utter pain of being dark
and woman,
living among men who despise
the "nappiness" of head & the
hue of skin sunbaked before birth.

the unimaginable hurt of being dark
and short and man,
living among images of vikings
tall and conquering
"angel-like" roaming the earth
seeding the wombs of the vanquished coloreds.

the war was fought
when being natural became anti-self & unkind,
the war was confusing
when we lied to ourselves to convince
the nonbelief in us,
the war was in disorder
when practice became embarrassing,
the war was lost
when self-hatred emerged as a force greater than the
scorn of sworn enemies.

beauty and being beautiful is not the question.
all people desire beauty.
a full people needs love,
music and flowers in their lives.
whose love remands the answer?
whose music determines the call?
whose beauty decides the winner?
whose culture dictates the dance?

what is the color and texture of your flower?

The End of White World Supremacy

The day, hour, minute
and
second that the
chinese
and
japanese
sign
a
joint
industrial
and
mililary
pact.

Searching

1. Sisters

in moonlight and after
beautiful women speak in tongues and
answers

where is the music?
where is the passionate fire promised?
running
with the men—loudly
backward and fisted
fastly and crudely becoming the
enemy of silence
enemy of love and vision

friend of despair and destruction
tonight and often
many and more of the womanblack are
alone
and searching with children
some
creating networks of hatred
for the limitations in their lives
robbed of laughter and joy
challenged by biology and babies
as the men
keep company with others and themselves.

2. Empty warriors

the men,
occupying bedrooms and unemployment lines, on corners, in bars, stranded between middle management and bankruptcy, caught in warped mindsets of "success in america," the kind taught to first generation immigrants at local trade schools and jr. colleges, taught to people lost and unaware of history or future, ignorant of the middle passages.

the men,
occupying space with men and motives, in prisons, in safe houses, shooting up with juice and junk, many with hairless noses and needle-marked toes, searching for missing history, searching for the when and how of "making it in america."

the men,
escaped and taken, twice and three times absorbed in life and sharing, absorbed in locating the mission and magic, the manner and muscle, the answer and aims, walking the borders between smiles and outrage.

3. Transitions

in moonlight and after,
beautiful women,

respected women become elders of the storm,
riders of the hurricane,
keepers of the volcano,
warm and worked,
caught and embittered
often blaming
themselves for misery planned before their birth,
for hurt conceived by slaveholders on wall street,
executed prior to foreparents' arrival to consciousness.

4. Arrivals

of the women clean and cured,
of the men sensitive and sound,
all focused and calm,
listeners of a distant wind
love full and wanted
they
did not wait
& knew in the aloneness of early hours
that
snow was temporary and transient
    understood that evil could not be conquered
    on knees with folded hands,
    understood that ten decades of
    colorless rice, enriched bread and sugar
    would weaken a people,
    understood too that slavery, if it is to work,
    has to be accepted by the enslaved.
snow is temporary and heat does boil water.

5. The gathering

gathering as they do with
their water and weather,

their heat and blankets,
their thoughts and hearts,
wrapping their children and songs
in the mysteries of their men being butchered
beyond recognition.
some rushing
to the wilderness of
urban consumption and corporate takeovers,
in the midnight of a wasted culture of pornographic values,
in the indecisions of life and loving.
others coming with care
seeking
quality in the confusion of mistaken loyalties,
demanding
quality of responses,
quality in the searching,
quality in the giving and loving,
quality in the receiving
beginning anew.
fresh.

Poet: Gwendolyn Brooks at 70

as in music,
as in griots singing,
as in language mastered, matured
beyond melodic roots.

you came from the land of ivory and vegetation,
of seasons with large women guarding secrets.
your father was a running mountain,
your mother a crop-gatherer and God-carrier,
your family, earthgrown waterfalls,
all tested, clearheaded, focused.
ready to engage.

centuries displaced in this land of denial and disbelief,
this land of slavery and sugar diets,
of bacon breakfasts, short suns and long moons,
you sought memory and hidden ideas,
while writing the portrait of a battered people.

artfully you avoided becoming a literary museum,
side-stepped retirement and canonization,
gently casting a rising shadow over a generation of
urgent-creators waiting to make fire,
make change.

with the wind in your hand,
as in trumpeter blowing,
as in poet singing,
as in sister of the people, of the language,
smile at your work.

your harvest is coming in, bountifully.

Magnificent Tomorrows

(For Queen Mother Moore, Karima White, Sonia Sanchez, Mari Evans, Ruby Dee, Assata Shakur, Julia Fields and Janet Sankey)

1.
flames from sun
fire in during rainbow nights.

the women are colors of earth and ocean—
earth as life,
the beginning waters,
magnificent energy.

as the women go, so go the people,
determining mission,
determining possibilities.

stopping the women stops the future.
to understand slavery, feel the eyes of mothers.
there lies hope even in destruction, lies unspeakable horror or
fruitful destiny.

we
are now in the europe of our song,
non-melody with little beat or hope.
current dreams are visionless,
producing behavior absent of greatness.

2.
without great teachings,
without important thoughts,
without signifcant deeds,
the ordinary emerges as accepted example
gluing the women
to kitchens,
afternoon soaps
and the limiting imagination of sightless men.
producing
a people that move with the
quickness of decapitated bodies
while
calling such movement
divine.

possibilities: listen to the wind of women, the voices of big mama, zora neale, sister rosa, fanny Lou, pretty renee, gwen brooks, queen nzinga and warrior mothers. all birth and prophecy, black and heart warm, bare and precise. the women detailing the coming collapse or rise. the best and bent of youth emerging. telling triumphantly. if we listen, if we feel & prepare.

3.
if black women do not love,
there is no love.
if black women do not love,
harmony and sustaining humanity cease.
if black women do not love,
strength disconnects.
families sicken. growth is questionable &
there are few reasons to conquer ideas or foe.

as black women love,
europe gives way to southern meals.
as black women mature,
so come flames from sun,
rainbows at dusk.
sculpture of elizabeth catlett and
music of nina simone.
as women black connect,
the earth expands, minds open and books reveal the possible
if we study
if we feel the flow & secrets of our women,
if we listen,
if we concentrate,
if we carefully care,
if we simply do.

Always Remember Where You Are

(For Zora Neale Hurston)

1.

it seems as though she had been
planted outside northwestern high
next to the basketball court on 86th street
behind her weather-worn blue buick
seated on a rusting folding
chair where she sold cookies, candies, history,
causes, chewing gum, vision, corn chips,
soda pop and advice to teenagers with
26-year-old mothers and grandmothers
under 40. most of their father's music
ceased during viet nam and the fbi's
war against black men who dared to
question the saintliness of congress and the
imperial presidency.

2.

She sold wisdom from her weather
worn buick bought for her by her son,
a former NBA basketball star. he had
earned NBA records and money in new york
during the 60s and 70s flying high above
hoops and reality only to slip on a
nickel bag and later fall into deadly
habit of sniffing his breakfast, lunch
and dinner. eventually his snacks interrupted
practice and games as his place in
the world became that of a certified
junky circling a basketball that
he could not bounce and a mother
he could not recognize, nor she him.

3.
As his records faded and his money
disappeared quicker than shit in
a flushing toilet, he returned home to
mamma, a pitiful casualty, unable
to write his name or remember the
love that got him out of dusable high
with scholarship offers from 50
universities, no questions asked.
that his mother cared and he was 1st team
all american high school and college is
now history. this mother, in the august
and winter of her time, with eyes
and smile frozen in urban memories,
sells sugar and dreams now from the
trunk of destroyed promises in america.

Poem Resulting From a Television Ad For *The Color Purple*

Girl
"you sho is ugly,"
broken too,
auctioned off.
sold and resold again & again
prostituted by
negroes passing & modern slavemasters
who smell gold,
smell VCR royalties,
smell cable TV rentals,
smell negroes willing to kneel, and suck again.

knowing that women "ugly" and non-ugly, "dumb" and
 undumb, daily at
typing pools, day-care centers, laundromats, card parties,
 avon lunches,
factory assembly lines and tupperware picnics share horror
 stories of
their lives with men and will dress in sunday's best to stand in
 minus 14
degree wind chill premiers to see themselves beaten and
 humiliated to
confirm fact and rumor of rough life and the insightfulness of
 d.w. griffith's *birth of* a *nation.*

the women of good words,
the women of history and content,
the women of balance,
the women who enjoy their men
are either lucky, lying or crazy.

lucky?
these women knew that black people didn't walk on water or
    come to
america first class twa.
to be in america is not luck but is a
little told chronicle of continental rape and hate.

lying?
the lie that america was bought
from indians on the trail of 1000 tears & that
colored people loved plantation life and
trees exist to hang black men from regardless of the
utterings of amos & andy, stepin fetchit and quincy jones.

crazy?
black people who refuse to mentally die
or buy are crazy. elijah muhammad, martin luther king,
malcolm x were complete aberrations & crazy.
crazy. paul robeson. triple crazy.
harriet tubman, fannie lou hamer, southern crazy.
marcus garvey, edward blyden, claude mckay
south of florida caribbean crazy.
margaret danner, larry neal, hoyt w. fuller, literary crazy.
bob marley, bessie smith, marvin gaye,
musically, musically crazy, crazy before contact with
    europeans crazy,
black people who refuse to mentally
die or buy into america's
nightmare are positively
crazy.

Woman with Meaning

she is small and round,
round face and shoulders connected to half-sun breast,
on a round stomach that sits on rounded buttocks,
held up by short curved legs and circular feet,
her smile reveals bright teeth, and when it comes,
her eyes sing joy and her face issues in gladness,
she is brilliant beauty.
she likes colors,

her hair, which is worn in its natural form, is
often accented with vivid, cheerful scarfs. her make-up
is difficult to detect, it complements her oak-colored skin,
suggesting statuesque music. her scent is fresh mango
and moroccan musk. her clothes are like haitian paintings,
highly noticeable during her rhythmic walks,
as she steps like a dancer.

she is a serious woman,
her values,
her ideas,
her attitudes,
her actions are those of a reflective mind.
her child is her life,
her people their future,
she and her child live alone and the brothers
speak good words about them.

the brothers,
married and unmarried, want to help her.
it is difficult to be with her and not
lose one's sense of balance,
one's sense of place and wisdom.
that is what caring does.
her aloneness
hurts and tears at the inside of serious men.
some of the older men have tried

to tie her heart into theirs but
the commitment was never enough.
her sense of honor and history,
her knowing of sisterhood and rightness
force her to sleep alone each night.

the brothers
continue to speak good words about her,
many
when thinking of
her smile.
others light candles and pray.
some send her notes, gifts and poems,
all
hoping for the unexpected.

Hoyt W. Fuller: No Easy Compromises

There is something magical about a person who has a passion for ideas. A part of the magic is that he or she is usually very serious and is a person with high standards and a definable purpose for living that is far beyond the ordinary. If such a person is willing and able to share his love—and in doing so, change others for the better—he needs to be remembered. Hoyt W. Fuller lived ahead of his time and, as is often the case of visionaries, he was impatient with mediocrity and ignorance. Yet, within the imperfections of growing up in America, he shared his music and mission with us to the end of his bright and influential life.

Hoyt Fuller's work influenced a generation of young scholars, activists, poets, teachers, writers and thinkers. His voice, quiet and consistent as editor of the important *Black World (Negro Digest)* and *First World* magazines, introduced Afro-American and African literature and writers to an international audience. His book, *Journey to Africa,* set the tone for a serious consideration and contemplation of that massive and complex continent. As teacher (adjunct professor at Northwestern and Cornell universities) and editor, he brought clarity to the turbulent decades of the sixties and seventies. True to the music of his time, he was the melody rather than the rhythm. His voice was direct and served as a road map for millions. He detested confusion in thought or language.

The quality that impressed me the most about Mr. Fuller was the maturity and thoughtfulness of his responses. It seemed as though most of his answers were logical and consistent with his actions. He seldom spoke from the top of his head and was Black (culturally, consciously and in color), before it was popular, and always in an instructive and non-dogmatic manner. There was a hard morality to his presence without the self-righteousness. He represented that which was decent, human and right in this world. Mr. Fuller was a true lover of life and words. He traveled among many languages and cultures and was an emotionally voracious reader of international literature.

The pronoun "I" seldom cluttered his lexicon, and his sense of *style* was in the league of Duke Ellington and Gwendolyn Brooks. He took on the bullies of the world using carefully structured sentences that displayed educated urban metaphors, exemplifying a serious mind at work. He exhibited preparedness and winning possibilities. His dedication to young writers and creators helped to launch hundreds of poets, essayists, playwrights, novelists, visual artists, photographers and thinkers into the international arena. Hoyt Fuller was a "cultural" father to an entire generation of Black wordusers. His uncompromising mind, his magic and music are missed. Few are able to sing his songs.

"compared to what," goes the song.
try example and originator.
try man of memory and legacy.
        man of destiny and future.
earthly visitor and runner among us,
suggesting *words* as mode and form,
        language morally precise,
demanding literacy and enlightenment,
as the ingredients for
beauty,
wisdom.

First World

(For Cheikh Anta Diop)

We were raised on the lower eastside of detroit,
close to harlem, new york, around the block from watts,
next to the mississippi delta in north america.
unaware of source or history, unaware of reasons,
whys or beginnings. accepting tarzan and she-woman,
accepting kong as king, accepting stanley-livingstone and
europecentric afrika, accepting british novels, french language
and portuguese folktales that devastated afrika's music &
magic, values and vision, people.

you helped restore memories,
gave us place and time,
positioned us within content and warnings,
centered us for the fire from the
first world:
original at dawn, founder of knowledge, inception. definer.
center of life, initial thinker, earliest, earliest order.
primary and wise, foremost, predominantly black, explainer,
mature pioneer, seer, roundrooted, earthlike, beginning tree,
cultivator, sourcegiver, genesis, entrance, tomorrow's light.
vision, unarguably afrikan.

Remarkable Music and Measure: Remembering the Fathers and the Sons

(For Chancellor Williams, Ossie Davis, Yosef ben Jochannan,
Hoyt W. Fuller, John H. Clarke and Hannibal Tirus Afrik)

these men
are alive & doing in this world.
all find the mediocre depressing and stimulating.

they function on sun & moon & mission.
their energy seldom dances within the
debilitating sight of others.
their expectations represent great challenge, clear motivation.

large moments exist between talkers and doers,
between original and carbon,
between infantile showboats and producers of brilliant
tomorrows.

these men take the negative and create winning potentialities,
confronting fears
and discouraging the gossip of fools or foe,
discouraging smallness in all.

their women are remarkable music and measure,
bright desert dust, rugged fruit bearers,
expectors, of clear options and family-first,
anticipating men, answers, results.

magic of the dark spirit guides them
over the dirt of europe and votive of afrika,
equipping them to recognize the enemy, whether barbarians,
priests or cabinet members in the government of assassins.

they understand the failure we strap to our own dreams.
as others & most do the robot,
they compose new melodies and
choreograph the warrior's prayer.
rulers and leaders,
followers of demagogues and noise makers
with brains of floating rocks forever seek them out.

not born great,
they decided early not to swim in the
butt prints of others

selecting to conquer ignorance and evil,
selecting to run with ideas as others and many
knee-danced and drove mercedes over the rainbows of our
children.

not born great,
they caused confusion in the tower,
worried captains of gun ships and
left large plants on this earth.

born like us, bronze and promising,
able to laugh and refuse greed in the wheat while
rejecting fairy tales and fashions from europe.

they are better, best and remarkable.
the measure of their music
is that certified fools and clowns
act intelligent in their light.

Honest Search

(For Bobby Wright)

with a mind as fast as a racetrack,
no wonder you were always running.

concerned about a people unaware of their own promise.

concerned about an answerless leadership lost
in material, status, pleasure acquisition

you did not dishonor the world, word or vision:
a fighter within the eye of the volcano,
a listener in the midst of the hurricane,
a lover unafraid of giving tears or laughter,
a scientist seeking bright and moving moments,
a deliverer of truths within the truths,
a tree rooted in history, beauty, permanence.
a good and honest man,
carrying wisdom.
carrying future.

we did not recognize greatness among us.

Moves

(For Wilson Goode)

a negro playing mayor and hardball,
playing dirty harry and the buck stops here,
forgot where he came from with an eye on
where he is,

forgetting the children dark,
the women black,
the men afrikan,
whose hair, diet and ideas clashed with
where they and he are.

in the city of bells and love
for certain brothers,
a negro
plays white and mayor,
makes history in america
by disregarding the bill of rights
while dropping bombs on
who he used to be.

confirming and confirming
that america is still number one
in the manufacturing of
niggers.

Pollution: Part I

a former jazz singer and
sideman to an imitation tap dance team,
recognizing his mediocrity
as a professional entertainer,
decided to use his gifts
in an area where competence is
uneven, less taxing and not measured
by melody or footmanship.

our singer-dancer
possessing the looks women adored,
having the rap men appreciated,
being the color negroes wished for,
endowed with the hair babies are born with,
insightful enough to peep the weaknesses
of his people,
changed his profession.

wilbert smith—
all 5' 11" of him—found a new name,
tailored his shirts,
bought a D.D. from a west coast jr. college,
picked up the
"most circulated book in the western world" and
found god.

Poet: What Ever Happened To Luther?

he was strange weather, this luther. he read books, mainly poetry and sometimes long books about people in foreign places. for a young man he was too serious, he never did smile, and the family still don't know if he had good teeth. he liked music too, even tried to play the trumpet until he heard the young miles davis. he then said that he'd try writing. the family didn't believe him because there ain't never been no writers in this family, and everybody knows that whatever you end up doing, it's gotta be in your blood. it's like loving women, it's in the blood, arteries and brains. this family don't even write letters, they call everybody. that's why the phone is off 6 months out of a year. then again, his brother willie t. use to write long, long letters from prison about the books he was reading by malcolm x, frantz fanon, george jackson, richard wright and others. luther, unlike his brother, didn't smoke or drink and he'd always be doing odd jobs to get money. even his closest friends clyde and t. bone didn't fully understand him. while they be partying all weekend, luther would be traveling. he would take his little money with a bag full of food, mainly fruit, and a change of underwear and get on the greyhound bus and go. he said he be visiting cities. yet, the real funny thing about luther was his ideas. he was always talking about afrika and black people. he was into that black stuff and he was as light skinned as a piece of golden corn on the cob. he'd be calling himself black and afrikan and upsetting everybody, especially white people. they be calling him crazy but not to his face. anyway the family, mainly the educated side, just left him alone. they would just be polite to him, and every child of god knows that when family members act polite, that means that they don't want to be around you. It didn't matter much because after his mother died he left the city and went into the army. the last time we heard from him was in 1963. he got put out the army for rioting. he disappeared somewhere between mississippi and chicago. a third cousin, whose family was also polite to, appeared one day and said that luther had grown a beard, changed his name and stopped eating meat. she said that he had been to afrika and now lived in chicago doing what he wanted to do, writing books, she also said that he smiles a lot and kinda got good teeth.

The Great Wait

(it is possible that those persons who feel the need to act against evil will be told to wait, be calm, have patience, don't get upset, be realistic, don't rock the boat, you are not so bad off, etc., etc.)

conscious tire of
waiting on waiters who wait for a living
as movers perfect the reasons why
others must wait.

movers say that waiting is an ancient art form
perfected by negroes waiting on something called *freedom*

that will surely come
if the waiters wait patiently in the kneeling position long
enough.
long enough is when the waiter's knees shine and
head automatically drops whenever waiters are in the
presence
of movers that tell them to be grateful
to have something to wait for.

movers say that afrikans can't even clothe themselves,
that the major occupation in central america is the
maintenance of cemeteries,
that the people of asia need to control their sex drive,
that the only people that *really* understand modern
technology are the south afrikaners and their brothers
on pennsylvania avenue and
that the major problem for others is that they do not
want to wait for their time.

most of the waiters are poor and miseducated.
waiting, like cocaine, is addictive.
people wait on welfare, workfare, healthfare, foodfare
and for businessmen and politicians to be fair.
waiters are line wise having spent a third of their lives
waiting in telephone lines, gas lines, light lines, bus lines,
train lines and unemployment lines.
waitin, waitin, tush, tush, tush.

waiters wait on presidents and first ladies to tell them
the secret of why waiting is better than
communism, socialism and hinduism,
why waiting is more uplifting than full employment
and is the coming tool to eliminate illiteracy and hunger.
waitin, waitin, tush.

western economists and sociologists have postulated that
waiting is the answer to family separations and ignorance.
that waiting will balance the budget and give waiters
the insight into why others care more about their condition
than they do.

the conscious world
waits on a people who have become
professional waiters.
the waiters' education clearly taught them
to aspire to become either the
waiter, waitee or waited.
for most wasted
waitin, waitin, tush, tush, tush.
popular consensus has it that
waiting builds character, cures dumbness and blindness,
waiting brings one closer to one's creator, waiting is intelligent
work,
waiting is the fat person's answer to exercise
waiting will be featured on the johnny carson show this week
disguised as
black urban professionals pushing the latest
form of waiting, "constructive engagement."
waitin, waitin, tush, tush, tush.
it is documented that
waiting will save the great whale population,
waiting will feed the children of the sudan,
waiting will stop acid rain,
waiting will save the great amazon rain forest,
waiting will guarantee disarmament and peace.
the major activity of waiters is watching television, sleeping,
eating junk foods and having frequent bowel movements.
waitin waitin tush tush tush tush

consciousness decays from
waitin on people with plastic bags
on their heads waitin
waitin on negroes that live for pleasure and money only waitin
waitin on a people that confuse freedom with handouts waitin
waitin on sam to straighten his spine and care for his children,
waiting on six child sue to say no,
waiting on $300 a day junkies,
waiting on a people whose heroes are mostly dead,
waitin on boldness from all this education we got,
waiting on the brother,
waiting on the sister.
waiting on waiters who wait for a living
as movers perfect the reasons why
others must wait.
waiting benefits non-waiters and their bankers.
most people are taught that
waiting is the misunderstood form of action,
is the act that is closest to sex and bar-b-q consumption.
waiting. waiting. waiting. waiting. waiting. waiting.
a truly universal art is practiced
by billions of people worldwide
who have been confirmed by their leaders
to be happy, satisfied and brain dead.

negro: an updated definition, part 368

(for clarence pendleton and diana ross, to be read
to the popular song, "born in the USA")

negroes (negroes/knee grows) pc., grows and devours itself; invented around 1619 in the americas by the british, french, spanish and portuguese. Also known as mulatto, creole, buck, aborigine, quadroon, bitch, mixedblood, stud, half-breed, uncle ben, aunt jemima, nigger and whatever.

BORN IN THE USA, THEY WAS BORN IN THE USA

negroes are treacherous and evil to own kind. major loyalty is to anything, anybody lighter than black. hates the color of coal, heats with gas or electricity, does not eat beans or fatback in public, hides from watermelon and neckbones. the greens they eat is spinach, and they dress in the fashion of calvin klein and anne klein II. males are mostly clean-shaved but are known to wear mustaches. females shave legs and are known to throw up at the sight of dirt under fingernails.

BORN IN THE USA, THEY WAS BORN

possessors of designer jeans, license plates and minds. negroes have been bought and sold around the world with minimum resistance. males and females are known to color their faces and spend a good part of their days staring in mirrors and pressing their heads. it is not unusual for them to have plastic surgery on their mouths, noses and feet. during the early part of the century, the males' necks were used to test the strength of ropes, and the females were considered, except for pigs, the best breeders in the world.

BORN IN THE

negroes live beyond their means and enjoy socializing with people that don't like them. great gossipers and soap opera enthusiasts. many run or jog from the word *racism.* politics gives them headaches, and afrikan history is about as important as country music. most bow and say sir to anything wearing a tie and will die for country and general motors.

BORN

negroes live mainly in england, france, the carribean, united states, brazil and other places where europeans built churches, planted potatoes and put up barbed wire. The men die early and the women are alone most of the time, even when the men are alive. many are stockholders in mcdonalds and ibm and are lovers of cowboy and space movies.

THEY ARE BORN IN THE USA

negroes were reborn in such TV shows as *webster, gimme a break, the jeffersons, different strokes, benson, amen* and *miami vice.*
they have currently captured the imagination of
the world and hollywood in movies like *a soldier's story, the color purple* and *native son.* love money
more than self, love money more than self.
Negroes, the people that gave the world
billy dee williams and diahann carroll,
wake up and go to sleep praying,
"Thank God for Slavery."

THEY WERE MADE IN THE USA.

Seeking Ancestors

(For the First Annual Egyptian Studies Conference, Los Angeles, California, February 1984, organized by Maulana Karenga and Jacob Carruthers)

1.
what it was before deathtraps
before *thriller* and *beat it,* beat it
before soaps and reagan being raised to the station
of new redeemer by grandchildren viewing progress as
calvin klein & sonys in the ear.

where are the wise words,
the critical minds,
the questioners of sordid deeds,
the drinkers of pure water,
the doers of large moments?

what it was before emma lou planned her entire life
according to the stars & big sonny wilson hung on to every
syllable spoken by rev. ike, believe in me, and palm readers
from the pentagon?

what it is
is amnesia in america,
is memory the length of private parts,
is junk food masquerading as nutrition,
is projects and tenements replacing pyramids & space,
is fad posing as substance?

what it is
is strength measured by what you drink,
what you drive,
how you dress,
the texture of your hair
and the color of your woman,
"working hard for the money."

in america
working hard for the money
can get you bullets in the spine,
cocaine in the veins or a gold plated watch made in japan.
young death is guaranteed only if you think.
thinking in brazil & uganda,
in pakistan & south afrika is considered
contagious and dangerous.

shame and shock have evaporated.
grown men take their daughters and
boys hump boys and we are told that this
is modern, is normal, is in and
in america
where vacant heads copy & buy and
nourishment is derived from pepsis & cokes,
as vikings suck the blood of black people
draining the vision from the real miracles of the west
as we all approach the time when honor and integrity are
obsolete
& preserved only in unread novels, unlistened music
as unattended grandmothers in michigan nursing homes
claim cats as family, friends and lovers.

2.
ever wonder where the circle came from
or who were the first people to use the triangle?
who were the original cultivators of the earth, who used
water of the nile to power minds and machines? what people
created music from instrument and voice and viewed the
building of cities as art and science? who were the
first to love because love contained the secrets of tomorrow?
look at yourselves.

there is magic in colors earth black & purple issuing in
browns upon greens & oranges & others producing yellows
and ever present blue, skylike rain & water & warm.
today,
it is sure and dangerous to be dark in this universe.
there are secrets in color design,
there are mysteries in the making of the world,
there are complexities in the doings of strangers against the
    world.
there are clear courses that most minds are not ready for,
will never be able to perceive.
the west does serious damage to the mind.

america is not for sale, it is the buyer.

3.
we need clear language,
able storytellers,
discoverers of crops and seeds.
we need
decipherers and investigators of ideas & promise,
foreparents
screaming music that will arm us
with wisdom of the first,
warnings of
surrogate mothers and gene pool fathers.
we need
memory & moments, melody and song.
expanding vision
in search of winning ways and noble tomorrows.

comin back clearin eyes stompin, steppin, bolder
takin the wind & whispers seriously, takin the
slave beyond copy as cure, coping as necessity,
liftin the self & selves beyond rumor & wigs,
carrying the beauty of thought to completion,
knowing that if we think it,
doin it is only extension and reward
seekin to eclipse the expected to better & best.
if we have to beat it, beat it, try beatin the enemy,
try beatin those who reduced people to excretion & mannequins.

we were once music and might growin steel
we were beauty & find often feeling first drivin fire
we were seer & solution lift on up emma lou.
quiet step step
willinthefire, will in thefire, will in the fire
step step "dance to the music" step "dance to the music"
    step step
quiet and contemplative,
clearly conscious of wrongness
turn it around big sonny w. believe that
"we are family, my brothers, sisters & me."

4.
we conquered other selves in us
we became before we knew
tradition evaporated as others and many
stole the magic and wealth of millions.
diluting the dark people's walk & way,
cutting out the soul & source extricating the spirit
assassinating the common way.

Conquerors of vastness were
unable to copy lean steam
drumbeat walkers dancers carrying
spirit as gut & drive,
spirit as purpose and future
spirit as loving find,
as will & way
seeking beauty & meaning
in the secrets of ancient wall paintings
& buried souls.

5.
we are here
combat weary and willing
now & singing
looking special devoid of defeat
fired energy & hope imagining the inconceivable
here
urgently seeking lost records
igniting possibilities.

in the light of Amon and ancestors,
in the step of the clear and conscious,
it is beauty most needed in this place
as we recall that
by relinquishing building secrets

we lost clear water & children,
we lost future & wisdom & continuity.
we lost ourselves

demand
that the few & wise of us,
monk & trane of us,
the careful & intelligent of us,
the hurston and dubois of us,
the silent and enduring of us,
the hansberry and woodson of us,
the conscious and loving of us,
to
recall the memory
recall the tradition & meaning
to rename the bringers
genius.
to quietly in the natural light of warm sunrises,
in the arms of loving smiles,
among the care of the consciously certain,
within the circle of the continued questioners,
to remember them ancestors all as
dark & talented.
as
gifted light
bringers of source,
bringers of silence,
bringers of remembrance.

Black Men (1991)

The B Network

brothers bop & pop and be-bop in cities locked up
and chained insane by crack and other acts
of desperation computerized in pentagon cellars producing
boppin brothers boastin of being better, best & beautiful.

if the boppin brothers are beautiful where are the sisters
who seek brotherman with a drugless head unbossed or
beaten
by the bodacious West?

in a time of big wind being blown by boastful brothers,
will other brothers beat back backwardness to better & best
without braggart bosses beatin butts,
takin names and diggin graves?

beatin badness into bad may be urban but is it beautiful &
serious?
or is it betrayal in an era of prepared easy death hangin on
corners trappin young brothers before they know the
difference between big death and big life?

brothers bop & pop and be-bop in cities locked up
and chained insane by crack and other acts
of desperation computerized in pentagon cellars producing
boppin brothers boastin of being better, best, beautiful
and definitely not *Black*.

the critical best is that
brothers better be the best if they are to avoid backwardness
brothers better be the best if they are to conquer beautiful
bigness
Comprehend that bad is only *bad* if it's big, Black and better
than boastful braggarts belittling our best and brightest
with bosses seeking inches when miles are better.

brothers need to bop to being Black & bright & above board
the black train of beautiful wisdom that is bending this bind
toward a new & knowledgeable beginning that is
bountiful & bountiful & beautiful
While be-boppin to be
better than the test,
brotherman.

better yet write the exam.

Black Manhood: Toward A Definition

your people first. a quiet strength. the positioning of one's self so that observation comes before reaction, where study is preferred to night life, where emotion is not seen as a weakness. love for self, family, children and extensions of self is beyond the verbal.

making your life accessible to children in meaningful ways. able to recognize the war we are in and doing anything to take care of family so long as it doesn't harm or negatively affect other Black people. willing to share resources to the maximum. willing to struggle unrelentingly against the evils of this world, especially evils that directly threaten the development of our people.

to seek and be that which is just, good and correct. properly positioning one's self in the context of our people. a listener, a student, a historian seeking hidden truths. one who develops leadership qualities and demands the same qualities of those who have been chosen to lead. sees material rewards as means toward an end and not an end in themselves. clean—mentally, spiritually and physically. protector of Black weak. one who respects elders. practical idealist, questioner of the universe and spiritually in tune with the best of the universe. honest and trusting, your word is your connector.

direction giver. husband. sensitive to Black women's needs and aspirations, realizing that it is not necessary for them to completely absorb themselves into us but that nothing separates the communication between us. a seeker of truth. a worker of the first order. teacher. example of what is to be. fighter. a builder with vision. connects land to liberation. a student of peace and war. statesman and warrior. one who is able to provide as well as receive. cullurally sound. creative. a motivator and stimulator of others.

a lover of life and all that is beautiful. one who is constantly growing and who learns from mistakes. a challenger of the known and the unknown. the first to admit that he does not know as he seeks to find out. able to solicit the best out of self and others. soft. strong. not afraid to take the lead. creative father. organized and organizer. a brother to brothers. a brother to sisters. understanding. parent. a winner. maintainer of the i can, i must, i will attitude toward Black struggle and life. a builder of the necessary. always and always in a process of growth and without a doubt believes that our values and traditions are not negotiable.

A Bonding

(For Susan and Khephra, August 20, 1989)

we were forest people.
landrooted. vegetable strong.
feet fastened to soil with earth strengthened toes.
determined fruit,
anchored
where music soared,
where dancers circled,
where writers sang,
where griots gave memory,
where smiles were not bought.

you have come to each other in wilderness,
in this time of cracked concrete, diminished vision, wounded
    rain.

at the center of flowers your craft is on fire.
only ask for what you can give.

do not forget bright mornings, hands touching under moonlight,
filtered water for your plants, healing laughter, renewing
futures. caring.

your search has been rewarded, marriage is not logical, it's necessary.
we have a way of running yellow lights, it is now
that we must claim
the sun in our hearts. your joining is a mending, a quilt.

as determined fruit
you have come late to this music,
only ask for what you can give.
you have asked for each other.

Mothers

(for Mittie Travis (1897-1989), Maxine Graves Lee (1924-1959),
Inez Hall and Gwendolyn Brooks)

"Mothers are not to be confused with females who only birth babies"

mountains have less height
and
elephants less weight than
mothers who plan bright futures for their children
against the sewers of western life.

mothers making magical music miles from monster madness
are not news,
are not subject for doctorates.

how shall we celebrate mothers?
how shall we call them in the winter of their lives?
what melody will cure slow bones?
who will bring them worriless late-years?
who will thank them for hidden pains?

mothers are not broken-homes,
they are irreplaceable fire,
a kiss or smile at a critical juncture,
a hug or reprimand when doubts swim in,
a calm glance when the world seems impossible,
the back that america could not break.

mothers making magical music miles from monster madness
are not news,
are not subject for doctorates.

mothers instill questions and common sense,
urge mighty thoughts and lively expectations,
are impetus for discipline and intelligent work while
making childhood exciting, unforgettable and challenging.
mothers are preventative medicine
they are
women who hold their children all night to break fevers,
women who cleaned other folks' homes in order to give their

children one,
women who listen when others laugh,
women who believe in their children's dreams,
women who lick the bruises of their children and
give up their food as they suffer hunger pains silently.

if mothers depart their precious spaces too early
values, traditions and bonding interiors are wounded,
morals confused, ethics unknown, needed examples absent
and
crippling histories of other people's victories are passed on as
knowledge.

mothers are not broken-homes,
they are gifts
sharing full hearts, friendships and mysteries.
as the legs of fathers are amputated
mothers double their giving
having seen the deadly future of white flowers.

mothers making magical music miles from monster madness
are not news,
are not subject for doctorates.

who will bring them juice in the sunset of their time?
who will celebrate the wisdom of their lives,
the centrality of their songs,
the quietness of their love,
the greatness of their dance?
it must be us,
able daughters, good
sons their cultural gift,
the fruits and vegetables of their medicine.

We must come like earth rich waterfalls.

Yes

for those that want:
every woman a man
every man a woman,
every person an education and willing work,
for all people
family, food, clothing, shelter, love,
frequent smiles and children swimming in glorious happiness.

for every elder a home, blooming health, few worries,
good teeth and fun-filled thank yous.
for all people,
liberating culture,
the full love of laughing children who
have been bathed in the caring eyes of
family, friends, nation.

for all people,
the inner glow that radiates peace and wisdom,
the confirming smiles of knowledge known,
the confident walk of music heard,
the quiet presence of having accepted and created beauty.

for Afrikan people
an unspoken understanding that
this is the center we gave the world

this is civilization.

Claiming Earth (1994)

Culture

The culture of a people is their definition.

The Afrikan/Black in us is the water, earth, air, fire and wind forming the core that produces the fuel energizing the spirits and souls that center our creation.

The sum total of a people's existence is exhibited in their culture, from the food grown, prepared and consumed to the clothes they make and wear, the god(s) they worship and the spirit manifested as a result of that worship, the music calling the drum in them producing the dance that glues them together in sharing movement and oneness, the visual art that replicates their souls and ideas for the others and themselves to see, the words—oral and written—marking their existence that forms the history and heritage of each moment catching all new creations in fiction and non-fiction, poetry disguised as song and drama in melodies that move the feet of the bodies toward the transportation that carries them throughout the planet especially among their own villages, towns and cities that ultimately harness the depth, the beauty, the ugliness, the technically unusable, the happiness, the magnificence, the rottenness, the kindness, the love, the rough-rawness, the refined carefulness, the unusual thoughtfulness, the occasional queerness, the quiet unexpectedness, an economy of fairness, the ripe laughter, the largeness and smallness of our souls, to the war and peace in each of us: confirming culture.

The culture of a people represents life, source, soul, spirit, saneness, silliness, science, smiles, seriousness and connectedness: family.

This familyhood confirms and confirms
in an undying love that is burned into the souls of each
newborn
binding them biologically and culturally
to life, source, spirit saneness, smiles, seriousness and
memory that
passes on immortality,
passes on the heartbeats of genius,
passes on respect for others,
passes on earthgrown love,
passes on the permanence of family,
community, nation, people, culminating in the unique
celebration of themselves.
spirited community

This is culture. replicate.

Haiti

(for the Haitian people and Randall Robinson)

in haiti at wahoo bay beach of port-au-prince
there are beautiful women in bathing suits
with men who are young, light-skinned and rich.
you are welcomed if you run with the right wolves.

in port-au-prince, on the other side of the water
fenced off from wahoo bay beach
a few children receive 19th century education in
one room shanties without running water or toilets.
their parents cook on outdoor woodfires and
pass waste in secret spots or community latrines.
they live in poverty within poverty and they elected a priest
to represent their dreams.
he promised food, clean water, education, wood, seeds,
fairness, democracy and peace on earth.

the people of haiti are angry with u.s. presidents.
the haitian military forced their elected priest to flee in the
night, with their dreams and prayers
in a quickly packed suitcase.

the people are uneducated, not stupid.
democracy is coming to south africa and
haiti drowns in white promises.
bill clinton talks in codes as
paramilitary terror squads beat patriotism into the people.
american businesses pay 14 cents an hour to the peasants
and
provide japanese toys and airline tickets to the elite.

the people of haiti are angry with u.s. presidents.
they take boat rides by the thousands
to cross a sea made of their dead for america.
most are returned on military ships,
unsuitable as political refugees.
we are told that *race* is not the problem
it is the island, it's not cuba.

the rich in haiti diet,
the poor starve and disappear if they complain too loudly.
randall robinson lived on water and tomato juice
his eyes sank into his forehead for a month.
his eyes are clear and so is he.

the new duvalierists rule a dirty capital,
when rain comes the people join the mud,
the rich drive jeeps made in the U.S.
the "MREs"—morally repugnant elite—are like elite
everywhere:
they do not feel for others,
they hide their eyes,
they wear foreign made clothes,
their children have private playgrounds and educations,
they live on hills and laugh at the dark people who don't
even own the night.
they speak the language of killers.

White People are People Too

(For Mead, Hillman, Bly, Densmore, and Multicultural Men's Work)

Most struggles have a way of homogenizing people,
of devaluing individuality
always looking at the big suffering revolutionary picture,
our pains inhibit seeing beyond our struggle,
beyond culture, beyond race.

race struggle can be cleansing and uplifting,
race struggle can be blinding and self-righteous,
race struggle seldom separates the evil from the ignorant,
"bad and not so bad, good and not so good, best and better,"
race struggle minimizes intrarace struggle.

parts of a lifetime are lost documenting the enemy.
in struggle
we only know each other and
each other is not the world

it is not in me to love an enemy
who has committed horrific crimes against children.
are crimes transferrable?
are crimes inherited by sons and daughters
who reject that history
and work for reconciliation and reparations?
can being Black and African-centered guide me to the
centering best of Asians, Europeans, Native Americans,
indigenous peoples, women, others?

it is in me to grow.
to walk among vegetation and cultures, to think.
it is in me to see that pain is colorless
it is in me to value the differences of others.

It is human to share,
I am not suicidal.

Rwanda: Where Tears have no Power

Who has the moral high ground?

Fifteen blocks from the whitehouse
on small corners in northwest, d.c.
boys disguised as men rip each other's hearts out
with weapons made in china. they fight for territory.

across the planet in a land where civilization was born
the boys of d.c. know nothing about their distant relatives
in rwanda. they have never heard of the hutu or tutsi people.
their eyes draw blanks at the mention of kigali, byumba
or butare. all they know are the streets of d.c., and do not
cry at funerals anymore. numbers and frequency have a way
of making murder commonplace and not news
unless it spreads outside of our house, block, territory.

modern massacres are intraethnic. bosnia, sri lanka, burundi,
nagorno-karabakh, iraq, laos, angola, liberia and rwanda are
small foreign names on a map made in europe. when bodies
by the tens of thousands float down a river turning the water
the color of blood, as a quarter of a million people flee barefoot
into tanzania, somehow we notice. we do not smile, we
have no more tears. we hold our thoughts in a deeply muted
silence looking south and thinking that today
nelson mandela seems much larger
than he is.

Gwendolyn Brooks: Distinctive and Proud at 77

how do we greet significant people among us,
what is the area code that glues them to us,
who lights the sun burning in their hearts,
where stands their truths in these days of MTV
      and ethnic cleansing,
what language is the language of Blacks?

she has a map in her. she always returns home. we are not
open prairie, we are rural concrete written out of history. she
reminds us of what we can become, not political correctness
or social commentators and not excuse makers for Big people.
always a credit-giver for ideas originated in the quiet of her
many contemplations. a big thinker is she. sleeps with paper
and dictionary by her bed, sleeps with children in her head.
her first and second drafts are pen on paper. her husband thinks
he underestimates her. she thinks we all have possibilities.
nothing is simplified or simply given. she wears her love in her
language. if you do not listen, you will miss her secrets. we do
not occupy the margins of her heart, we are the blood, soul, Black
richness, spirit and water-source pumping the music she speaks.
uncluttered by people worship, she lives always on the edge of
significant discovery. her instruction is "rise to the occasion,"
her religion is "kindness," her work is sharing and making words
matter. she gives to the people everybody takes from.
she is grounded-seeker. cultured-boned.
she is Black sunset and at 77 is no amateur.
rooted willingly and firmly in dark soil, she is last of the great oaks.
name her poet.
as it does us, her language needs to blanket the earth.

GroundWork (1996)

Foreword to *GroundWork*

Gwendolyn Brooks

Haki: artist, pioneer, "loyalist." Haki developed a *communicating* expression that suited his direct and earnest concepts. More than any other Black poet who became influential in the late sixties, he remained actively loyal to the richness of his faith in and love for Black people. He scolds them now and then, but only as a benevolent father would scold them—aching in his awareness of how much there is to hurt them, in themselves and outside themselves—aching in his wish that they maintain integrity and a decent Family loyalty. He has influenced many Black poets, Hispanic poets, and, strangely Caucasian poets who sensed a vibrant vigor in his dealings with language, and admired it, respected it.

Haki has said:

> What writers write tells to what extent they are involved with the real world.... Writers should be questioners of the world and doers within the world. Question everything. And don't be satisfied with the quick surface answers.... Bad writing containing the most revolutionary idea is, first and last, bad writing. A high standard must be met if the writer is to communicate effectively. The ability to develop a style that is clear, original, and communicative is what separates writers from non-writers.

Many years ago I said of his style and commitment (interchangeable) what is mercilessly true today:

> [He] knows that nothing human is elegant. He is not interested in modes of writing that aspire to elegance. He is well-acquainted with "elegant" literature (what hasn't he read?) but, while certainly respecting the advantages and influence of good workmanship, he is not interested in supplying the needs of the English Departments at Harvard and Oxford nor the editors of Partisan Review, although he could mightily serve as fact factory for these. He speaks to black hungry for what they themselves refer to as "*real* poetry." These blacks find themselves and the stuff of their existence in his healthy, lithe, lusty reaches of free verse. The last thing these people crave is elegance. It is very hard to enchant, with elegant song, the ears of a fellow whose stomach is growling. He can't hear you. The more interesting noise is too loud.

And, of course, Haki was always interested in reaching "those people."

Haki, at times, has been called a "racist." I define racism as prejudice *with* oppression. That is: you are permitted to detest green eyes. That's all right. That's *personal.* What you are *not* permitted to do is kill every green-eyed individual you encounter. That's *not* all right. That's OPPRESSION.

Haki is not a killer. He is a lover of humanity, of what is human. He is an interpreter and a protector of Blackness. He is a subscriber to what is beautiful in the world.

Long ago Haki defined Black poetry. He considered it a working beauty fully able to nourish and extend Black people. (That is the ultimate meaning of his essential definition.)

In this foreword I am *not* assaulting our mutual understanding that there are respectable Black uniquities. However, today many Black poets are flopping off in worrisome directions. Many of them do not know *what* to do or be. Many of them want above *all* things *not* to be Black. Black people who want above all things not to be Black are pitiable and comical people in the world. The poets among such *fight* Blackness with every punch and pout in their power. Such people are very busy imitating some of the new moderns, manufacturers of chopped-up journalism, dazed and dopey. Such people have been fondled and adopted by non-spunky white poets and critics who of course have no interest in preserving, in *enfirming* the bolts, the binders of Blackness. They would like Blackness to disappear altogether.

Said and says Haki: "The Black writer learns from the people.... Black artists are culture stabilizers, bringing back old values, and introducing new ones."

I long ago decided he is a further pioneer and a positive prophet, a prophet not afraid to be positive even *though* aware of a daily evolving, of his own sober and firm churning. He is a toughness. he is not a superficial toughness. He is the kind of toughness that doesn't just "sass its mammy" but goes right through to the bone.

1996

Standing as an African Man:
Black Men in a Sea of Whiteness

Where do I belong and what is the price I have to pay for being where and who I am?

Study the faces of children who look like you. Walk your streets. Count the smiles and bright eyes, and make a mental note of their ages. At what age do our children cease to smile naturally, smile full-teeth, uninhibited, expecting full life? At what age will memory of lost friends, and lost relatives, deaden their eyes? Where does childhood stop in much of our community? At seven, eight? How many killings, rapes, beatings, verbal and mental abuse, hustles, get-over programs, drug infestations, drive-by shootings/drive-by leaders must they witness before their eyes dry up for good and their only thought is, "Will I make it to the age of twenty-five?" When the life in the eyes of our children does not gleam brightly with future and hope, we cease being nurturers and become repairers of broken spirits and stolen souls. This is the state we are now in and too often it is too late.

Where do I belong and what is the price I have to pay for being where and who I am?

If you don't know, you can't do.

From whom do we buy our food? From whom do we rent our apartments? From whom do we buy our clothes, furniture, cars, and life-bettering needs? On whose land do we walk, sleep, live, play, work, get high, chase women, lie, steal, produce children, and die? Why is it that over a million Black men and 100,000 Black and brown women populate the nation's prisons? Is race a factor in a land where white people control most things of value? Is race a factor in a country where young Black boys and men are dying quicker than their birth rate? When do we declare war on our own destruction? Why is it that the Blacker one is the worse it is? Who taught Black people that killing Black people is alright and sometimes honorable?

This is Our Charge!

Study the landscape. Read the music in your hearts. Remember the beauty of mothers, sisters, and the women in our lives who talked good about us. Remember when we talked good about us. Remember when we talked good about them. Understand the importance of ideas.

This is Our Mission!

Pick up a book. Challenge the you in you. Rise above the limited expectations of people who do not like you and never will like you. Rise above the self-hatred that slowly eats your heart, mind, and spirit away. Find like-minded brothers. Study together. Talk together. Find each others' hearts. Ask the right questions. Why are we poor? Why are our children not educated? Why are our children dying at such an unbelievable rate? Why are we landless?

What does land ownership have to do with race? What does wealth have to do with race? Why do we hate being called African and Black? What does Africa mean to me, us? Why is Africa in a state of confusion and civil war? Why is there no work in our communities? What is the difference between a producer and a consumer? What do we produce that is sold and used worldwide? Whose knowledge is most valuable for the development of Black (African) people? Would I kill myself and others who look like me if I loved myself and those who look like me? From where does self-love come? Who taught me, us, self-hatred? Is selfhatred an idea? Is self-love an idea? To whose ideas do we tapdance? With whose ideas do we impress each other? Are African (Black) ideas crucial to our discourse and development? Can a Black person be multicultural if he/she does not have his/her culture first? When do we declare war on ignorance, intellectual betrayal, self-destruction, pimpism, weakening pleasures, European worldviews, beggar mentalities, and white world supremacy? Is race an idea? When will we use the race idea to benefit us?

Where do I belong and what is the price I have to pay for being where and who I am?

We belong among the people worldwide who look like us. We belong to a world where we produce rather than consume. We belong to a world where the measurement of Black beauty and worth is internal, cultural, and confirming.

We belong where our education is not anti-us.

We belong among African men who are brothers and brothers who are Africans. How will we recognize them?

You will recognize your brothers
by the way they act and move throughout the world.
there will be a strange force about them,
here will be unspoken answers in them.
this will be obvious not only to you but to many.
the confidence they have in themselves and in
their people will be evident in their quiet saneness.
the way they relate to women will be
clean, complimentary, responsible, with honesty and as
partners.
the way they relate to children will be
strong and soft full of positive direction and as example.
the way they relate to men
will be that of questioning our position in this world,
will be one of planning for movement and change,
will be one of working for their people,
will be one of gaining and maintaining trust within the
culture.

these men at first will seem strange and unusual but
this will not be the case for long.
they will train others and the discipline they display
will be a way of life for many.
they know that this is difficult
but this is the life that they have chosen
for themselves, for us, for life:
they will be the examples,
they will be the answers, they will be the first-line builders,
they will be the creators,
they will be the first to give up the weakening pleasures,
they will be the first to share a black value system,
they will be the workers,
they will be the scholars,
they will be the providers,
they will be the historians,
they will be the doctors, lawyers, farmers, priests
and all that is needed for development and growth.
you will recognize these brothers
and
they will not betray you.

The Mission of a Good Man

(For Robert J. Dale at fifty)

we must read this man differently
dark-skinned children are at the center of his heart.

he possesses a desperate joy,
few pleasures, easy laughter,
he takes time to hear
little voices.

his thoughts are reclusive, private, complex.
he lives among a community
that understands & calls his name often and
thinks that he is a mountain,
thinks that he is rice milk & precious stone.
they see him the way he sees our children. honestly.

his interior is tree lined, African wheat grass, mountainous.
he has a suffering smile that understands voluminous truths.
he must make a payroll twice monthly,
    make deals with pants-wearing roaches with
    deep immune systems & bent smiles requiring him
    to bathe & meditate frequently. he says,
    for our children we must claim part of the map,
    geography is not european, is not white, must not
    be foreign to us.
we must receive this man accurately, traditionally.
dark-skinned children are at the heart of his center.

his heart is African.

The State's Answer to Economic Development

it is the poor
that populate Las Vegas & riverboat casinos
where neon lights & one-armed bandits never die
yet draw the young
and aged whose lives
seem exhausted & bored beside
the lights,
the games,
the entertainment,
the unchances,
the early hope
where everybody can afford
a hotel room to drop a suitcase
with fresh greyhound tags notating
the midnight ride from California & elsewhere
with $300 in their left shoes
that they think
will win them a life.

So Many Books, So Little Time

(For librarians & independent booksellers)

Frequently during my mornings of pain & reflection
when I can't write
or articulate my thoughts
or locate the mindmusic needed
to complete the poems & essays
that are weeks plus days overdue
forcing me to stop, I say cease
answering my phone, eating right, running my miles,
reading my mail and making love.
(Also, this is when my children do not seek me out
because I do not seek them out)
I escape north, to the nearest library or used bookstore.
They are my retreats, my quiet energy/givers, my intellectual
refuge.

For me it is not bluewater beaches, theme parks
or silent chapels hidden among forest greens.
Not multistored American malls, corporate book
supermarkets, mountain trails or Caribbean hideaways.

My sanctuaries are liberated lighthouses of shelved books,
featuring forgotten poets, unread anthropologists &
playwrights; starring careful anthologists of art & photography,
upstart literary critics; introducing dissertations of tenure-
seeking assistant professors, self-published geniuses, remaindered
first novelists; highlighting speed-written bestsellers,
wise historians & theologians, nobel & pulitzer prize winning
poets & fiction writers, overcertain political commentators,
small press wonderkinds & learned academics.
All are vitamins for my slow brain & sidetracked spirit in this
winter of creating.

I do not believe in smiling politicians, AMA doctors,
zebra-faced bankers, red-jacketed real estate or automobile
salespeople or singing preachers.

I believe in books,
it can be conveniently argued that knowledge,
not that which is condensed or computer packaged, but
pages of hard-fought words, dancing language
meticulously & contemplatively written by the likes of
    me & others,
shelved imperfectly at the levels of open hearts & minds
is preventive medicine strengthening me for the return to my
clear pages of incomplete ideas to be reworked, revised &
written as new worlds and words in all of their subjective
configurations to eventually be processed into books that
will hopefully be placed on the shelves of libraries &
bookstores to be found & browsed over by receptive
booklovers, readers & writers looking for a retreat,
looking for departure & home,
looking for open heart surgery without the knife.

Too Many of our Young are Dying

moments represent a lifetime.

our hearts lose sunshine
when our children cease to smile words
and share with parents their passionate pain.
our children, in the millions
are dropping from the trees of life too soon,
their innocent hearts and bodies
are forced to navigate within modern madness,
searching for life and love
in the basements of a crippled metropolis,
a disintegrating culture   too soon.

are we not all earth & lakes & sun?
are we not all mamas & babas to their young music?
their lives are not abstracted bragging rights,
we must never stop listening to their stories & songs.

when our children
do not share their young pain
it is a sign of our closed ears and punctured hearts
do not misread the silences in their eyes,
they are seeking sunshine from us
immediately.

What Makes Him Happy

this woman who loves black & white photographs is
brightfaced, blessed with deep-rooted & perspicuous eyes,
carries one hundred & thirty-five pounds of tall,
lean beauty draped on African bones uses
liquid soap that smells of peppermint or almond;
drives her car barefooted.

she appreciates the difficult differences
between Toni Morrison and William Faulkner,
understands that the free market is really a family affair,
has tasted and lost profound love and experienced
the pain and miracle of giving birth.
this woman runs a mile in under nine minutes
and believes that billie holiday, john coltrane &
louis armstrong are alive & still swingin, says
she loves vegetables, brown rice, nectarines & her son.

she relaxes with films that need subtitles,
music that requires a mind and her man
who is comfortable with complexity and enchantment.
she is contemplative about romare bearden's signature on his
paintings,
& has a smile that evokes volcanoes in men.
she has god in her heart but doesn't brag about it,
prefers baths to showers & sweetens her body with
olive/aloe oil.
her home is art-full as are the five rings decorating her fingers
& ears,
her hair is shaped close to her head which she cuts herself,
she has a museum of a memory & articulates her love and
thoughts firmly and passionately while listening to
billie, trane & pops collaborating
in black & blue eight-scale harmonies
the music, the traditions & the *way* of our tomorrows.

A Calling

(for Rev. Frank Madison Reid III
on the occasion of 25 years of service in the ministry)

we are short memory people,
too willing to settle for artless resumes of
rapid life   brief prayers   cappuccino.

our young adapt to contemporary clothing without question,
as we fail to acknowledge brilliance among us
displaying a hesitancy to tell this preacherman, this good
 brother
how his journey has become our journey.
in him is ordered-calm, deep thought, quality-love, a probing
 mind.

are pastors inspired to read Baldwin, Morrison, Diop,
Chomsky, Said and Brooks? are their ears prepared for
Monk, Aretha, Trane, Chuck D and music screaming from the
tongues of hypocrites? can a serious minister be known for
anything other than knowing God's name, being clean, loving
his family and saying double yes to fried chicken dinners?
cultural essentiality?

we are short memory people,
you have been planted among us
artfully seeded in Black earth to illuminate the texts,
shepherd our prayers, spiritualize our commitments and
help us seal the holes in our souls.

some arrogantly shout that this is your job,
in kind smiles and rather meditatively, others voice
we don't remember you ever filling out an
employment application.

HeartLove: Wedding and Love Poems (1998)

Maintaining Loveships

There are many paragraphs in a life of love. I say "paragraph" because the stanza of poetry is still foreign to most of us. Love is a living river running slowly north to south, traversing the entire human continent. Love is like the Mississippi River experiencing all types of weather, hot to cold, warm to cool, frigid to steaming hot. Find the weather of the person you love, monitor it often. Or like the river's weather, adjust your body temperatures to accommodate the other in your life and adapt to your own definitions of happiness, stability, and seriousness. Remember that love is not a swimming contest, and most of us will never learn to backstroke. Learn to swim upstream together.

Bonding—mating, and preferably marriage to another—is or can be music. (Much of the time, in this culture, it is regrettable noise.) However, this bonding can be the best of the early Supremes, Miracles, Four Tops and Nat King Cole. Some of us. measured our early happiness with each new cut by the Dells:

"Stay in My Corner." Coupling is also Bessie Smith, Billie Holiday and, yes, Nina Simone—as they sing with tears in their eyes, "Am I Blue?" We choose our dancing partners. We can either two-step, tap, do modern, African, the breakdown, or get in line and pulse. Whatever tune we choose will demand work, require navigating the personal river of the other, require the sharing of the most intimate spaces. We may be southern in our spirit, yet, too often, our struggle is to neutralize the northern winds blowing ice into our lives. Think in bright possibilities.

To the Men

Women are different in so many beautiful ways. I wonder if we men really ever sit down within our own questions and ponder the complicated melodies of the woman/women in our lives? Do we ever try to put our feet and souls into their shoes and spirits? Each woman is her own color, is her own stream, is her own season, and has her own personal weather report. We must listen to our women. We must know the winds of our women. Often these winds come with hurricane force, but mostly they arrive smoothly so as not to take either of us off center. The women in our lives are the balances that keep our families from falling too far off course. If there is to be "war," let it be against superficial assessments of women. Do not fear intelligent, self-reliant, independent, strong-willed, and culturally focused women. Seek them. Most of these women have strong backs, questions and answers. They harbor ships of love. They also hold within them the pain and happiness of large families and culturally defined histories. The most serious of them think in long distance and careful sentences. If they are with children, they function always with a clock in them. Most of them carry the pulse of their children close to their hearts. They also carry the smiles of the men they love tightly in the vicinity of the same heart. We must begin to carry the spirits of our women in us. We must open our mind's eye to the great possibilities that serious mating represents for our future. This is HeartLove.

To the Women

Men are beautiful in so many different ways. They come with unorganized heartbeats. They come, often ready to learn, ready to be taught a different rhythm. Like their toes, the size and shape of their hearts are hiding complicated fears. Young men fear women. They hide their fears in muted language and quiet cool. At dances, they hold up walls with their backs, a mean lean carefully shaped to give off messages of "I'm ready." Generally with one or more of their brothers they signal that, "We're ready." "Ready for what?" is the question. Too many men function overtime in ways to impress other men, mainly their fathers or mentors, brothers, uncles, grandfathers, teachers, or coaches. They buy into the "impressions" business too early. Often the men talk in codes. Men do not beat around the bush, men beat the bush. Most men do not talk or sing to the woman/women in their lives the music that is pulsating in their minds. We think that we are lovers, or we want to be lovers, but seldom contemplate the meaning of love. Too many of us have been taught "love" by our peers and the street. Too often this is translated into the physical only. Women represent children, commitment, sharing, and long-distance conversations about tomorrows and fears. But, we do not listen. Too many men come ill-prepared for love, for sharing, for deep-river rides, having spent too much time in the northern hemisphere of their minds. Men need understanding, good instructions, and magic in their lives. Women represent all of this to us. This is HeartLove.

To the Men and Women

Marriage, mating or bonding is not a vacation or a prolonged holiday. Eighty percent of a marriage is work, compromise, adaptations, changes, intimate conversations, laughter, sexual sharing, confusion, joy, smiles, tears, pain, crises, re-education, community, apologies, mistakes, more mistakes, new knowledge, and love. If children are involved, include parenting and repeat everything above twice for each year of the marriage. If the marriage lasts more than fifteen years, the couple should add wisdom and many, many thank-yous. What about the other twenty percent? I presume that even in the most successful marriages, the couples will sleep.

Remember, the deepest hurt is the hurt inflicted by lovers. To remain lovers is hard work; it is not natural. Mating/marriage is cultural. Most things grow old. The key to beautiful tomorrows is involvement in a loveship that ages gracefully. We are bound to make mistakes in our loveships, but the lesson is to learn and grow from them. Always listen to your mistakes, learn from your mistakes.

If Black women do not love, there is no love. As the women go, so go the people. Stopping the woman stops the future. If Black women do not love, strength disconnects, families sicken, growth is questionable, and there are few reasons to conquer ideas or foes. If Black men do not love, shouting starts, the shooting commences, boys fill prisons, and our women grow gardens off to themselves. If Black women and men love, so come flowers from sun, rainbows at dusk. As Black women and men connect, the earth expands, minds open and our yeses become natural as we seek HeartLove.

DarkRooted: The Joining

(For Marilyn and David Hall, June 23, 1990)

it is said each morning before parting, before meeting
the wind, the two of you clasp suntouched hands &
sing a quiet prayer for the continued wholeness & safety
of the other. anchoring. it is known that your four hands
touching softly complete the first circle, mending
the two of you quilt-like into an unending image of
long-distances
earth trees. in this kente-cloth man who is brother to
his community lies deep well values, wind-swept valleys.
mountains. broad memory, historical pain, committed
joy. energy. determined force. i've seen his father.
in this batik-cloth woman whose beauty graced our eyes
there is crystal-hope. renewing grass spirit, watered fruit,
heartbeat cool, active brain, willing searcher.
serious runner. i've seen the people of her homeland.
we listen to the sunlight burning between your hearts.
we confirm the enchanted beat of your calling.
as in water conversing with sea rocks we come
touch-tongue,
we come joyfully to your circle,
duplicating the quest. you are yes. anchored african trees.
darkrooted. ones.

Answers: This Magic Moment
(For Gina and Chester, *August 18, 1990*)

now that you have young love
insist upon the dawn,
its mornings bright with sun and rain
that summon up continuity.

now that your love is bonded and
culturally confirmed, do not forget:
first meetings, great and early laughter,
preparation for first dates, delicate touches and
kisses that quicken heartbeats, love notes and
phone calls into the midnights' dawns. do not forget
promises; there are always pure promises of,
"forever yours."

now that you are one and one. matched.
remember the path that joined you.

now that you have traditional clarity and
are blessed with conscientious givers among you,
do not forget world without light or hope,
do not forget brutality, hunger, raw violence
visited upon children.

share the beauty in your eyes this day,
grow into mature love, leaving little for granted.

insist upon the dawn,
its mornings bright with sun and rain,
summoning rainbows and continuity,
summoning you here. brilliantly beautiful,
caring, content, young lovers,
growing into your promises,
confirming life,
confirming us,
giving an answer.

Breathing the Breadth of the Other

(For Lynn and Ron Rochon, August 22, 1993)

same love different decades.
we've seen the sun
rise
melting loud promises of our twenties.
the young do not love carefully,
the young innocently love, often,
the young *live* with wishes of no boredom.

you are mature young
a decade past romanticism,
years on the other side of searching,
months away from intimate hunger,
weeks from assigning blame,
days removed from contemplating advice from
  relatives,
within seconds confirming, we are ready!

these are your commitments:

a. listen first, listen last, communicate.
b. when angry, hit the couch in private instead of each other.
   measure each other's pulse seven times a week; do
   not buy a pulse meter.
d. divide the housework
      B.C. (Before Children)
        you[1]: garbage, dishes, bedroom, car, kitchen,
              mopping, weekly wash, cooking, shopping,
              no pets.
        you[2]: living room, bathroom, halls, cooking, car,
              sweeping, shopping, weekly wash, kitchen,
              argue for a cat.

A.C. (After Children) revise everything
e. encourage growth in each other. intelligence may
marry stupid, but brains don't stay with pinheads.
f. parent against the culture; if you spend $100 on
Nintendo, your children will become what you deserve.
g. do not take current beauty for granted. big eaters
are wrong. fat is not pretty nor healthy.
h. grow into greater love, nothing stays the same.
challenge the beauty in each other. fight for
understanding.

we've seen the sun
rise
in you
knowing the bones in her back,
feeling the tenderness of his feet,

same love, different decade,
breathing the scent of each other
breath to breath
sustaining the music of bright expectations
life confirmed. complete.
one.

Long Distance Lovers

Long distance lovers are those
who against the laughter
of doubts and anti-commitments
have hung tough
in a
civilization of perpetual partings
and wounded children

Quiet Mountains to Your Elegance

(For Carolyn and Charles on 25 years of marriage, September 19, 1993)

Yours is a regenerative descant.

This community has witnessed your maturation,
this community has participated in the birth and
  nurturing of your child,
this community has embraced your design,
this community has grown in the glow of your
  commitment.

Now that you have chosen to rejoice
in this quarter century of your love
we too renew our song.

We grow quiet mountains to your elegance.
yours are right memory, precious culture,
intricate calling, bonding,
affirming the Africa reach in us.
The exactness of your love replenishes the drumbeat in
  our steps.
Come as calm weather, muted in the understanding
that within decades of tumultuous stirrings
your melody is original antique,
determined answering, a smile.

Let this be our legacy,
our melody.

Translations

(For Gerry and John Howell, August 27, 1994)

She has unearthed your center
it is attached to the heart of
this woman.
Does she know your history,
has she deciphered your language,
has she made any sense of your diet,
does your reading of books frighten her?

Does she know that you have brothers
with different last names?

You come to the union as experienced practitioners
pained, gutted, illuminated, with children,
cleansed, wiser.

She will bring balance to your life.
What will you give her?

Try the promise of loving longevity
consultant happiness,
measured music of the Dells and Four Tops
indigenous beauty,
try the abandonment of weakening habits.

There are mountains in the two of you
climb each other regularly
watch for mudslides and cracks in the rocks.
Your life-line is love and
intimate distance spaced by
silent yeses confirming
"this magic moment so different and so new"
your voices,
perfectly pitched, natural.
Sing your songs.

Contemplating Full Orchards

(For Bakari Kitwana and Monique Jacques, November 26, 1995)

New York City is not a place to watch
the sun or grow a forest. agreed.

I speak from the tongue of a father,
a brother, as one who has known deep love.

This marriage is not an exam. You are now
entering the rooms of living mysteries where
prophesy reveals itself as knowledge and mother-wit.
this is the clearest contingency for love:
        commitment to differences, listening, compromise,
         assigned prescriptive silences,
         learned laughter, artful music and essential values.

in fresh marriages you are exposed
like new seeds in earth,
like delinquent gossip from children,
like well water to the earth's organisms.
define your memories gracefully.

sweet, sweet lovers
crowd your bed in each other.
rise each day with distinctive voices
contemplating full orchards draped in
bountiful moons of mastered touching,
accepting unpredictables,
expecting well-placed joy. agreed.

Memories are Made for Poets

(For Sharon Franklin Taylor and Useni Eugene Perkins, November 30, 1996)

in our adolescence we played at love
the kind that surfaced for too many pretty faces
attached to bodies that stopped one's breath   always
surrounded by innocent laughter that continued
until the rings were firmly placed
on the left side of our hearts.

memories are made of this.

in this season of ripened watermelons,
pre-driven cars and year-round vegetables from
  California
we now accept breathless prayers
while gently exchanging thread, bread and long life
with this elegant woman who knows God and you.
she believes you are the river running into her desert.
we are here to confirm the richness of her earth,
of her decision.

the truth is that this poet does not wish to age alone
and is known by many and most
to recognize succint beauty and deep love
especially if such love is shining luminously upon him.

The Reconstitution of all their Days and Nights

(For Benard King and Nequai Taylor, August 23, 1997)

are the lovers
soon to be husband and wife
ready to ride their words and deeds of obligation?
have they been schooled in the art of long nights
in and out of each other's arms?
have they tasted the bittersweet days of doubt and boredom?
what of the great possibility of children, yes
children with exposed hearts and innocent eyes
demanding the reconstitution of all of their days and
        nights, forthcoming?

tell them loudly that the love of each other is not enough!
that knowing, that family, that towering expectations,
that community steeped in luminous tradition
coupled with the laws and lows of deep valleys
harboring the necessity of memory, meaning and
touch all reaching
for the perfection of new days as promised in muted signs
only if they listen and love, do mindful work
        and love, speak good words
        and love, share meaningful values
        and love, grow into each other responsibly
        and love,   to love deeply like earthmusic dancing
life from the drums of our dreams, beating rough water,
beating ripe wind, beating bright sun,
drumming these young hearts into family.

The Preparation Chant

(minister)

in the hollow night the bells ring,
in the basement under dim lights the bellmaker sings,
in the closet, in the house across from the church the
 minister makes ready,
in the hot breath of a child, the sister to the bride,
 a smile is seen,
in the mixed steps of the brother to the groom
 a dance is forming,
in the words of the father we are here in love and love,
in the actions of the mother seen at 6:00 a.m. running
 into the church,
in the questions asked by children waiting to eat,
in the mission of *this* man and *this* woman memorizing
 their commitments,
in the quiet of their community contemplating
a party, quilt and prodigy.

(bride and groom)

Wait:
on this occasion of pure water, rain, river runs,
lakefront beauty, waterfalls, dreams of warm baths,
it is the right clean,
the telling of our stories, the ocean of Black memory that must
be underpenned, strengthened, made holy, praised, stretched
higher than the expected.
the two is one. sun filled prerequisite for family,
for future, for accepting secrets reserved for careful, careful
lovers. we join the community.
open eyed, deeply considered having studied *the* texts
and listened to our elders.

(maid of honor)

Why:
it is observed, some say that it is written,
others talk of permanency and the need for quality
reproduction. nonaccidental births.
refreshing music, history understood,
a politics of mutual respect in a society of knowers,
builders, artists, musicians, writers, poets, teachers,
pastors, chiropractors, herbalists and
volunteer gardeners who teach that farming is
fundamental to civilization.
producing can-do people not afraid of kindness or
melody or sweet yeses.

(best man)

Start:
before the introductions, before the knowledge of God,
before the attraction of opposites,
before the melting of hearts,
before the empty sidewalks intersect your centers.
define your common music, construct a future
into right-propositions, proposals, preparations and expectations.
kneel to a quality life with a person better than you are,
rise sweet summer,
rise with the wisdom of grandmothers,
rise understanding that creation is ongoing,
immensely appealing and acceptable to fools
and geniuses, and those of us in between.

(*minister*)

in the coming day light,
in the willful act of sharing bed and fruit,
in the commitment of supreme sacrifices for the couple's good,
in accepting the carelessness and ignorance of youth
  and past lives,
in the first questions of survival, sameness and civility,
in the promises of deep passion, pasture, passage and work,
in the activism of protecting culture, people,
  ideas and clean water,
in the spirit of that which is greater than we are allowed
  to know or be,
in the privacy of two people who have exchanged
  wood, fire, earth and pancakes,
in the oneness of shared hearts acknowledging responsibility,
holy words and family.

(*bride and groom*)

we now carry each other's bags, histories, vegetables, dreams,
common concerns, furniture
and end each others sentences with more periods
than question marks.
as we make our house sacred,
prosperous, complimentary and joyous.

The Only Time

the only time a man
can tell a woman
he loves her too much is when
he doesn't mean it.

Love Gets Too Much Credit Until It Finds You

you don't find love it finds you
not that love is hidden or unavailable
it's on its own mission searching for receptive souls.
love cannot be bought, sold or ordered with dinner,
cannot be charged on gold cards or revolving accounts,
cannot be bartered with food stamps, coupons or promises,
cannot be redeemed with cashier checks or money orders.
love is seasoned and concealed in fine fire,
delicate music and accessible secrets that are quilted
to the tone of distinctive voices wrapped in unconditions and
clear commitments
created for unique lovers who have matured
and are prepared to receive the most precious of stones
allowing love to tango its cultured language generously
and unencumbered into the essence of those
who are blessed.

Tough Love

his soul knows no calling,
hears few kind footsteps.
he talks street & prison with right hand on his privates,
his pants hang low on his hip bone,
his language is protective & guttural,
he sees with one eye,
his walk is drum-dance,
he runs with the roughroad tribe,
wears black glove on left fist.
has never known a personal smile from an adult,
his knowledge is popular, urban & short.
he discovered moon, sun & flowers at 20,
the elder in his life is 26 and like him
knows he is in trouble.
he's seeking a distant memory, a calling

last week a smiling woman called his name,
she wasn't carrying weed or guns or junk food.

She Never Grew Up

She lost herself in *people* magazine beauty.
family and strangers started telling her
how beautiful she was before she was born
she absorbed their words at birth & never let go.

her color is mango black wrapped around innocent
green eyes.
she had a smile that was invented for her teeth.
the beauty confirming words clouded her memory
and impeded her walk.
she had deficient family to protect her.
at 29 she was an old woman.
men had given her everything that
she & they thought she needed.
they stole her youth
unmarried with 8 children
she didn't know the intimate history of her lovers
they all told her, repeatedly
how beautiful she was.

the color of mango black with green eyes
she could not see the lies from men who
always swore that they deeply loved her just before
they parted her legs,
rode her like a horse,
took her juice
left their seed &
never said good-bye.

Why She Loves Him

she seldom would admit to him the reasons she was
attracted his way (not necessarily in this order):
looks, hair, tone of voice, content of his conversation, body
scent, his infectious smile,
manners, kindness & ideas. the drape of his clothes,
the quietness of his intentions & interior, care for
others, the questions he asked,
his understanding of multiple realities, his culture &
politics, his insistence upon paying for dinner,
movies & music while dating.
he is unpredictable, well traveled with a large
mind & is unpretentious. the way he smiles
at children & gravitates toward them,
his advocacy of extended family, love of exercise,
walking, love of land.
he doesn't smoke, drink, do drugs or sleep around,
does not think it right, necessary or safe to have sex
on the first, second, third or fourth dates,
he feels that birth control is his responsibility too, clean, loves
to visit bookstores, libraries, farms,
museums and art galleries, read books,
quarterlies and magazines that have more text than
pictures. adores visual art, music, movies and theater.
respectful of women's dreams and vision.
he doesn't eat meat, fish, chicken or dairy products.
productive and economically independent,
not jealous, mentally and physically sound,
an intense caring lover and yoga practitioner. the
spiritualness of his utterances and
his presence quiets her.
the way he communicates without words is precious, and
she knows the exact location of his heart.

Laini

nurtured like her mother
wondrous,
contemplative & self absorbed.
she assigned herself a capacious journey.
new york city is a frightening certainty.
i cried when she returned
whole & enlarged & well.
still avoiding vegetables & housework.

For Mariama
Spelman Commencement
(May 22, 1995)

The sun has blessed you.
this ritual of light,
this necessary coming out,
this gathering of sisters, mothers, grandmothers,
this awakening,
this journey,
this deciding step,
this quality walk,
this gathering of family, extended family, people,
this welcoming rootedness,
this earth warming call,
this Black high jump,
this continuation of Leslie, Alfre, Alice, and Johnnetta,*
this double-dutch of ready-women,
this calm before the *yes,*
this Africa across the seas,
you are our deep calculation,
embrace your numbers
come to this moment,
run to the new century without apology or slowness.
you are affirmation and clean-sound
mind your wealth internally and
never forget your name.

**Leslie Richards, Alfre Woodard, Alice Walker, and Johnnetta B. Cole*

In Our Tradition

(for the brothers)

his woman is sitting on the back porch,
insects feed off the sweat of her lean body,
they have just finished making love.
she hurried out of the room
to cry
away from his smiles & smell.
after the flood of '95
she had promised herself that before
she loved him again
she would take to the fields, break bread with nuns
look wolves in the eye & kneel before the sea of light
to armor her heart away from his touch.

her breath young & spirited,
her eyes lucent & unequivocal
betrayed the armor about her heart

it is he who promised her heartlove
it is she who questions the love in
his heart.

Alone Much Of The Time

The women he experienced and enjoyed life with
were fine, intelligent, children loving & smiled naturally.
Most were intuitive, self-starters & understood balance.
he avoided women with multicolored finger nails,
all the answers,
processed or finger waved hair styles,
smokers, drinkers, excessive talkers,
soap opera & talk show enthusiasts while
side-stepping women who wore clothes
glued to their bodies like balloons to air.
he didn't care for gossipers, nonreaders, big
eaters or women who were cultureless
and believed that the only use for money was to spend it.

Risk Everything

I

at thirty-six you had tasted and tested life.
it had not conformed or confused you.
you could count your losses and loves on either hand,
a slow count. one love for each decade minus the first. in your
twenties you were blessed with a son with a man who had
detoured to a corner of your heart
without experiencing sun, healing
water or the voices of enlightened ancestors.
you traveled south and birthed a boy genius. this is to say you
always total your journey, could read a map at night and were
never without cab fare, your mother taught you her pain and
laughter, your
grandmother said, "men needed excuses." your father proved
her correct. your aunts schooled you in the lies of women. it
was left to you to
locate the intimate and intricate truths. your best girl
friend taught you how to fix
cars that you drove as if your soul was glued to the steering
wheel of better destinations.

you found that men were like unchartered continents
most are undeveloped nations,
often tribal in their limitations,
too many unable to reach their own knowledges
or questions. having your own son to raise,
you refuse to suffer for boys in grown folks clothes.
in your fourth decade you allowed a man into your life who was
not looking for you.
he spoke in poems and strange food.
he looked at you for a full year before he said yes.
he realized that you were a compass, a liberated zone, careful
and sure. discriminating. lean with love.

II

you take my ebony stone and i take yours.
breathe on it, touch it to your heart. like stones we
are not new to earth or love, we've planted seeds at
midnight.
we approach the sun cleansed. whole. awaken to
shape a memory.
no longer young young our expectations are like the
stones:
hard melody, created in sweet heat.
everlasting. focused.
shaped in deep histories by the unimpressionable
medications of struggle and deep rooted greens.
we are the fundamental witness to each other's
requirements. supportive and thankful.
these stones are not to be cast away. ever.
they carry spirited devotion and tender joy
they are our markings and maps,
they are our delicate signatures.

Often Hard to Believe

(For my sons Don, Bomani & Akili)

there are thinking, loving, giving, good & kind men
among us. there are men who consider others first &
more, who are secure,
generous, well-adjusted, liberated, competitive,
competent & contemplative. around us are creative,
talented & confident, big eaters & men who fast.
in our communities are children caring, women caring
& loving, partying, intuitive, hard working & joyous
men occupying the frozen memory of all. within these grounds
are men who cook, clean, build & marry.
resourceful, peaceful, peace loving & peace giving men toil the
earth together.
on their knees are spiritual, meditative, deep thinking &
praying brothers.
gathered musically here are healthy, sportsminded,
sexually sensitive, strong,
profoundly loving & cultural men
who understand & practice reciprocity.
they know the hurt, hearts & missions of women,
they feel the bones, secrets & hearts of men,
they anticipate, defend & nurture the innocence in
children.
in their psychology are defiant warriors existing between
turbulence & honor.
seldom highlighted are the bold men who articulate & carry
the fears of others.
among men are dreamers, doers & doubters who will not

betray a trust.
they are fathers & parents who love so deeply that they are
often misunderstood.
in their quietness is patience, calmness & forbearance that
some read as weakness,
impotence & vulnerability.
in all of this they naturally smile & occasionally
belly-laugh.
these beauty-seekers safeguard civilization & we need to be
reminded of their open-hearted presence in
abundance among us.
often & more they run against the accepted &
encourage definitions of ignorant hard hats, drunken soldiers,
arrogant professors & immature politicians
who swim in egocentric heat &
the rhetoric of fools.

Parting Lovers, A Closing with Renewing Possibilities

Part One

There is more in the missing and the giving than in the
receiving. When love leaves, melody leaves, songs cease,
laughter becomes measured and brightens one's face less often.
Touch or being touched becomes highly discriminatory.
Certain touches are avoided. When love leaves,
a tearing takes place; it's like the center of one's heart being
ripped apart and exposed unfiltered
to sand or acid, like pollution. Sleeplessness
follows, one's inability to eat, and the sudden loss of weight is
inevitable for many. Others put on weight. The gaining
impacts the body: "junk food" and guilt
take the place of internal cleansing. When love is missing or
detained, there is a constant hit in the pit of the stomach,
simulating an indefinable emptiness. The loss of love is the
losing of a precious part, like being lost in action,
the mission other in you. For serious lovers,
for contemplative lovers, for lovers who understand the
silklike concentration of energy and spirit required, it will take
the noise and force of hurricanes, the lava of volcanoes, and
the disconnectedness of earthquakes to confirm the undoings
of this loveship. The quieting of this kind of love is not an
often occurrence, once in a generation, maybe twice in a
lifetime. Such love is heart-rooted, sexually measured (hot),
thoughtfully shared, consistent, a slow and deliberate love
which will take the cultures and breathless thoughts of loving
others to demand its transition.

Part Two

Where end to end becomes beginning to beginning. The releasing of mind, soul, and spirit. The best cure for transitional love is to leave lovingly. To refocus and communicate, digest and internalize the crackings and earth-movings in your hearts. The ultimate healers for parting lovers is rest, is meditation, is re-evaluation of one's loveship. Healing requires waiting time, demands thinking time, needs liberating and insightful music. Healing is a sharing of pain with a trusted friend talking it out. More waiting time. Avoiding blame. Reconstructing of beautiful memories. Rebuilding thoughts. Conversations with one's self. Meditation. Deep study and creative productions. Exercise. Fasting. Cleansing. Cultural inner attainment. Surrounding one's self with nature and music, art, literature, dance; the quiet beat and rhythms of new life. Searching softly for the simple rejuvenative powers of nature. Reach for colors that are reflective. Search actively for certainty, smiles, and learned exactness of blooming new love. Take your time in the searching. Rising in this vast world are renewal possibilities. Spring, at planting time. New heat coming. Soon.

Part Three

If parting is necessary
part as lovers.
part as two people
who can still
smile & talk & share
the good & important
with each other.
part
wishing each other
happy
happy life
in a world
fighting against the
men and the women,
sisters and brothers
Black as
we.

Voices with Loaded Language

(For Bobbi Womack and Thelma Myers, December 26, 1993)

you are not really friends to me
more like teachers, mothers, close nurturers,
i have listened to you for twenty-three years and
my enlargement has become quieted and determined
reflecting your words to me.

not quite stone,
you are more like rock-bone blended with flowers
of rainbow designing-black brownish-orange leaves
ordering up yellow suns
aiding your rising each morning
to strengthen our spines,
to make temporary treaties with tree-uprooters
bent on the annihilation of your off-spring,
the seasoning of your extended families.

you chose questions,
you quilted responsibility into my shoes,
your touch, darkly-soft, muted my anger
tuning it into focused toil,
permanent fruit. duty-deeds. resulting labor.
you are, as they say, "right on the dime," stone right.
I bring you flowers in the language of your teachings:
always consider your race positively,
contemplate deeply on your culture,
do not try to reason with sworn enemies.
be child-centered in your family making,
be deliberate in your work.
meditate on bright tomorrows.
keep love central to your life.

Quality: Gwendolyn Brooks at 73
(June 7, 1990)

breath,
life after seven decades plus three years
is a lot of breathing. seventy three years on this
earth is a lot of taking in and giving out, is a
life of coming from somewhere and for many a bunch
of going nowhere.

how do we celebrate a poet who has created
music with words for over fifty years, who has
showered magic on her people, who has redefined
poetry into a black world exactness
thereby giving the universe an insight into
darkroads?

just say she interprets beauty and wants to
give life, say she is patient with phoniness
and doesn't mind people calling her gwen or sister.
say she sees the genius in our children, is visionary
about possibilities, sees as clearly as ray charles and
stevie wonder, hears like determined elephants looking
for food. say that her touch is fine wood, her memory
is like an african road map detailing adventure and
clarity, yet returning to chicago's south evans
to record the journey. say her voice is majestic
and magnetic as she speaks in poetry, rhythms, song
and spirited trumpets, say she is dark skinned,
melanin rich, small-boned, hurricane-willed,
with a mind like a tornado redefining the landscape.
life after seven decades plus three years
is a lot of breathing.
gwendolyn, gwen, sister g has
not disappointed our anticipations.
in the middle
of her eldership she brings us
vigorous language, memory,
illumination.

she brings breath.

Being Here
(For Willie Green DeBerry, 1913–1994)

this is our findings:
he knew how to carry water,
love a wife, rear children, crack nuts,
name a daughter after himself,
inquire about the friends of his children,
provide beans and beets, shoes, questions, safety &
obstacles.
he was a tree.

his dying did not disable us
his creative preparation rooted our souls
providing not a living will but
a will to accept the life one has lived.
it is his sojourn that is remembered:
he was rock and bone, joy fed his heart,
they said he loved like a father,
his smiles and anger were tied to a greater good,
let's say he was blackman as anchor.
(in a land that did not allow him to be a captain)

he was our center
he lived the color green.

Volcanoes in the Souls of Children

(For Gwendolyn Calvert Baker
and the 1995 Chicago State University Graduates)

we have learned to sleep on bare mattresses,
we measure our tomorrows against the deaths of
    eleven-year-olds
acculturated to the violence of Haiti, Somalia, Bosnia,
nonprescription rocks, and Stateway Gardens.*

why is self-hatred considered normal among us?
why are our children angry?
what motivates the failure fields in their eyes?
why, among strangers, is there raw passion in their
    hatred of us?

we refuse victimhood,
the depreciation of young minds is not to be rewarded!
only until we understand the offerings
can we appreciate rejection.

each decade there is a revisiting of Black intelligence.

it is not the logic that is repudiated in the rule of
'i' before 'e' except after 'c', it is the assertion of
teachers who believe that our learning rules of language is
    insignificant
in our speaking, writing, and understanding.
who are the measurers among us?
    who certified their knowledge?
    why do we have to beg and fight
    for that which others expect as normal nurturing?

* public housing on the South Side of Chicago

we reject victimhood,
great teachers discover their hearts early,
knowing that it is difficult to climb mountains without
visiting them.
practice brings permanency.
this is our calling. we are essential to each other's
crops. we are the rain, the sun, the deep dark, dark
soil renouncing the, short life of concrete and the
cemented messages in its cracks. We are the bonded
meditative silence reading the future in each
other's eyes. celebrated vision. we are the yeses,
the can-dos, the give me a challenge-chance, the
mountains builders, the quiet creators who understand
the innate children erupting earthwide and refusing
to be prey or martyr, repudiating foreign assessments.
first, belonging to each other, back-watchers.
quick minds dancing within the fire and mud. ready
for the wind. riding our own memories, history, future.

All Children are Precious

(For Barbara A. Sizemore, May 9, 1997)

it is not uncommon to see her
in unexpected moments smiling at the loudly
  impossible.
the great mission in her life is measured
by making believers out of angry experts
who use toilet tissue to write their books and reports
on the largely impossible melodies,
they confirm noise, she hears music

strangers feel that her affection
is illegible but apparent.

her love is a Blackbold quilt
wearing the palm prints of children questioning
the direction of their fingers
the colors in their eyes and extreme ideas.
however, they are not opposing forces
their hearts are consumptive, calm and clear
when caring is present.

our children see the lies and failure in the eyes
of teachers who have given up.
our children survive cultural ignorance, soda pop,
potato chips and sweet cake breakfasts, each other
and people with earned degrees.
what are the ethics of children without self-knowledge?

she sees children as sacred places,
she has a repairable heart and
the quiet word on the street is that
Duke Ellington would have liked her smile.
in it gleams her greatest theme
the love of our children and the articulation of
their possibilities.

Why You are Here

(For Clifford Watson, February 8, 1998)

We are cut from the same tree
not logs, scraps of wood or toothpicks
but
molded as sculptured future by rock cutters
translating their art on to the roots
of long life, baobab trees having
endured the hurricanes, volcanoes and
earthquakes of
sprinting in America.

Our lives have never been at peace.

You have communities that love you.
We do not say it often enough.
With nourishment of millet and lentils
you have been our tall structure
an eloquent fire, sacred and on course.
We now keep each other's scrapbooks and smiles.

jimmy lee

jimmy lee is my dad,
my mothers told me so
my birth certificate states it,
his mother, my grandmother confirms that he is,
my aunt, his half-sister swears it to be,
my sister, his daughter believes it to be true.

on the street i am known as the son of mr. lee.
i have his height, artistic bent, independent spirit,
love of music, size 11 1/2 feet and an
uncanny ability to spot and tell a lie quicker than a
fastball taking on speed toward a rookie at
bat for the very first time.

jimmy lee is my dad,
he calls me son whenever he wants something,
this is the only evidence that i have of his fatherhood,
it has been a profound lesson and
i have never liked baseball.

Courage

(For Betty Shabazz, 1936-1997)

how does one proceed with half a heart?
what is the message in this transition from
body to spirit to the quiet recesses of our minds,
what should we take from this passing?

there are people who think that their lives are *the* truth.
we walk blindly in the city and the city is all we know
as ignorant people talk about how ignorant other
   people are,
this woman would smile with extended hand and
   heart,
her soul had experienced the white night of loss.

the culturally honest and spiritual among us
are always lied to and laughed at.
in their loneliness they seldom speak
we do not understand them.
we fear their peace and presence,
we fear their questioning the lies in us,
we fear their liberation.

courage is not leaving the battle until the last child is
      accounted for,
courage is saying no to the gossip of fools, friend and foe,
courage is examining the laws and souls of sworn enemies,
courage is creating a life of good values, kindness and small
      deeds.
courage is this woman, Betty Shabazz, daring to cross
      the crack in the concrete
drawn by dull-witted prophets who
mistrust the truth of their own god.

Brad

(For Walter Bradford, 1937–1997)

We met during the explosive decade of the sixties. Both of us were on fire. Young and ready to attack evil as we knew it. Both of us experienced the military at the end of our teen years, which prepared us to be impatient around children with guns and boys in black playing military. We kept our criticism to ourselves because we were still young, full of hope and energy and robust tomorrows.

We were poor and extremely grateful for Chicago's community colleges—a place where we first met and encountered the challenge of structured intellectual life.

Gwendolyn Brooks, Hoyt W. Fuller and the brothers and sisters of OBAC* carried our voices. Their workshops helped us to refine our narratives. Writing poetry was to be our way out. We had fire-words to share with each other and the world. And, somehow we knew that we would make a difference.

You made a difference. There are hundreds of men and women who knew you by "Brad" and they too realized that you were exceptional and on loan to us. You could organize a Chinese puzzle and make sense out of Black people born into fear, bondage, confusion and a European system that negated their very souls. Your chocolate smile will be missed and I'm not alone in my sadness.

*Organization of Black American Culture

This Poet: Gwendolyn Brooks at Eighty
(June 7, 1997)

this poet, this genuine visionary,
this carrier of human spirit,
this chronicler of the Blackside of life,
this kind and gentle person is the reason
we lend our voices to this day.

that other poets have championed good writing
and literature, have exposed evil
in the world, have contributed mightily of personal resources
to the young, to the would-be-writers,
to students and to the institutions of common good
is without a doubt. however,
the only poet who has made it a mission
to incorporate all of this and more into a wonderful and
dedicated lifestyle is Gwendolyn Brooks.

without press releases, P.R. people or interpreters
from the academy the great work of this quiet poet
has touched a city, this state, our nation, and the world
her poetry, her children's books,
her essays and her autobiographies have given us an insight
into the complexities of the Black human condition
that few writers can match, yet we all try
she *is* our standard
seventy years of writing do make a difference.

we gratefully and gracefully walk in her shadow,
not because she needs or requests that we do so;
it is that her work,
her outstanding contribution to Black literary music
in this world that demands the best from the least of us.
at eighty she needs no introductions or encouraging words.
at eighty the notes she writes to herself
are more comprehensive and in larger letters.

at eighty her walk is slower and her eyesight less certain.
at eighty she loves silence, is never voiceless or alone,
at eighty, Blackness remains her star and
she alerts her readers always to the huge possibility
of knowing one's self, others,
and the mystery and joy of a full life.

she has approached 320 seasons
on her own terms.
she has taken the alphabet and structured a language.
she has walked thousands of miles carrying her own baggage.

she has done the work she aimed to do,
children call her "Mama Gwen" and memorize her lines.

that which is "incomplete" is at her home
on the dining room table, in neat piles
enclosed in all size packages,
open and unopened,
here and only here is where she will always be behind

she is the last of the great
handwritten letter answerers and
she will not be able to keep up with this volume of
love.

Etta

(For Etta Moten Barnett at 96)

Etta, not accepting exclusion or
the concept *can't* leaped creatively and courageously into
the 20th century. her talent, eloquent and grand, evoked
sun, moon, boiling water and 12-grain bread. Solid
she was known to harbor mountains in her heart,
her prodigious artistry conquered the agnosticisms of
minute-minded women and smiling men as lesser souls
buck-danced to the promises of colored stardom. Soon.
Etta at ninety-six is our clear memorandum,
an endearing spirit who took her dreams and songs,
her dance and drama and gracefully grounded a
cultural signature on three generations and a continent.
Solid. as she is.

if you lose your optimism you're in serious trouble

(For Leon Forrest, 1937–1997)

i never knew the
coal that burned dark between us.
i understood your reinvented fire.
appreciated the dance, music and optimism in you.
recognized the writer, lover, professor running in you.
quietly this evening
i wished we had had winter-fights
lengthy talks, small arguments or deafening
disagreements stretching into the night of our imaginations.
i'll miss those nonconversations between novelist and poet.
i'll think of you while thanking you as i and others
continue our majestic journey
paging through the inspiring puzzles and prize
of your language.

Grandfathers: They Speak Through Me

(For W.E.B. Du Bois and Paul Robeson)

His father's father prepared him to bite his tongue,
power-listening became his gateway to information
and race knowledge.
his mother's father embraced him fully with large hugs and
words of "can-do" possibilities
in a time of darkness and treachery.
I was their blood mixture, their bone,
their claim to immortality and song.

grandfather graves declared white
people deficient, diseased and dangerous,
he had scars documenting it, he,
an african-black laborer could fix anything
moving that had a motor, a self-taught mechanic
who was gang beaten at 22 for correcting a white man at a
chevy dealership at a time when the accepted
attitude in arkansas for negroes in the presence
of whites was head bowed, eyes deep to the ground. quiet.
defeated.

grandfather lee a bronze colored
detroit minister of the baptist persuasion
never worked a day for white folks, god talked to him early
and he kept his smile.
he pastored to a community where eyes and work seldom said
no or "can't do," starting from a store front, growing into a
used movie theater, to building from the earth up,
into a 1,500-seat stained glass, concrete and fine wood
cathedral, this became an answer.
god was his mission, his people his melody
and neither *quit* nor *quiet* were in him.
he anchored bronzeville, negotiated with white stones, had
what his congregation called good back-up, the solid feed of
osun, obatala and shango.

at six i was at their knees consuming words, jerks,
silences and secrets.
at eleven i was taken to the woods and left with knife, water
and a map, manhood was coming. soon.
at thirteen i was taken to the pulpit,
given the bible, songbook and silver watch,
jesus was in the air and always on time.
at fourteen i discovered richard wright, louis
armstrong, chester himes, miles davis, langston hughes,
gwendolyn brooks and motown. i was branded crazy, insolent
and world-wounded for the questions i asked and for the
burn in my eyes.
as a young man i carried many knowledges,
ran between two cultures,
cleared my head in the military and libraries
and cried for the loss of my mother.
i kissed girls and black politics on the g.i. bill in college and
was exiled into black struggle in the early sixties.
i learned to ride the winds of battle.

as a man i choose poetry, love and extended family.
i selected black independence, institution building and
the cheery eyes of children as my mission.
i breathe the smoke and oxygen from the fires of my
        grandfathers,
i have their slow smile, quick mind and necessary wit, i wear
their earth shoes and dance with their languages,

i speak in the cadences of southern trees,
holy water and books,
i carry their messages and courageous hearts,
my eyes are ancestor deep, bold and intrepid,
i whisper their songs as mantras.
my music is accelerated blues, the four tops and trane.
it is they, my grandfathers who taught me the notes and
rhythms and as the son of their sons
i'm not missing a beat.

Books As Answer

(In recognition National Black Book Week, February 23–March 1)

there was only one book in our home
it was briefly read on sundays and
in between the lies & promises of smiling men
who slept with their palms out & pants unzipped.
it was known by us children as *the* sunday book.

rain and books & sun and books to read
in a home where books were as strange as
money and foreign policy discussions
and I alone searched for meaning
where rocks & belts & human storms
disguised themselves as answers, reference and revelation.
and I a young map of what is missing and wrong
in a home empty of books, void of liberating
words dancing as poetry and song,
vacuous of language that reveals pictures of
one's own fields, spirits, cities and defining ideas.
and I without the quiet contemplation that meditative prose
demands
was left free to drink from the garbage cans of riotous
imaginations,
was sucked into the poverty of cultural destruction & violent
answers.

until
someone, a stranger, a dark skinned woman with natural hair,
in a storefront library laid a book in front of me
and the language looked like me, walked like me,
talked to me, pulled me into its rhythms & stares,
slapped me warmly into its consciousness and read,

rain and books & sun and books,
we are each other's words & winds
we are each other's breath & smiles,
we are each other's memories & mores,
we build our stories page by page
chapter by chapter, poem by poem, play by play
to create a life, family, culture & a civilization
where it will take more than sixty seconds
to tell strangers who you really are,
to tell enemies and lovers your name.

Peace Starts Inside You

smile. breathe deeply, inhale. hold. exhale.
envy no one erase jealousy from your mind, heart &
words. speak & think good of self & others. awaken
the life spirit inside of you. breathe deeply the good in
you. smile. seek wholeness & calm. breathe.
plant good thoughts of peace & knowledge. smile often
as you breathe forgiveness and reciprocity. search
the silence in you that releases the noise that contains
the grays, whites, plastics and clocks blocking the
life force in your morning stretches. slowly breathe & smile.
breathe away ignorance, revenge, incompetence & mediocrity.
work your inner-self. breathe & smile life into your cells.
eliminate corrupt thoughts, words & actions. study peace.
smile. breathe yes into your life, to love. to family.
    to happiness. to children & children & children
    becoming the reflection of you.
discover stillness. vegetation. water. earth. breathe. health. joy.
smile. silence. breathe deeply, inhale. hold. exhale. smile. life
stillness. smile for good work, deep study, wellness.
quiet consciousness
calm within the quiet,
peace be still
smile & breathe
release. relief.

Tough Notes:
A Healing Call for Creating Exceptional Black Men
(2002)

A Poet's Call

it has always been easy
to get to my heart.
there is no other way of stating it.
the best poets are lovers,
are receptacles for pain, joy, injustice
and the innocent smiles of children.
we trust too early and easily,
we read potential in the countless faces of evil,
we carry many, many wounds.
we are often crippled yet some heal quickly
only to open their hearts to stories our
    children can see through.
the right words can send us on unlimited journeys.
the hurt in children's eyes releases fury
    in our soul and fists,
Black girls' mistreated hair brings tears.
I do not wish it to always be this way.
to care too much can damage one's spirit
yet, the secret to the longevity of significant poets is
we never give up on love, poetry and
the smiles of the young.

Black Women Have Been our Answers, No Matter the Questions

the women are colors of earth and ocean
earth as life,
the beginning waters
magnificent energy.
as the women go, so go the people
determining missions
determining possibilities.
stopping the women stops the future.

without great teaching,
without important thoughts,
without significant deeds,
the ordinary emerges as accepted example.
gluing the women to kitchens,
afternoon soaps,
and limiting the imagination of sightless men.
producing a people that move with the
quickness of decapitated bodies
while
calling such movement
divine.

Possibilities: listen to the mind of women, the voices of big mama, zora neale, sister nora, fanny lou, pretty renee, gwen brooks, queen nzinga, and warrior mothers. all birth and prophecy, black and heart warm, bare and precise. the women detailing the coming collapse or rise. the best and best of youth emerging. telling triumphantly. if we listen, if we feel and prepare.

Fathers and Sons:
The Healing Call

we the men of twenty-four-seven at dawn
of Nat, Garvey, Dubois, Medgar, Malcolm and King,
of swift tongues, fast hands and educated ears
must rise to the answer before dawn.
we are the quiet in the fire of unforgiven streets,
we are the hands beating the come home drums,
we are the home surrounded in father-love, yeses & stop watches,
we are the poetic spirit making life worth living.

this is our call,
to boys who earned their names suffering spit & fist.
scale your dreams
avoid the dust of manufactured fairy tales,
bury evil choices and mandate a working truth,
unscar your todays with a loving advocacy of tomorrow
trust the sun, moon, grass, blooming flowers and clean water,
defeat the devil's wars, burn the torturers play pager,
write your own truths, herein lies the challenge:
how far will good go in this age of lotteries and mega churches?
how far will justice travel in the breath of polluted
judge, priest, police, lawyer and politician?
how far will peace advance in the rhetoric of clowns?
what role will wisdom play in the desert of bogus thought?

this is our call,
sponsor our sons, fill the emptiness in their questions.
this is our theology: defeat the devil's plans
answer the s.o.s., save our sons with f.o.c., fathers on call,
we are sacred answers for the deserted hearts of
boys becoming men.

Reparations:
The United States' Debt Owed to Black People

Debt is owed to African people for centuries of unpaid
forced labor, suffering,
death in the tens of millions and the systematic
seasoning and
victimization of an entire race of people.

Debt is owed for the willful and brutal separation of
African people from their
land, mothers from children, husbands from wives
and families, children
from fathers and mothers and a whole people
from their African land, culture and
consciousness that defined them and gave them
substance and
memory.

Debt is owed for redefining all African people, women,
men and children as
slaves and sub-humans not deserving of salvation,
universal love,
kindness, human consideration, education and fair
compensation for all
forms of labor.

Debt is owed for the designation of African people as
property, three-fifth
humans whose only use is to slave from sun-up to
sun-down, for slave owners, therefore
reduced American people to the category of animals
accorded less care than that of pigs,
sheep, cattle and dogs.

Debt is owed for the inhuman treatment of Africans
forced to slave for the sole
benefit of Europeans, Americans and others
for leftover food, clothes
and sleeping space and whose worth and value
was determined by their
production in building wealth for Europe, America
and their people.

Debt is owed for the brutal, ordered, encouraged and
unrelenting rape of
African women by white human (aka slave) traders
and owners, thereby producing a
nation of half-black, half-white children whose
color, status, history and consciousness
branded them forever as bastards, thereby creating
a color, class and cultural
consciousness that to this day continues to rip the
hearts out of African
people maintaining a vicious circle of self-hatred,
self-destruction and denial in them.

Debt is owed for centuries of ruthless, planned and
destructive looting and
wholesale theft of Africa's people, land and mineral
wealth for the sole
purpose of creating wealth for Europe, the United
States and their
people.

Debt is owed to Black people for centuries of merciless
treatment, mendacious
reordering of the historical record and torturous
psychic damage.

Debt is owed for systematically stealing the cultural
memory from African people, for
the denaturing and renaming them thereby
creating a people unaware of
themselves and whose history and person is now
synonymous with
slavery and slave.

The successful creation of the "Negro" people in the United States is the tortuous American tragedy. This white supremacist metaphor started in this land with the ethnic cleansing and genocide of American indigenous people, renamed Indians and/or Native Americans. Thereby, let it be stated forcefully and without doubt or hesitation that the United States was founded and developed on two holocausts, that of the indigenous people and that of the enslaved Africans. Now, today, in this new century and millennium it is documented, confirmed and agreed upon by all thinking and well meaning people that—

Debt is owed to Native Americans and Black people forced:
to laugh when there is nothing funny,
to smile when they are in pain,
to demean themselves on stage, in film, television and
videos,
to dance when their hearts hurt,
to accept delusion as truth,
to lie to their children in the face of contradiction,
to pray to a God that does not look like them,
to pay compounded interest on the wealth they
created,
to sell their souls for acceptance in a fairy tale,
to mortgage their spirits for another people's history,
to support white peoples-affirmative action with
centuries of Black labor and taxes,
to create America's music and be denied the fortunes
made for others,
to see clearly and act as if they are blind,
to act stupid in the eyes of a fearful rulership,
to say yes when they really mean No!
to go into battle to maim or kill other whites
and non-whites
for the benefit of whites.

What does America owe Native American Indians and
Black people?
What is the current worth of America? Or
count the stars in all of the galaxies and multiply in
dollars by 100 billion,
For a reflective start.

Run Toward Fear

Fear

It is the poets who run toward fear.
They are what we read,
think and speak,
fighting for greater possibilities
than the words of tabloids and broadsheets where
Texas and London compare notes as
cries of 9/11 loudly emerge out of context
connected to dust on the throats of
authority and might disguised
as camouflaged revenge in the night
from small heads of an imperial
news speak.
back page the greed of Enron, WorldCom
and Halliburton. clustered
vampires needing fresh blood
rally against a mosquito whose flesh
is dark and oily, slippery and deadly
as our homeland colors are manipulated
between yellow, orange, red and re-election.

In Another Land

their parents' eyes no longer glow
they are water full and deplete
anchoring horror and hunger scarred faces.
children weighted down with loss of families, friends,
trust, homes, land, work, local scent, livestock,
dignity and a country where indigenous schools
fail to prepare children for refugee status
or quick exits with grandmothers in wheelbarrows and
pregnant women driving tractors on one-way roads.

Kosovo is like Rwanda, Bosnia, and other recent histories,
small men with guns and putrid ideas
spit in the face of sanity, reason and why.
today's leaders stand before maps and spin lies
as televised and tortured children
wade through natural and manmade mud
while quietly praying for bread, meat, blankets,
revenge and clean water, with only their
questioning minds and culture,
empty stomachs and warm hands,
shattered doubts, history and dreams.

this is how new hatred is created
how centuries of ugly
memories are introduced to pre-teens and babies
whose smiles have disappeared or are broken
frozen in the tears of parents and elders who
whisper of a future, of possibilities
in the privacy and temporary protection of donated tents.

**Remembering the children of Kosovo*

Legal Lottery

the only men I saw
reading the starr report
on president clinton were lawyers.
they were not reading for facts on whitewater,
travelgate or sexual insights on the use of cigars.
they weren't necessarily interested in impeachable crimes.
they read each word
of every sentence of every paragraph
looking for, eagerly in search of,
the secrets to a fifty million dollar payday.

Chicago is Illinois Country

we are the breast and chest of this nation,
four seasons on the shores of hope
where ideas and fresh water feed
hearts and land in this century's city,
all aware that we can be illumination,
velocity, bread, breath and motion.

we, the carriers of deep earth, sun, snow, desert
and red clay, collided in search of soul and finality.

there are recent padlocks on our memories.
neither infidels or unbelievers   we are loosely
camouflaged and choreographed dancers.
out of necessity and accelerated foresight,
we arrived as unsettled bones and motion.

calm   we are not
satisfied   we are not

our music is the accretion of
multiple tongues into one language
the indomitable spirit harmonizing in
must do theaters where second as in city or state
is absent from our vocabulary and intentions.

we, carriers of all cultures,
invented untried futures
gathered the sane vitality of distant spheres
to narrate an illuminated vision and motion
in this city,
in this state,
in the breast and chest of this nation.

Illinois Humanities Council establishes the Studs Terkel Humanities Service Award, November 6, 2002

Art

1
Art is a prodigious and primary energy force. Children's active participation in music, dance, painting, poetry, film, photography and the indigenous crafts of their people is what makes them whole, significantly human, secure in their own skin, culture and abilities. Thus, generating in them unlimited possibilities.

Art is fundamental instruction and food for a people's soul as they translate the many languages and acts of becoming, often telling them in no uncertain terms that all humans are not pure or perfect. However, the children of all cultures inherit their creators' capacity to originate from the bone of their imaginations the closest manifestations of purity, perfection and beauty. Art, at its best, encourages us to walk on water, dance on top of trees and skip from star to star without being able to swim, keep a beat or fly. A child's "on fire" imagination is the one universal prerequisite for becoming an artist.

2
Magnify your children's minds with art,
jumpstart their questions with art,
introduce your children to the cultures of the world
through art,
energize their young feet, spirits and souls with art,
infuse the values important to civil culture via art,
keep them curious, political and creative with art,
speak and define the universal language of
beauty with art,
learn to appreciate peace with art,
approach the cultures of others through their art,
introduce the spiritual paths of other
people through their art.
keep young people in school, off drugs and
out of prison with art,
keep their young minds running, jumping
and excited with art.
examine the nurturing moments of love,
peace and connecting differences with art.

3
Art allows and encourages the love of self and others. The best artists are not mass murderers, criminals or child molesters; they are in the beauty and creation business. Art is elemental to intelligent intelligence, working democracy, freedom, equality and justice. Art, if used wisely and widely, early and often is an answer and a question. It is the cultural lake that the indigenous rivers of dance, music, local images and voices flow. Art is the waterfall of life, reflecting the untimely and unique soul of a people. Art is the drumbeat of good and great hearts forever seeking peace and a grand future for all enlightened peoples. For these are the people the world over who lovingly proclaim, "give the artists some," kind words, financial support, yeses from your heart, knowing intuitively that there will be creative reciprocity in all that they give us. Why? Because fundamentally art inspires, informs, directs, generates hope and challenges the receiver to respond. And finally, and this is consequential, the quality of the art determines the quality of the responses.

What Do You Say?

replacing fools and crooks
with other fools and crooks
is to the democratic legislative process
what salt is to the seasoning
of over cooked neck bones.
they both kill.

Wasted Life

he spent fifty years
of his life
trying to convince
white people that
he was as good as they were.
he not only failed
but
didn't learn anything
from the experience except
to strategically forget his name and
lie in long sentences.

We Need Not Whisper

We need not whisper
this to neighbors or friends.
We need not kneel or hide our emotions
at this hour.
We need not fail to call up the history of Black flight
caught between success, BET and the
color of gold and coal.
We need not shuffle or polka
to accordion music in 6/8 time.
We need not cry or grin in silence
as white bullets rip the spine, split the brain and
shatter the dreams and lives of our children.

We have new definitions.
We are the off spring of Shaka Zulu, Nat Turner,
Ida. B. Wells, Duke Ellington, Paul Robeson, Rosa Parks,
Martin Luther King, Malcolm X, Ella Baker, Harold Washington,
Gwendolyn Brooks, gospel and blues.
We are not new Negroes reacting to the rap of
unsmiling and misguided sons and daughters modeling
over priced starter jackets from the GAP, Wall Street and MTV.
We are bright definitions and
accepting quietly the murder of our children
is not one of them.

In memory of Amadou Diallo, Tyisha Miller and others.

Gate Keepers

the seeing is in the listening
it is where you walk and sleep that matters
it is the Black and why in the question that demands answers,
it is the done deal before the critique.
gate keepers run from moments to tell
truth to children or power,
truth they deem better if delivered
in anthropological language
that caused their mommas
to apologize to God and family for
sending their only child to Harvard
to be educated and to find himself.

Missed Information

too many people say
they in love
with each other,
they cars,
they houses, they churches,
they fingernails laced with diamonds,
they love oprah & montel & pig feet
eaten in secret because it ain't cool
to eat the feet of pigs in public
especially by those who wear tailor-made dresses
and pinstripe suits.
they say love makes them do it
love is the "o" and "y" as in only you
which is believable if you are 14
and separated from your mind and soul
which is a legal excuse if you were
educated in the public schools of houston, detroit, chicago
or new york.
"I love you" the famous last words of
tom's uncle bobo to lincoln just before
he took back they 40 acres and a mule,
condoleeza, bobo, bertha and collin are in love,
they proud too,
that's another story.

Laws of the Street

if someone among the men
assemble on the corner of 47th & ellis
in front of bj's bar,
all talking shit and spit
looks like he wants to attack
you
it is best to fire on him first
with the fury and force of a thousand guerrillas
not to just knock him down
but to firmly plant in his mind
hard reasons
for not getting up.

Can You Write a Non-Struggle Poem?

Can you write a poem not about politics, culture, economic
struggle or the possibilities of drinking unfiltered water?
Can you put words of rhythm together that do not comment on
the warmth and cold of indigenous teas and corporate coffee or
the conflict of words, worlds and actual life? Is it possible to
render musical language into the yin and yang of acupuncture
healing points, the yeses, nos, and questions of accepted
thought, the rich and poor of potatoes, bean and rice eaters
without surveying the landscape of corrupted lifestyles and
hideouts of platinum credit card holders? Must your poems
always remind us of the tortured citizens, the nation's homeless,
urban schools and assembly line workers? Why write about
million dollar condo owners and the culture of food stamp
users in the same line? Is not the economics divide between
women and men a known quantity, and what of the super egos
of politicians, public intellectuals and medical doctors rendered
in free verse? Is not the arrogance of America's imperialism,
the elitism of professors misusing language and ideas
expected, just as that of preachers, priests, rabbis, monks and
imams interpreting the world of God unquestionable and
naturally poetic? What of the aloneness and fear of children
dancing between broken families, state and private agencies
looking for clean love and healing human touch as subject
matter for serious poets? It would truly take a master poet to
link tax loopholes of the rich with the wars over oil, water, dark
earth, neck-bone eaters and the F.C.C. giveaways. Poetry, we
are told doesn't play well in the company of the military and
prison industrial complexes or that of retired generals quickly
joining the executive work forces of Boeing and General
Electric. You forget that poets are not lobbyist, or
ambassadors for reason. They are dreamers and talkers and
love chasers. They need to concentrate on reading and writing
poetry and let the professionals continue to mismanage words,
the world and wonderment.

Amiri

baraka
"always
come in a
            place
later."
rushin to catch words that came before him
tho that don't much matter,
him got his own words, music, dance, dramatics
& bright ideas even if some of them used cars
& don't work.   but baraka works
works harder than 15 men his age,
da, da da, do   who been around
long enough to tell his time
in places where people have tried to
beat the beat & tempo out of his talk & walk.
monk, trane & duke played secrets
that saved him and us even if we didn't
accurately hear their da da, doos
baraka did. they spoke musically to him.
he gave us his many languages & genius.
his comin in time is getting better & best & less late,
even for this sage still makin up stories
actin on his own stage & firing truthpoems
that compel liars & politicians to exit early and often.

For Amiri Baraka

Baraka II

i saw *The Dead Lecturer* in a Chicago airport.
pacing, fast walking probably quick thinking about
unfinished projects like plays, poems and essays about
"successful" negroes supporting Bush & Ghost
and the secrets of whites with rhythm and
mass graves in Rwanda;
mostly *Tales* of *The System of Dante's Hell* out of school
really way past graduate courses taught
on the rough-neck streets
of Newark. A kind of *Funk Lore* in 3/4 time.
recently, i saw *Black Fire, In Our Terribleness*—older and
small but still a witness with missing teeth, grayer hair with a
fast smile in a blue shirt, accentuated by a smokin Egyptian
print tie—on the south side of Chicago.
Spirit Reach with his *Hard Facts* was alone and
standing close to a pay phone without an assistant,
credit or debit cards, without lovers of literature or *Jello*
supporting him. No *Kawaida Studies* here.
his aloneness frightens me, approaching him I wondered
why this genius of serious music,
of transcendent literature wasn't
surrounded by readers, fans, collectors of fine words on pages
seeking instructions and autographs.
It's Nation Time is still asleep.
where were the *Blues People* and *Black Magic* folks?
S.O.S. for the *Slave* ships and *The Motion of History* souls.
where were the consumers of best sellers, few sellers & the
new line of negro confessional booty-call stores. maybe
they just didn't notice this *Wise, Why's, Y's* poet,
this lover of language, passionate protector of
sound and the laughter of children.
maybe they were blinded by their bones of contradiction—
and pimp juice traversing their veins. they looked past this
original and complicated seer of Black life, this *The Moderns*

updated, reworked beyond *Transbluesency,*
there will be no *Eulogies* here,
no *Preface to a Twenty Volume Suicide Note,*
just an older and able African son going *Home,*
pacing the floor at Midway Airport
on the southside of Chicago, thinking and
alone with a swift—smile.
"whats happenin bro?"

Baraka III

it's difficult to be talented
& genius
yet, often called crazy to your face
in a place that rewards moneymakers
who build and worship skyscrapers as monuments
to the individuality of dollar
bill collecting and preemptive war making
& whose poets and artists are viewed
as handicapped, a bit mad with water colored hands & ideas.
artists who work at beauty, wear words
bathed in nature & music,
talk in complex sentences, odd metaphors & swinging
feet are confusing to themselves and others.
they also think too much about
the nature of flags and forests,
the truth of institutions & religions
of language and lawyers, bankers & brokers;
the why & who of homelessness,
the question of collateral damage and
the battle between cultures, races & classes out of school.

actually, being a complete artist
in a place that worships skyscrapers, money, war,
misconceived thought and hummer2, over children
requires a bit of madness.

Why Shani?

Old folks say that the most
courageous and committed people
are tested incessantly,
given the most intricate mountain to forge,
the deepest forest fires to quiet,
the harsher hellholes to navigate.
this journey does not inspire struggle
just unlimited offers of another path
to reconsider opposing injustice,
to stop working for the children of strangers,
to cease cleaning the wounds of the battered,
to abandon poetry.

to rise from unanswerable pain
requires a history beyond the acquisition of things,
demands work on the other side of self and self.
you have labored and researched the catalogs of the world
& refused to be separated from the poor and poorer.

your love for us is uncorrupted and contagious,
grounded in your arts, activism and the familial.
we reciprocate.

For the Baraka Family

Remembering Betty Shabazz

i, a poet, a weaver of life, an unfinished soul in motion still
a closet dancer who greyhounded between
detroit and chicago
on the same roads
that Malcolm Little, Malcolm X, El Hajj Malik El Shabazz
traveled the identical highways
that Betty, Betty Shabazz, Dr. Betty Shabazz questioned still
i, a poet, an observer of life met Betty,
a giver and nurturer of black winds and earth,
airborne at 33,000 feet over pennsylvania in the year of 75

i, a poet whose voice was confirmed, layered & enlarged
after hearing
a "young shining prince," before we knew
we had the sons of kings and queens among us whispering
African truths that gutted the whiteness in our bellies & minds

i, a poet with watered eyes proclaimed cultural love for black
memory, future,
family and to Betty Shabazz: a genuine work
in progress devoted to
six plus more of her blood and bones. still

i, a poet, a weaver of life's tales found a gift at 33,000 feet
a stand for something spirit in st. john knits, sipping vernor's
ginger ale

a soul in motion electric sliding to the music
of "I'm every woman...
it's all in me," forever observant of predators selling sister love,
baby love
and a woman's place, a woman's place. still

i met a woman not a victim,
i met a sister not a tragedy
i met a warrior-teacher not a professional widow,
i met a baobab tree standing permanently against
human hurricanes & earthquakes still
she was city and voice and insightful storm,

a drop-dead shopper only to give most away,
viewed young people as possibilities, psychic nourishment,
undeveloped innocence mother thoughts still
she had grown into gianthood
did not fear nameless faces anymore
her prayerful language accented
"hey, girlfriend" or "my brother" burns in our memories still
peace be still dear Betty
who found the good in us and praised it
I'm every woman, woman, woman,
it's all in me still.

for Maya Angelou, Ruby Dee, Laura Ross Brown, and Susan L. Taylor

Bones

she riffs in less than fifty words
poems that unveil a peoples' bones.

improvising veto-proof likeness
she cleans neighborhoods of celebrated ignorance
among the weak, wicked and wise,
among the wounded, weary and brief winners.

with oxygen lines,
with a vernacular voice and memory
she sings, swims and dances to the merry movements
of the underlooked, bloodflow, heartdrums
and blistered feet of betrayed generations.

this museum of a poet is not about
impressing enemies, friends or lovers,
her urges are to write gladness, grief and melodies,
always probing for trustworthy tales
of her deep-south multitudes.   acutely
aware of the exaggerations of politicians,
public intellectuals and the criminally rich
she is our brilliant testifier.

For Lucille Clifton

A Mixture of Rain, Rice and Silence

men seldom reveal their hearts to other men
you are listener and conscious galaxy
not quite stone
more like pieces of a royal mountain
where flowers, rainbows, memory and rich earth integrate.
your singing and dancing made me
look like an original member of the Temptations
yet,
you are a mixture of rain, rice and silence,
one who practices faith, breathes truth and labors
confirming that a moral life is not a dull life for
a basketball player who is gentle with children and
the broken hearts of the wounded forgotten.
they say you love your people,
they say you are authentic and rare,
they say you are calm and storm and love the law,
like Marvin Gaye I call you brother, brother
infinitely more than a footnote
much like a carefully worded
prose poem searching for our collective heart.

For David Hall at Fifty
May 26, 2000

The Journey

the missed steps are the most frightening
the unsureness of the calling
wondering if there will be
a hand, a will, a way, a plan
yes, a people
who understand the almost
impregnable face of whiteness
in all of its veiled and public permutations.

if Black people are America's hopeful metaphor
imagine for a moment, just a moment,
the utter responsibility of Black Leadership,
officers without a focused army,
ill equipped for the details of polluted speech,
deciphering small print, questionable deal making,
disguised remunerations, an adulterous culture and
objectionable amendments to Democracy.

statesmen and women who seem stateless
struggle over Black bones,
　　　　Black memory,
　　　　Black hope and promises
　　　　Black conscience, territory and integrity.
herein is the journey
be not broken words, deeds or
stale flowers on unmarked graves.
claim justice,
demand vigilance of courts and kindergartens,
resist evil in all colors and configurations,
do not fear truth, criticism or Black love.
speak knowledge.
do not whisper in the ears of enemies,
because of elaborate egos, attitudes and corruption.
betrayal is an easy door at noon or midnight,
rejecting corporate bounty is the backbone exam.
speak courage forcefully
remember you are our fire and water,
　　　　　　　our light and wind,
　　　　　　　our voice and answer,
　　　　　　　our agent of warmth, wisdom and sun.

you are our language, spirit and definitions.

love is where we emerged,
love is where we will travel,
love is at the pilgrimage end,
is the reality guiding your work.
the reason we negotiate mountains and persevere.

run like lions on the hunt,
others think that they know us.
that too is our ace, our secret, our bond.
leadership may only last a season
let the rain come,
we are the earth.

For The Congressional Black Caucus Thirtieth Anniversary Celebrations, September, 2001.

We Family

We family,
we friends,
we neighbors,
we assemblage of smiling folk
mostly strangers at this gate
gathered south to confirm
this cornerstone of cultures,
this joining of names and spirits,
this remarkable sharing of water
deep breathing, gold, grandmother tales,
bread, music, cloth, life's fragments and genuine love.

Your fathers are pleased and joyous,
your mothers are tearful and earthful,
those gathered are thankful,
all are concerned and most earnest in their
good words, well wishes, exact advice and gifts.
the flowers are happy, the air invigorating
today's passion is meditative and prayerful.

This sacred ritual of ocean crossing,
of consenting hearts, families and traditions
is the blessing
is too a warning, hot soup. sweet pastry, green cultivation,
lusted waterfalls, untamed climate, quiet talk, unknown steps,
complex hours, birth,

yams, bold darkness, abundant wellness and histories.
this clasping of hands,
this smiling silence,
this rooted journey of two African souls
has spirited us home this day.

Our extended stillness and thoughts
second these original lovers
who are prompt and prepared,
suitable and equipped for life's arrangements and traditions.

Of those here gathered
we urgently assert and affirm that
we be family,   now and now
unremittingly.

For Janet Danielle Hutchinson and Bomani Garvey Madhubuti Lee,
married on September 15, 2001 and for the Hutchinson
and Madhubuti families.

Our Daughter On Loan

you were not to be ours forever,
yours was a short map.
some say a liberian circle
there is little human logic to your pilgrimage.
we must not deem it incomplete,
we do confirm that it was brief.

the day the sun bloodied,
the moon disappeared,
interrupting great promise and progress,
magnificent expectations.
visual artists painted muted yellows,
poets and musicians were silent and
fiction writers and dancers joined hands and tears
the second your breath stopped.

your history was still in discovery
as grandmothers, big mommas and babas declared,
"you were on loan to us,"
not a borrowed book or pawn shop watch.
your visit among us is still mystery and melody,
"tweety" birds with rhythm in their eyes.

your mother is a southern river,
your father a strong stone with baggage,
your family is Black stories, deep crops,
gathering winds, Black hurricanes in waiting.
you were washed in love and possibilities,
sun bathed in smiles, tunes and cultural signatures.
why you leave us so soon?

For Kevani Zelpah Moyo
(1982–1999)

Black Earth

she was rich memory, melody and best words,
urgent fire riding sun, moon and red dust,
a hat wearing big momma with an iowa ph.d.
Poet of solid songs, cotton fields and Mississippi gumbo,
messenger of our south, Rising.
if truth be liberated, her work navigated the student's spirit in
us.
she left literature, smiles, and ironwood wisdom.
she prepared us to see Black Earth.
daylight at the river's edge always
ready to extinguish square curves and invisible scars.
she was our railroad,
southwind and portrait,
our earth fed tree, soul rooted and able,
clearly a spirited dancer in a land not expecting us to
rise.

For Margaret Walker Alexander, 1915–1998

When 21 is More Than A Number

we all knew them,
they were our children, Chicago's brightmoments.
their deaths stole our hearts and
tragically touched a nation.
their memory occupies our dreams,
our waking minutes and the
seconds of our deep contemplations.
we are now in the rough tomorrows
of pain, outrage and reordering.

these young people,
these daughters and sons,
these developing geniuses at the
apex of their calling
would demand a renewed commitment
to smiles, safe territory and the noticing of simple pleasures:
grass, sun, the unhurried walk of the elderly,
the magical laughter of the innocent,
dancing to the melodies of love,
embracing the education of young seekers,
the taste of fresh grapes, watermelon, peaches and water.

as unthinkable as it seems today
we remain the wind and lake of their missed lives,
we are the answers to their unasked questions,
we are the on-goings, get-ups and critical yeses of future days,
we are the westside/southside of their walked streets,
we are the souls, spirits, and source of their beginnings.
do not render their lives irrelevant
they would want us to magnify the
alphabet enlightening the tongues of children.

For the 21 young people who perished in Chicago's E2 Night Club on February 17, 2003

Eighty-Three is a Wise Number

The weather does not age, it
changes
bringing peach and hurricanes,
water
and sun for planting, walking
and smiles
extending people to long life,
maybe.

I've grown up in your magic,
shadows and words,
I've seen you manage pens,
paper, poor eyesight and gift
giving.
I've measured the recent dip in
your walk,
noting the way the wind leans
you into its current
and I worry.

What if I'm not there to catch
your arm
to gently steer you away from a
fall, missed step
or from harm's way

but you've always been your
own clock
and as the seasons disappear
and rise
you know exactly what time it
is,
beating the beat in storms not
of your making.

for Gwendolyn Brooks at 83

Gwendolyn Brooks Illinois State Library: The Naming, June 6, 2003

your ancestry is book country,
able bones crossing the atlantic ocean to discover
white pages, protein and protégé in the midland.

in my first days of learning I remember eyeglasses that joined
  your smile.
I recall your fingers, long, thin, delicately brown and touchable,
suited for turning book pages, appropriate for ink sculpturing
  on paper.
fingers connected to memory, a people, a culture,
  Chicago and this state.
using the language of 47th street, Springfield and Cambridge,
  your poetry
silences us with its narrative love-songs, ripe-sources
  and bone-truths.
poems that governed the weather, invented eyes the colors
  of wheat, sky, coal,
cabbage, soybeans and yes, creating images out of empty
  pockets and kitchenettes.
art that reversed massacred thought, healthy words renouncing
ignorance, providing a
landscape of glorious literature
emphasizing lineage, liberty and validation.
your discourse is of children, the four seasons:
poetry that deciphers myths.
your writing: the impulse to arrive at meaning, life-ringing
  idioms, bright-calm
all accenting wisdom that affirmed in us the kindness
  of your grand spirit,
the friendliness of ideas, melodies and soap operas,
of water, sun and clean fire. your language is of
the necessity of carrot juice, broccoli and fattening chocolate,
of solitude, good pens and fine paper,
the labor of writers, poets, musicians and under-fed artists,
of librarians, libraries, books and break-even bookstores,
the support of printers, editors and struggling book publishers,
of book festivals, newspapers, magazines and twice-a-year
  quarterlies,

the requirement of contemplation, dialogue with others
  and reading on trains,
of legislators thinking outside the prism of dark suits
  and half-stories.

our ancestry is book country and rich earth,
galloping souls and skillful deal makers.
we are becoming the portrait of your right words.

Word Founder

he who takes the notes and
lost pages of the bitterly grounded,
he who files the failed memories
of the physically and psychologically beaten,
culturally enslaved and misrepresented billions;

he who documents the life stories of the people
whose voices are compromised each millisecond
of each second of each day
from sun high to moon light—
a people whose loud and clear whispers,
screamed and heartfelt autobiographies
bounce off the muted ears of a corrupted scholarship;

he who comprehends the unique power of story-telling
and intimately interprets the concepts
that voice a people's narratives
especially the lifelines of Africans whose saneness
was stolen, hijacked and colonialized
by Euro-Americans disguised as authorities,
saviors and, of course, revelation, as well as, the blessed
descendents of the descendents who created civilization,
popcorn, rubber bands, the wheel and something called race
and measured intelligence;
he is welcomed Word Founder.

to you—meticulous in researcher,
attentive listener and prudent recorder—
we say, yes.   To your mind's eye,
your calm commitment, authenticity;
love of truth,
we, the beneficiaries of your peaceful calling,
singular oeuvre and numerous struggles
say, yes.   To you, our able sage and seer—
original, rooted and serious educator,
a mountain of optimism and faith,
a hurricane of energy, spirit and Black love,
a volcano whose fire has quieted and is rested
let the chorus sing
yes—ashe,
yes—ashe,
yes—ashe,
ashe, ashe, ashe.

For Jacob H. Carruthers (1930–2004)

Water

we are the stories we are told,
they create boundaries in our voices.
we answer to names that are not ours,
African bones are buried on foreign soil and
our children are taught by people who do not
love them.

enter the mountain of truth
enter the rain drops of wisdom
enter the valley of right voices
enter the waves on the dark sea
enter the geography of a new continent
enter the enlightenment of Black
enter the quality of first thought.

He arrived in June, left in February
he farmed and fished for eighty nine years.
he created circles, mutual light
hands that touched prayer,
words that reordered memory,
ancestral stories of The Black Messiah,
he started a nation of believers who believed in themselves.

they say he is resting in Beulah Land.

For Jaramogi Abebe Agyeman
First Holy Patriarch
Pan African Orthodox Christian Church
August 1, 2003

The Sea in Your Language

she came to Urbana loving literature
stayed to start a movement among wheat, soybeans & vacant
smiles
words always precede battle and battery
even where the language is not broken, torn or wanting.
Amidst the English-English you do not disappoint.
Revelation: it's rough being a woman, Black, slim, immaculate
with a brain as quick as fire in their tongue and ours.

Radical surgery allowed you to walk away from fear
making you incapable of treachery or grinning rhetoric.
Words matter. Some cut like big Willie's razor, bloodless.
others come deceptively like Vietnamese art, long history, short
notice.
twenty years of working in white shadows
qualifies you for a double zero preceding your name.
Your memory is of banished bones and promises.

Did I say she is the sea in you and me, and
morning tulips, red spirits, rainbow colors. Wow!
Our kind of woman. Running buddy. Sister. Genuine.
Announce her as valuable earth, hatwearer with a killer smile.

For Sandra Gibbs
November 20, 1999

Heart Work

Art has its own answers and name,
has beauty, insight and great questions too.
the poem is the unheard inquiry,
a foreign language in English and off rhyme
torturously taught by P.E. teachers
to a population bred on commercials and war games,
where the loud aesthetic is the nation's weapon
limited only by the zeros on its dollar bills.
You go substratum to decipher
the secrets of poets, musicians and hand painters.
Poetry has blanketed your heart and
your heart is like that of "Lincoln West," "Strong Men," and
"Mollie Means"
running alone on *A Street in Bronzeville* and southern back
roads

For the Teachers of Poetry

Useni

at 70 he still collects medals
for the ten minute mile he runs with a soft smile,
knowing that he is one of three
in his age class in the race
who can
beat the sixty and under upstarts
who think that he is younger
than he claims.
reluctantly they eat his dust
and marvel at the beauty of his wife,
not aware of his real life
as poet.
tradition has it that most poets
have good looking women close by.
it is part of their job description.
yet, this useni man
does have a respectable career
where young men call him baba,
study his books and
quietly listen to the rhythms of his words,
seeking insight into his deep humanity
and running secrets.
i fail to inform you that this poet
is in league with Baraka, Wilson, Hansberry,
Hughes, and Ted Ward in capturing our
endless souls for the stage.

he is our anticipation,
life with an open heart of affirmations,
my love for him is earth grown,
spirited and brotherfed
we are wondrous of his gifts, longevity, and bad eating habits.

For Useni Eugene Perkins on his seventieth birthday
September 13, 2003

Aunt Mayme

there was this distant desert a half century away,
on the negro door to "jew town" at chicago's 14th and hastings,
on a one house street with a broom factory on the corner,
there stood a home, with walk over stairs connecting sidewalk
to hope,
where summers and other drop-off times were spent
with a loving aunt, many children and an uncle
larger than doorways named jesse james.
he wore guns, had a majestic smile on a large
bald head. he adored his family and worked all the time.

our days were spent collecting metal and saleable junk
in secure alleys where work was not begging for jobs
but inventing employment, making do with ideas and nothing.
knowing that if everything is everything,
then nothing is nothing.
except we, my sister and I, had aunt mayme for precious
moments with uncle jesse who worked all the time.

during summers and some autumns at irregular
drop-offs, my sister and I received uncommon love,
full meals, deep warmth and learned the location of family
from aunt mayme, a host of first cousins
and that giant of a black man with guns,
a winning and intelligent smile,
pre-MJ bald head
with promises and safety in his eyes.

on her 75th birthday, February 1, 2003

Duke

was it Duke Ellington
who said that
music was his mistress?
she musta been
fine
wore red, read poetry and prose
could swing naturally,
danced a lot and didn't need
too much sleep.

Tee One in a Complex World

this woman
does good when good is unnoticeable or advertised,
she carries rocks to the dams of beavers,
writes memorandum of possibilities for single mothers,
vows publicly for the security of children,
hears the prophets' voices from the roots of oak trees,
would give you her leg
if she didn't have to walk.

this woman
can read a smile in evil,
studies the earth's waterfalls,
understands iambic pentameter,
reads the sacred texts of Africa and Israel,
she sings the lyrics of Shirley Horn
while monitoring the intricate speech of her progeny
who converses in coded alphabet and colors.

her kisses are climactic
an oral lover who has a fondness for carrot juice.
she memorizes the sensitive nerves of her men and
attends to the feet of the difficult musician on her block.
her decisive word to him was no
as she prepared to travel foreign waters
to kiss new trees.

this woman is artful earth opening for the seeds awaiting her.

Maya: We Honor Our Own

your voice bridged genre,
in concert with Malcolm, Killens, Baldwin and Brooks
it matured us,
stamped us to ourselves,
impelled a recognition that had been contradicted
by priest and anthropologist,
by banker and architect.

your voice, able, harmonious and emphatic,
willfully free and angular
dared to confront our fears,
invade our interiors and weak utterances.
Maya, a wandering call back,
our precise reminder.
no longer a test pilot,
welcome
poet who can boogie-down.
you are among the last of the great trees,
high questioner, master wordgiver and witness.
you've paid our dues,
there is no copy, clown or apology here.

we find home in your presence.

For Maya Angelou, Howard University – Heart's Day 2004

For R. Kelly

if you have daughters?
how you gointa
protect them
from the somebodies just
like you?

Wynton

that boy musta been listenin to Pops
he plays trumpet real good
just like Satchmo when he hot,
my grandfather announced.
I agreed and more.

the trumpet seems like it is
sewn to his lips
cause he plays like
Sterling Brown reading his poems.
and we all know poetry comes from God.

For Wynton Marsalis

Butt for Sale: The Gateway to Factualization

rising quickly under the umbrella of scholar extraordinaire
professor greats, dr. heavy loose greats, aka jump greats to
close associates, friends and spelling buddies, recently of yale,
cornell, duke and now residing permanently at the cambridge
of America.

rising energetically to the undeniable
challenge of Black-Blackness
and African-centered ideas running amuck
from uncertified upstarts,
captain greats, the queen of rebuttal, designated hit man,
the protector of rap & sap, the answerer to out
of order negroes,
honorary defender of the forgotten misogynist 2 live crew,
rappers who wouldn't recognize a syllable that was pro-Black
women if it bit their tongues as they struggled against the devil
to scream money without the B_____, F____ & N____ words
that decorate & inflate their male insightfulness.

now, rising cleverly on the western horizon super scholar for
hire, wordsmith on the negro-right, chairperson
and proclaimer of white truths, coming like a dull
razor cutting clear speech, dr. jump, the last word, eloquently
ascending from the lower middle east-side of Manhattan
where real men are made and turned-out with the frequency of
run away children forced into prostitution, comes the most
sought after H.N.I.C.[1] the world has known since the
unquestioned rhyme, reason & puppetry of the marvelous
stepin fetchit, is dr. heavy loose greats.

climbing ruthlessly and uninhibited on the op-ed pages of
"All the News That's Fit to Print"[2] is professor jump
who is crowned prince of B for Black studies, Black with an
enlarged A, as in anti-African thought, dr. greats is in
the house residing as the advocate of white, Zionist and
wahhabist il-liberal ideas of advanced thought. professor
greats, the respected expert on everything colored, negro,
Black, African, afro-American, brown, unwhite, mulatto and
coon is the gifted yes-sir-boss of the new century.

give him his due as he rises against the sun, sons and
daughters blessed by the sun who dared to question the
illegality and brutality of enslavement, dare to examine ideas
unsanctioned or confirmed
by the official canonicals, dare to fight acts that have
disfigured Black minds and bodies:
acts & ideas that produced the unspoken,
under-studied or acknowledged holocaust
of the African middle passage and beyond.

dr. greats rising happily and comfortably against the dark
people who battle brain mismanagement hourly,
rising strategically with a clown's grin to be anointed by
"all the news that's fit to print," "the new yorker" and cambridge
of the east as authentic and accredited Black, afro-American
and authority on watermelon seed spitting.

professor greats is on board to uncover the "anti-white,"
"anti-jewish," therefore ungodly, unrighteous conspiracy
of Blacks who think, he and his assistants are on a
mission to uproot the "Black demagogues" and
"pseudo-scholars"
who must be neutralized, must be cut off at the knees,
as in kneel niggers; must be white-out. dr. greats, one among
many who are maid boys and economically armed to clean
the corridors of Black/African intrusion once and forever.

greaterman ascending in perfect pitch, possessing a technical
magnetism and imagination, the newest star of negro studies,
the honorary European of the left, right and center.
the corrector, the yellow highlighter for the west, untouched by
ancestor worship, shoddy scholarship and rib eating contests.

greaterman running uncensored and alive, last seen
at cambridge mini lecturing to wide-eyed future
directors of M16, CIA and the ghost of viking
barbarians in dark suits all learning close textual
reading and listening. We have greaterman joyously jumping
to the beat of alien women in heat and skipping to the polka
of white rulership demanding confirmed articulations
of former slaves.

greaterman, the clarence thomas of modern grantsmanship,
is able to leap long sentences in simple utterances, able
to survey African civilizations in a brief phase, able to
disarm and dismantle young scholars with a mere glance and
promises of book contracts, able to terrorize untenured
assistant professors in unmusical prose, collaborated by the
primary sources on the back of cereal boxes as he films the
entire continent of Africa and its people in a tee-shirt.

dr. heavy loose greats, aka jump, reborn on the
yes plantation of sambo university, is now the
unquestioned, unchallenged sovereign on the negro.
he plays daily and deadly in the legitimate journals,
magazines, newspapers, broadcasts, colleges and courts
of the euro-world.
yet and yet,
jumperman is unwelcomed in the eyes
of Black children and incarcerated boymen,
is forbidden to eat at the table
of African mothers & fathers who
anticipate the horror and prepare for the cowardly carnage
that certified niggers do
yielding white hatchets,
dripping Black blood.

Notes
1. Head Negro In Charge
2. see Op-Ed page, *New York Times,* July 20, 1992

What We Don't Know

how do full time talkers,
"human rights" organizers & spokespersons who
have never known employment,
never dirtied their hands at
carpentry, garbage pick-up, nursing,
window cleaning, plumbing or
butchering fried chicken that widens their waist-lines
live so well?

Should they not share the secrets of the militant
unemployed who change town cars yearly,
vacation in exclusive communities,
demand private planes and sex partners,
solicit front-row seats at fights,
super bowls, all star games,
Las Vegas openings' and pork chop eating roasts?

the large perception is that we are
led by men (& a few women) who bathe in integrity,
who are believed to be walking in the footsteps of Malcolm,
Martin, Medgar and Parks,
yet they tailor their suits and ideas,
bishop over failing colleges and victim-talk,
pop-up for cameras and microphones
as perfectionist in the art of one-liners and people politics
strategically misusing the race card.

how do full-time God talkers
become millionaires in America
be they Christian, Jews or Muslim?
what we don't know is
some bodies in the moments and minutes of daylight, after hours and
blinking eyes
must be
in the capital and corporate offices of money
making side deals with the devil.

For the Consideration of Poets

where is the poetry of resistance,
    the poetry of honorable defiance
unafraid of the lies from career politicians and businessmen,
not respectful of journalist who write
official speak void of educated thought
without double search or sub surface questions
that war talk demands?
where is the poetry of doubt and suspicion
not in the service of the state, bishops and priests,
not in the service of beautiful people and late night promises,
not in the services of influence, incompetence and academic
    clown talk?

Afterword

Lita Hooper

What is Haki Madhubuti's legacy? Poetry, surely. But more than that, his work is evidence of the labor and commitment that is demanded of activists and literary giants. This collection offers us the arc of his development as a voice—reactionary poet to reflective wordsmith. Merciless at times, Madhubuti is always in the process of exposing, celebrating, educating, indicting, satirizing and, most often, loving. That he loves black people is obvious. He does so through his selfless offering of healing words of wisdom and dynamic action plans rooted in history. But his love extends beyond American ghettos and gentrified urban enclaves, beyond the lost and wandering homeless, beyond hip-hop divas and fearless thugs serving time or holding down street corners spinning rhymes. His love is universal, reaching into the Diaspora like a cyclone to gather us up and return us to our true selves.

What will follow this collection? How will this voice continue to expand, rise up to meet new social changes and challenges? Certainly, the most recent poems included here are indicative of his continuing effort to recognize the heroes and sheroes whose lives and work will not be forgotten. As usual, this new work speaks to the cultural issues at hand, how black people's realities are affected by the ever-changing political landscape of the world. What we see is Madhubuti at his best—placing at the center of his work the people who inform his vision and who are, therefore, inspired by it.

Luckily there is so much more to come from this self-appointed protector. It is certain that he will continue to illuminate our shortcomings, which scuttle in the darkness as we dance and sing and die on a leased stage, our traditions checked at the door. These poems, his gifts, are unconditional. We need only take the time to unwrap each one, remembering Gwendolyn Brooks' profound words: "...we are each other's/harvest:/we are each other's/business:/we are each other's/magnitude and bond."

Lita Hooper is an Associate Professor of English at Georgia Perimeter College and author of three books, including *Art of Work: The Art and Life of Haki R. Madhubuti.*

Haki R. Madhubuti

As poet, publisher, editor and educator, Haki R. Madhubuti has been a pivotal figure in the development of a strong Black literary tradition, emerging from the Civil Rights and Black Arts era of the 60s and continuing to the present. Over the years, he has published more than 28 books (some under his former name, Don L. Lee). Madhubuti is a proponent of independent Black institutions. He founded Third World Press in 1967. He is also a founder of the Institute of Positive Education/New Concept School (1969), co-founder of Betty Shabazz International Charter School (1998), Barbara A. Sizemore Middle School (2005), and DuSable Leadership Academy (2005), all of which are in Chicago.

An award-winning poet and recipient of the National Endowment for the Arts and National Endowment for the Humanities fellowships, American Book Award, the Studs Terkel Humanities Service Award and others. In 2007, he was named Chicagoan of the Year by *Chicago Magazine.* In May of 2008, Madhubuti was honored with a Lifetime Achievement Award from Art Sanctuary of Philadelphia. In 2009, he was named one of the "Ebony Power 150: Most Influential Blacks in America" for education. In 2010, Madhubuti was awarded the poetry prize at the Ninth Annual Hurston/Wright Legacy Awards for his book, *Liberation Narratives.*

Haki R. Madhubuti is the former University Distinguished Professor and professor of English at Chicago State University where he was the founder and director-emeritus of the Gwendolyn Brooks Center and director of the Master of Fine Arts in Creative Writing Program. Currently, Madhubuti is the Ida B. Wells-Barnett University Professor at DePaul University.